THE PHILOSOPHY O

THE PHILOSOPHY OF THE LIMIT

DRUCILLA CORNELL

ROUTLEDGE NEW YORK AND LONDON

Published in 1992 by

Routledge
An imprint of Routledge, Chapman and Hall, Inc.
29 West 35 Street
New York, NY 10001

Published in Great Britain by

Routledge
11 New Fetter Lane
London EC4P 4EE

Library of Congress Cataloging in Publication Data

Cornell, Drucilla.
    The philosophy of the limit / Drucilla Cornell.
      p. cm.
    Includes bibliographical references and index.
    ISBN 0-415-90238-X.—ISBN 0-415-90239-8 (pbk.)
    1. Deconstruction. 2. Ethics. 3. Law—Philosophy. 4. Justice
(Philosophy)   I. Title.
B809.6.C67   1992
149—dc20   91-34524
                                        CIP

British Library Cataloguing in Publication Data

Cornell, Drucilla
   The philosophy of the limit.
   I. Title
   190

ISBN 0-415-90238-X
ISBN 0-415-90239-8 pbk

For Jacques,
with thanks for his friendship

Contents

Preface

In the past four years I have developed an ethical reading of what has come to be known as deconstruction. I proceeded to a discussion of how the ethical reading of deconstruction related to the philosophy of alterity of Emmanuel Levinas. I then further explored how a correct understanding of this relationship could help us in examining questions of justice and of legal interpretation. As my own conception developed in the course of these essays, it became more and more evident that the word deconstruction did not adequately portray the special kind of quasi-transcendental analysis that I attributed to Derrida and that I argued had important implications in the field of law. The recognition of the inadequacy of the word deconstruction led me to rename Derrida's philosophical project the philosophy of the limit. As is usually the case, the event of renaming prodded me to reconsider fundamental aspects of my own earlier work. Thus, although six of the chapters are based on essays I published in the *Cardozo Law Review*, the *Yale Journal of Law and Humanities*, and *Social Concept*, they have all been substantially rewritten.

Many people have helped me over the years in developing the ethical configuration I portray in this book. Bruce Ackerman, Stanley Fish, Frank Michelmann, and Barbara Herrnstein Smith warrant my special thanks for their constant intellectual support and excellent criticism of my writing. I also need to thank Jonathan Culler and Cynthia Chase for providing me with such a hospitable intellectual environment when I was a research fellow at the AD White House. They provided me with an important forum in which I could present my work. Richard Bernstein was also a very careful reader of all the drafts of the essays that have become the basis of this book. His intervention taught me important lessons. My colleagues at Cardozo, Arthur Jacobsen, Michel Rosenfeld, and David Carlson, have been a constant source of encouragement as well as of thoughtful commentary. My continuing debate with Seyla Benhabib has led me to rethink many of the central ideas in this book. Our collaboration as well as our endless discussions have led me to clarify my own position. Judith Butler has played a crucial role in her excellent commentaries on various versions of these essays. My assistants, Deborah Garfield, Collin Biddle, Kathy Kemp, Byron Mattingly, and Whedbee Macabee, gave me invaluable help. Not only did they assist me in each step of the production of this manuscript, they also offered me invaluable editorial advice. They are a constant reminder of just how much one has to learn from one's students. In the end, there are no adequate words of thanks for their commitment and intellectual energy. As always, I want to express my appreciation to Maureen MacGrogan who has given me so much as an editor, an intellectual interlocutor, and particularly as a friend. The day-to-day emotional and intellectual sustenance provided to me by my husband, Greg Defrietas, has been invaluable to me throughout the conceptualization and actualization of this book.

But there is one person whose friendship and support has come to symbolize for me the infinite respect for the other I evoke in this book. My friendship with Jacques Derrida has been a gift for which there could truly be no adequate thanks. His constant support and "positive mirroring" have given me more than I can say. My recognition of the significance of the role his friendship has played in my life can only be indicated by the dedication of this book.

Introduction:
What Is Postmodernity
Anyway?

This book aims to establish the relationship of the philosophy of the limit to questions of ethics, justice, and legal interpretation. I here introduce the phrase "the philosophy of the limit" in order to rename what has come to be called deconstruction. I engage in this process of renaming because this new designation should allow us to be more precise about what deconstruction actually is philosophically and, hence, to articulate more clearly its significance for law. The philosophy of the limit, then, by refocusing attention on the limits constraining philosophical understanding, rather than on negative preconceptions engendered by the notion of "deconstructing" as that concept has been read and misread over the years, draws attention to two aspects of deconstructive theory crucial to any apprehension of contemporary philosophical practice in its association with legal studies. First, deconstruction, reconceived as the philosophy of the limit, does not reduce the philosophical tradition to an "unreconstructable" litter, thus undermining the possibility of determining precepts for moral action; rather, it exposes the quasi-transcendental conditions that establish any system, including a legal system as a system. This exposure, which in Derrida proceeds through what he calls the "logic of parergonality,"[1] demonstrates how the very establishment of the system as a system implies a *beyond* to it, precisely by virtue of what it excludes. The second aspect of deconstruction more accurately described by the notion of limit is related to what Charles Peirce in his own critique of Hegelian idealism called secondness. By secondness Peirce indicates the materiality that persists *beyond* any attempt to conceptualize it. Secondness, in other words, is what resists. Very simply, reality is not interpretation all the way down. As we will see, Derrida continually points to the failure of idealism to capture the real. The limit of any system of meaning is, for Derrida, graphically represented to us in death. As a result, for Derrida we may know secondness only indirectly, for example in the death of a friend or lover, but the indirectness of this knowledge does not diminish the force of its impact. Derrida's engagement with the problem of secondness is actually foundational to his more obvious interest in the relationship to the Other. In his discussion of Levinas and Heidegger, Derrida reads

Levinas' ethical philosophy of alterity as demanding that we recognize the being of the Other and the Other as ~~Being~~[2] if we are not to revert to the rejection of materiality as unholy and to the mystification of the Other. This mystification, incidentally, can be seen in Levinas' own symbolization—via the figure of the pregnant mother—of the ethical relationship to the Other. Derrida's insistence, then, on secondness is crucial to his own aspiration to heed the call of the Other.

It is important to note here that Derrida's deconstructive exercises are unique in the way in which the limit of any system is exposed. The uniqueness of Derrida's own philosophical positioning is that it does not attempt positively to describe the limit as an oppositional cut, or merely as the system's own self-limitation so that the system can perpetuate itself as a whole. If Derrida were positively to describe the limit as an oppositional cut, he would be reinstating the traditional assumptions and dichotomies he seeks to deconstruct. The force of *différance* prevents any system—the classical system in this book will be Hegel's system—from encompassing its other or its excess. The Other for Derrida remains other to the system. My argument will be that Derrida's project is not only to show us why and how there is always the Other to the system; it is also to indicate the ethical aspiration behind that demonstration. For Derrida, the excess to the system cannot be known positively; hence, there is no beyond to what he would call the undecidable. We must try, if we are to remain faithful to the ethical relationship, to heed its otherness to any system of conventional definition.

This book will attempt to reformulate the juridical and legal significance of this recognition of the limit of idealism, if idealism is understood to give us a system that can successfully incorporate what is other to the system and thereby erase the system's contradictions. More specifically, I will try to show the significance for legal interpretation of Derrida's own understanding of justice as an aporia that inevitably serves as the limit to any attempt to collapse justice into positive law. Indeed, the significance of understanding justice as the limit to any system of positive law is the first reason I am renaming deconstruction as the philosophy of the limit.

My second reason for engaging in this process of renaming is this: I hope to change the terms of the debate between thinkers of so-called "modernity" and "postmodernity." As we will see in the forthcoming discussion I do not believe that Derrida or Levinas, the two thinkers most intimately connected with the project of this book, are correctly identified as "postmodern." More importantly, the very term "postmodernity," although relevant in the realm of aesthetics, loses much of its richness when carried over into philosophy and legal studies; "postmodernity" easily falls in with a particular perspective on historical and philosophical development which cannot do justice to the complexity of Derrida's and Levinas' work.

The argument that we are now in "postmodernity" necessarily implies a progression from the premodern to the modern to the "postmodern." Such a conception, at the very least, presupposes a teleological notion of historical development that can be described precisely enough to delineate the transition from one period into another. For example, Jürgen Habermas makes a distinction between the modern and the postmodern that rests on the teleological development from *mythos* to *logos*, which in turn demands the separation of the Right from the Good. The set of normative ideals characteristic of the Enlightenment marks a turning point in philosophy and in political and legal life. This change from *mythos* to *logos*, so the argument goes, elevates public reason rather than community prejudice to dominion over our political life. Public reason, in turn, allows for the rational legitimation of shared normative ideals. Habermas argues that this move from *mythos* to *logos* is the key aspect of modernity, a modernity which he then claims as the very basis of an enlightened political and legal ordering. For Habermas, as already suggested, such a political order separates questions of Justice from questions of the Good. Instead, the Enlightenment, by rationalizing public norms and, more specifically, by institutionalizing the rule of law as a recognizable set of rules and procedures, promotes the Right to a position of priority. This move to rationalize public norms in the rule of law is the very crux of modernity and the Enlightenment ideals that mark modernity as an historical period.[3] In Rawls' recent work, the ideal of public reason and a cognizable system of law with established rights is understood to be inherent in the very idea of constitutional government. Both Habermas and Rawls argue that it is only by respecting the ideal of public reason and by establishing basic rights and guaranteed procedures applicable to all citizens equally and understandable by the public as a whole that we can truly be said to have moved from the rule of "men" to the rule of law.[4]

Despite this similarity between Rawls and Habermas, however, their recent works diverge over whether Justice and the Good can be rigidly separated. For Rawls, the centrality of tolerance blurs the distinction. Tolerance is the basic political value upon which constitutional government is founded. Tolerance *recognizes* that certain areas of human engagement should be free from state intervention. Human beings must be free to pursue competing forms of life and divergent moral commitments. But these pursuits must not infringe on the basic rights and other forms of constitutional protections that are guaranteed to all citizens as a matter of law. Unlike Habermas, Rawls does not speak in terms of historical periods, but his understanding of the "constitutional essentials" inherent in the "overlapping consensus" embodies the historical reality of constitutional government. An "overlapping consensus" clearly involves an interpretation of the political significance of the Reformation. Indeed, tolerance is the political value behind the Reformation's insistence that the state should not be given the power to control religion, let alone to establish one particular religious view as the state religion. In terms of American constitutional law, we recognize the value of religious tolerance by imposing measures which prevent the government from establishing a state religion and by guaranteeing the freedom of the individual to practice his or her religious convictions under the First Amendment. For Rawls, even though religious warfare is no longer as prevalent as it was at the time of the founding of the Constitution, the political issue of tolerance is by no means outdated. On the contrary, Rawls believes many of the heated political and moral debates of our time are religious battles, sometimes thinly disguised, sometimes openly expressed. Think, for example, of the battles over abortion, homosexuality, and pornography.

It would greatly oversimplify Rawls' recent work to assume that it relies, at least in the traditional Kantian sense, on the division between the Right and the Good. Of course, it should be noted here that Kant's own insistence on this distinction only pertained to the sphere of morality, and not to the hustle and bustle of political and legal juggling. Rawls' "overlapping consensus," by means of which we are able to elaborate "constitutional essentials," does not merely represent a *pure* procedure to establish what is Right, which then becomes the very basis of the rule of law. Substitutive moral commitments are part of what make up our "constitutional essentials." These "constitutional essentials" enjoy a quasi-transcendental status in the sense that they are understood as the prior *basis*—meaning here prior to the actual day-to-day political struggles which set the guidelines and the limits of majoritarian politics—of the rule of law. In other words, equality now understood as a limit on majoritarian politics is given an historical dimension, but in such a way as to protect the need for a procedure to legitimate established guidelines, irreducible to the particular conventions of a particular society at a particular time. But this procedure is not de-ontological in the strict sense of the word. Rawls, and as we will see also, Thomas Nagel, struggles to develop a new way of thinking about justice which would avoid reducing ethics and norms, on the one hand, to a simple appeal to the conventions of a particular community, or, on the other, to a de-ontological approach, the strong counter to conventionalism which seems to deny history and the significance of our developed legal and moral conceptions. Constitutional essentials are based on the overlapping consensus of what our constitutional government has stood for over time. This overlapping consensus, in turn, defines the ideal of equality upon which Rawls understands the Constitution to rest. Rawls' "constitutional essentials" certainly can allow for the promotion by the state of certain values—for example, specific interventions to compensate for the educational disadvantage of African Americans. In this sense they allow what have traditionally been designated as questions of the "good life" to be recognized by the law.

The liberal concern with the limits of state intervention into the lives of individuals and members of groups experimenting with different lifestyles can best be understood through the title of Thomas Nagel's recent work, *Partiality and Equality*.[5] In this essay, Nagel tries to think through how to establish limits to the equality before the law that must be guaranteed to individuals if the legal order is to be legitimate (even though the concept of legitimation is not Nagel's own language). For Nagel, individuality demands partiality. Each one of us has specific ambitions and talents to which we are inevitably partial. In order to have an adequate understanding of justice, then, we must begin with the recognition of individual partiality. It is important to note here, that for Nagel partiality is mandated by individual differences. He is not *directly* speaking to the *partiality* of the state to certain forms of life. My addition to his argument is that any meaningful *legal* recognition of even individual partiality—take, for example, the commitments of the artist—will demand the *partiality* of the state to support these endowments—for example funding for the arts—if this recognition is to be given content. As a result, I am arguing that the recognition of individual partiality cannot be separated from the partiality of the state to divergent moral and personal commitments. An example from Nagel which shows the connection between the two forms of partiality is the protection of homosexuality by the state: If the individual's sexual life is to be protected, the state must favor the homosexual over the Puritan who would repress him or her. I believe this reading is true to Nagel's understanding of the role of law and morality, as well as to his insistence that some division between the private and the public must be legally protected. This insistence on the limit of equality in the name of partiality obviously differs from the traditional rationalist view, which argues that the government must remain neutral to all forms of life. Under this conception of neutrality, the very idea of partiality to certain forms of life would be suspect because it would necessitate that the government evaluate which form of life was better. Further, such an evaluation would be condemned because it logically implicates something like a conception of the Good in order to ethically, legally, and politically affirm which form of life is better. Nagel's recent work attempts to negotiate this impasse between the Right and the Good by asking, How do we rationally decide which forms of life and moral commitments the government can be partial to without altogether undermining a concept of normative legitimacy as the basis of a legal system?

Nagel's concept of reasonableness helps us to answer that question without introducing a strong conception of the Good in the sense, for example of Aristotle or his modern interpreter, Alasdair MacIntyre. Under Nagel's conception of reasonableness, we weigh the extent of the wrong and the degree of the suffering of competing parties, each of whom represents a different moral commitment, against one another. Who, following the previous example, is wronged more profoundly and suffers more intensely, the homosexual who is repressed or the puritan who believes that homosexuality is evil and must be repressed? This conception of reasonableness allows us as moral agents and, more importantly, the law and the state to decide between competing moral visions when there is clearly no public consensus on the issues involved. But it also obviously allows government "partiality" to certain groups over others. It is evident, then, that the very idea of partiality allows certain questions of the good life to be legally addressed as we attempt to determine what is legitimate partiality. Yes, legitimacy also implies that partiality not be left to the latest whim of the community. But even so, the very notion of partiality denies the rigorous separation of questions of the good life from questions of justice.

To summarize, American liberal analytic jurisprudence has long since moved away from a rigid commitment to a de-ontological theory of the Right which, if strictly interpreted, would prevent "substantive" questions on what kinds of forms of life should be protected and even promoted from being considered as questions of justice. This move has implications for the debate between the "new communitarians" and the "liberals," as well as for the discussion between liberals and critical theorists. The "new communitarian" argument against liberal analytic jurisprudence assumes that this position rests on an abstract conception of Right which in turn implies a view of the person which supposedly has nothing to do with one's concrete self as situated in a community.[6] The argument then proceeds to challenge the divide between the Right and the Good because this very separation implies the abstract view of the person. Instead of abstract theories of the Right, the new communitarians would have us rely on the embodied, concrete norms of our actual communities to guide us in our legal and political commitments and disputes. But once we understand the direction that analytic jurisprudence has taken, we can also see that, at least as it has been defined, the debate between the "new communitarians" and the liberals, understood to rest on the traditional distinction between the Right and the Good, is rendered moot. In other words, legal scholars should no longer pit an appeal to tradition-constituted inquiry,[7] which defines the Good against a de-ontological analysis which rigorously separates Justice from the Good. They need no longer search for *pure* procedures assumed to be just, as long as the proper procedures for debate are in place, precisely because they leave substantive questions, including substantive rights, to the arena of politics. Instead, they should ask what is a legally *legitimate* tradition and community, a question that cannot be *absolutely* separated from certain further questions such as what is morally acceptable and which forms of life would we like to see promoted in our community. In Nagel's language the question of justice can no longer be definitively separated from a discussion about which forms of life we should affirm through partiality.

There is also no doubt, however, that both Nagel's understanding of reasonableness and the Rawlsian conception of the political value of tolerance do put certain limits on *mythos*, particularly if *mythos* is understood to include religious commitments that are allowed to dominate the state legislative process unchecked by legal restriction based on the ideal of public reason. Rawls' own thinking on what constitutes public reason is complicated indeed. For now, I am using public reason in the very simple sense that the "religious" or moral commitments of individuals and groups must be examined by other criteria than the current norms and myths of a particular community. It may well be the case that a community believes in the myth that homosexuality is "evil." Such a myth is often bolstered by an appeal to God. The ideal of public reason serves the purpose of helping us to decide when such myths illegitimately threaten to suppress individual rights and legitimate group experimentations. The word "legitimate" implies the institutionalization of minimal normative standards which prevent a community from degenerating into violence against groups or individuals, such as homosexuals and women, who are not defined by the community's myths as fully "human," and, thus, as "true" participants in the community. "Constitutional essentials" in Rawls serve the exact purpose of providing the minimal normative standard both for legal legitimacy and for the protection of the community from its own prejudices.

But the emphasis on tolerance also denies that myths can be completely cleansed from political and even legal life, which is the second difference between the thinkers of analytic jurisprudence and Habermas' conception of an enlightened political and legal order which separates myth from political and legal life (if not from social life).[8] Indeed, the very emphasis on *tolerance* implies that different myths, religious commitments and moral beliefs are unavoidable and inevitably continue to maintain a hold on human beings. Isolating the notion of a tolerance of difference, in other words, would not be necessary if various groups did not cling so stubbornly to intolerant ideologies—for example, combative, fundamentalist religions. In a country such as the United States, where a substantial proportion of the population are fundamentalist Christians struggling for the incorporation of their religious views into political life, it would be difficult to argue that we have achieved anything close to complete secularization. Rawls, too, in his latest writing, realizes just how far we are from the completed process of secularization in politics and even in law.

This realization and its corresponding emphasis on tolerance may well explain why there has been little or no discussion of historical periodization within analytic jurisprudence. Rather than focus on the ideals of modernity, there has instead been a re-envisioning of the ideals understood to be inherent in constitutional government. Clearly there are shared presuppositions between analytic jurisprudence and the thinkers of modernity such as Jürgen Habermas.[9] These presuppositions obviously include an emphasis on public reason and some theoretical elaboration of minimal conditions of justice that justifies a limit on communitarian myths. Given these shared presuppositions, a number of thinkers influenced by Habermas stress his relevance to debates within American jurisprudence.[10]

Critics of "postmodernity" like Habermas himself have not realized that these same presuppositions are shared by the writers who have been lumped together under the tag "postmodern." On the other hand, due to the clichés that have come to be associated with deconstruction, the usefulness of deconstruction to a conception of a legitimate legal and political order has been dismissed.[11] Jacques Derrida has recently made his position clear in his statement that "nothing seems . . . less outdated than the classical emancipatory ideal."[12] He has also insisted on the centrality of public reason in the university system as a guard against one of the focal myths of modernity. That myth, as he understands it, elevates technology, and with it instrumental rationality, to the position of a new God. And on the issue of divergent lifestyles, even his critics[13] recognize that there is an emphasis in Derrida's writing on tolerance of difference. Furthermore, as we will see in the second chapter of this book, he is certainly suspicious on ethical grounds of communitarianism, if the "new" communitarianism is understood, that is, to resolve ethical, political, and legal questions of the day by invoking the current conventions of a given society.

On the whole, critics of postmodernity have overlooked the ethical and political affinity of Derrida's writing with recent, liberal analytic jurisprudence. I use "affinity" deliberately; there are also significant differences between the writers of liberal analytic jurisprudence and the thinkers labeled as "postmodern." For now, however, I want only to note that this insistence on shared presuppositions would seem strange, indeed, to Derrida's critics who accuse "deconstruction" of being unable to help us *in any way* to think concretely about justice, law, and politics.[14]

The error of "deconstruction," so the argument goes, is to remain mistakenly caught up in the attempt to philosophically spell out the "constitution and institution of politics in Western culture"[15] prior to actual politics. This error then, is responsible for Derrida's emphasis on a quasi-transcendental analysis rather than on the empirical research necessary for resolving social debates on the level of actual politics.[16] Instead of completely disagreeing with this interpretation of "deconstruction," I will show why the continuing emphasis on a quasi-transcendental analysis is crucial to justice and, more specifically, to a conception of justice that promotes, not just allows, legal transformation. Throughout this book, I will suggest that the central difference between liberal analytic jurisprudence and deconstruction lies in their divergent opinions on the desirability and possibility of thoroughgoing social and legal transformation. This difference turns on what I will describe as the unerasable moment of utopianism which is inherent in "deconstruction" and in the writing of Emmanuel Levinas on the ethical relation. The liberals such as Rawls and Nagel are undoubtedly more suspicious of utopianism.

But this difference certainly does not imply the appropriateness of the identification of "postmodern" thinkers with the rejection of the most basic liberal presuppositions. This set of rejections has been repeated only too often: the rejection of public reason, universal ideals of justice, and the rule of law, as well as the suspicion of all forms of social stabilization, even when couched in terms of community ideals. I have already suggested that Derrida himself has explicitly endorsed the traditional, emancipatory ideals he purportedly rejects. So these rejections certainly do not follow from what he writes. Of course, the more profound criticism proposes that in spite of his political commitments, Derrida's philosophical enterprise actually contradicts the very emancipatory ideals he would like to support. Levinas' work is less frequently attacked because it is less well known to Derrida's critics. In answer to these critics, I will explore how

Derrida's specific deconstructionist interventions, and deconstruction more generally, once it is reconceived as the philosophy of the limit, are the expression of an ethical positioning perfectly consistent with his stated political convictions. But in a more comprehensive manner, I will also argue that it is the intersection of the writings of Jacques Derrida, Jacques Lacan, and Emmanuel Levinas that provides us with the "new" ethical configuration I portray in this book, that is, an ethical configuration new in its difference from both the critical social theory of Jürgen Habermas and the analytic jurisprudence of Nagel and Rawls.

But let me return to why I call this intersection an ethical configuration. Several years ago, I argued that the relation between the "modern" and the "postmodern" could be understood as a constellation, borrowing the phrase from Theodor Adorno. I will discuss in detail Adorno's metaphor and its ethical significance in the first chapter of this book. Now, however, looking back over this argument, I would like to suggest that there are difficulties with the transferring of Adorno's and certainly of Walter Benjamin's metaphor of constellation to the context of the debate over the relationship between the "modern" and "postmodern." Constellation is obviously a term borrowed from astrology. The relevance of its origin lies in the fact that the clustering of stars into a constellation allows some access to the thing itself, the stellar bodies; in other words, the constellations constructed by the astrologer from without, like words in language, allow us to decipher the realm of things in their historical relations, that is, the constellations which they bear within themselves. Further, a constellation is not constructed or designated by a set of normative ideals or their supposed rejection; thus, it stands outside of the debate over how historical periods are defined in terms of changes within the realms of justice, law, and politics.

In Adorno, as we will see in the first chapter, the metaphor of the constellation has specific ethical content. To briefly summarize here: Adorno's metaphor of constellation is associated with the ethical position which critiques idealism for smothering the object in a conceptual apparatus. Put differently, constellation allows one to decipher the truth of the object without imposing an outside definition. Feminist literature, for example, frequently relies on constellations as means of deciphering women's experience as objects of masculine desire in such a way as to reveal a truth behind that experience which differs from the definitions generally imposed on women's experience by the gender hierarchy.[17] Constellations, in other words, allow the experiences of women to be decoded.

But historical periods are not just deciphered, they are always in part constructed. As we have seen in the debates over what constitutes the "modern" and the "postmodern," these categories are also normatively constructed. Consequently, the metaphor of the constellation is problematic in the context of this debate since its power relies on the assumption that the object to be deciphered is already there prior to the decipherment, that is, it cannot account for the normative intervention of the debators themselves. As a result, I have rejected my earlier formulation.

In fact, there are two additional reasons to be suspicious of this attempt to describe the continuity of the "modern" and the "postmodern" via the metaphor of the constellation. I have suggested already that the metaphor of the constellation cannot adequately account for the constructedness of the attempt to designate historical periods. Even if one assumes that there is no rigid divide between the "modern" and the "postmodern" and, therefore, that the best way to challenge the rigid divide would be to somehow show the connection, this attempt still implies an acceptance of historical periodization. Yet, if there is one theme that unites Derrida and Levinas, it is the rejection of the belief that there exist normative or descriptive criteria that can be used to successfully distinguish historical periods one from another, particularly if this periodization is teleological in form. This rejection does not mean that their work is ahistorical, or that they deny the possibility of transformation. Things can and do change; they merely question a view which couches change in terms of rigid, historical periodization. The rejection of periodization implies a challenge to a teleological conception of history that has remained implicit in the debate; for even when the form of the debate attempts to show the connection between modern and postmodern, this attempt still implies the designation of historical periods. For a theorist of modernity such as Habermas, on the other hand, the need to distinguish between periods is crucial if one is to adequately defend what is essential to an enlightened political order. The emphasis is not on connection but on distinction. For example, as I have already suggested, the distinction between the premodern and the modern is thought to rest on the teleological development from *mythos* to *logos*. But whether or not connection or distinction is emphasized, the tendency in the debate has been to constitute the postmodern in terms that I reject.

It is undoubtedly the case that the writers I discuss in this book—Jacques Derrida, Emmanuel Levinas, and Jacques Lacan—reject the idea that the movement from *mythos* to *logos* has been or *can* be completed. Indeed, they have ethically critiqued the view that this move has been completed on the grounds that this view is itself mythical. I begin the book with a discussion of Theodor Adorno precisely because he was perhaps the first thinker to expose the Enlightenment, understood to represent the completed move from *mythos* to *logos,* as itself a myth. This myth is dangerous from an ethical standpoint because it denies its own mythical structure, parading as the universal truth of *mankind* and, thus, foreclosing in advance the very legitimacy of its challengers. In both Adorno and Derrida, the exposure of myth—and, in Derrida's case in particular, the exposure of the mythological structure of the origin of legal authority—is itself ethically inspired because it seeks to portray the danger of upholding current ideals as unshakable truth. It is important to note that the argument that the movement from *mythos* to *logos* cannot be completed, even if it accepts that all myths are not repressive—I have argued that myth is a powerful *critical* tool in feminist theory[18]—does not endorse *mythos* rather than *logos*. It is not a retreat into what is designated by teleological conceptions of history as the premodern.

However, given the challenge to this selfsame teleology, the very usefulness of the term "postmodern" is also called into question—one reason, of course, why I believe it is acceptable to begin this book with Adorno, even if Adorno's work clearly "predates" the work of the writers who are labeled "postmodern." Worse yet, the argument over whether or not one should endorse the "modern" or the "postmodern" is often a poor excuse within current debates for academic mudslinging. These "code-words," which overwrite important moral, ethical, and legal disputes, are by now worn out from overuse. At this point, they function primarily to obscure subtle, theoretical differences between disputants and, therefore, do not help *enlighten* us about the ethical and political stakes in the debate. There is, then, a rhetorical reason for questioning the continuing usage of these terms.

But does that mean that there is no content to what has come to be called the "postmodern"? Is there nothing to it except academic haggling? The answer, I think, is no. This leads me to my justification for reformulating the intersection between Derrida, Lacan, and Levinas as an ethical configuration and rejecting my earlier formulation of the relation between the modern and the postmodern as a constellation. I want to suggest that the "postmodern" should be understood as an allegory and that, as such, it represents an ethical insistence on the limit to "positive" descriptions of the principles of modernity long-elaborated as the "last word" on "truth," "justice," "rightness," etc. I will return in the Conclusion to why I have relabeled deconstruction as the philosophy of the limit. This definition of the postmodern as an allegory which expresses the desire for a beyond to the current definition of Enlightenment ideals explains why I begin with Adorno, whose critique of all forms of positivism is clearly the forerunner of "postmodern" writings. Although in the Conclusion I will stress the difference between Adorno and the ethical configuration I evoke in this book, his contribution must be noted.

This emphasis on the limit and, as we will see, on the portrayal of justice as aporia is crucial to these marginalized groups whose well-being and very lives may depend on legal transformation. Thus, it is not a coincidence that the cases I discuss in order to demonstrate the legal power of the ethical configuration I evoke involve the rights of women and of homosexuals. Indeed, Jacques Lacan is included as a contributor to this ethical configuration precisely because an aspect of its "newness" lies in its emphasis on psychosexual dynamics and, more specifically, on the crucial importance of questions of sexual difference to problems of justice and legal interpretation. One *particular* formulation of the public/private distinction is thus challenged so as to allow questions of the gender hierarchy as they relate to women and to homosexuals to be noticed by the legal system. At the same time, I certainly do not reject the centrality of the distinction itself to a legitimate legal system.

Because I have advocated that the "postmodern" is an allegory, we can now understand yet another dimension of my choice of the word "configuration." An allegory necessarily involves figures and figurations, in this case, that depict the limit of institutionalized meaning and established communitarian norms. For example, in chapter 3, I have painted Derrida's own ethical positioning using the figure of the *Chiffonnier*. To summarize, then, I portray a configuration which gives body to the allegory of the ethical limit on any "positive" normative description of what constitutes modernity. Even if this "limit" is not to be understood as a "new" historical period, even if the ethical configuration I offer cannot be rigidly separated from the "modern," it can still help us think about justice and legal interpretation differently from the conceptions that have dominated analytic jurisprudence and critical social theory. As we will see, for marginalized groups, this is a difference that makes a difference. But let me turn now to the portrayal of the intersection of Derrida, Lacan, and Levinas as an ethical configuration that has important implications for the definition of justice and for a concept of legal interpretation.

1

The Ethical Message
of Negative Dialectics

> The need to let suffering speak
> is the condition of all truth.
>
> —Theodor Adorno, Negative Dialectics

1. Introduction

In *Negative Dialectics,* Adorno critiques Hegel for betraying the most radical implications of his own dialectic in the name of a comprehensive, encircling totality. This critique, the ethical dimension of which I hope to reveal, gestures toward a deconstruction, which is nevertheless an appropriation, of Schopenhauer's ethic of pity. In referring to Adorno's project, I use the word "ethical" deliberately. Adorno's suspicion of the normalizing effect inherent in the generalization of one behavioral system of "rules" led him away from the attempt to *determine* a morality and toward a more properly ethical conception of the relationship with the Other. For my purposes, "morality" designates any attempt to spell out how one *determines* a "right way to behave," behavioral norms which, once determined, can be translated into a system of rules. The ethical relation, a term which I contrast with morality, focuses instead on the kind of person one must become in order to develop a nonviolative relationship to the Other. The concern of the ethical relation, in other words, is a way of being in the world that spans divergent value systems and allows us to criticize the repressive aspects of competing moral systems

In his critique of Kant, for example, Adorno addresses the mode of subjection he associates with the Kantian subject of morality. He critiques the kind of person we are called upon to become if we are to do our moral duty under his own *interpretation* of Kant's categorical imperative. Like the early Hegel, Adorno is concerned with the ethical relationship in general. Adorno seeks to uncover just how one engages with the other in a nonviolative manner so that the Hegelian aspiration to reciprocal symmetry and mutual codetermination can be achieved. He argues that a truly nonviolative relationship to the other is foiled by what he calls the dialectic of Enlightenment which, for him, subsumes the Kantian theory of the subject of morality.

In the story that Adorno tells in *Negative Dialectics,*[1] the Kantian subject, as a being of the flesh, falls prey to the endless striving to subjugate his own impulses and thus to secure the possibility of moral action. Reason is geared solely to the preservation of the subject, equated here with consciousness; because of Kant's separation of consciousness from the flesh, the subject is pitted against the object, which includes that aspect of the subject conceived empirically. Conceived in this way, the subject-object relationship necessarily gives rise to the master-slave dialectic. The master-slave dialectic is played out in our relations to nature, taken here to mean both against the external world of things, and against our internal "nature" as physical, sexual beings. Ultimately, the master-slave dialectic takes its toll. The thinking subject's striving for mastery turns against itself. The part of our humanness that is "natural"—sexual desire, our longing for warmth and comfort—succumbs to a rationality whose mission is to drive into submission an essential part of what we are. The subject itself becomes objectified, an object among other objects. Relations between human beings degenerate into manipulative interaction, the goal of which is to master the other. Relations of reciprocal symmetry and mutual co-determination, in Hegel's sense, are thwarted, if not completely destroyed.

As I hope to show, Adorno makes the point that without the recovery of a playful innocence achieved through the reconnection with the Other in oneself, one cannot become a human being capable of nonviolative relations to the Other. In this sense, his dialectic of "natural" history is "directive"; it calls on us to "be" differently in our relationship to the Other. The emphasis on the "natural," desiring subject, the importance in Adorno's theory of the dissolution of rigid ego dictates, the suspicion of the normalizing impulse in the call to duty, are anti-Kantian, at least on the traditional reading of Kant; but these emphases do not make Adorno's message anti-ethical. Adorno denies that the ethical must be based on the will to limitation and control rather than on the desire for fulfillment. He holds, rather, that the will to limitation, in the call to do one's duty, itself replicates the master-slave dialectic and eventually undermines the possibility of a nonrepressive basis for Kant's own understanding of the importance of goodwill in relations to others.[2]

The young Hegel was also specifically concerned with the "repressive" aspects of Kantian morality and, more generally, with the havoc unleashed by the Enlightenment's radical divide between subject and object, mind and nature, and body and soul. Hegel's system aims to reveal the state of reconciliation underlying a social fabric violently torn asunder. Adorno challenges Hegel on the grounds that Hegel's system turns against the very dialectical reciprocity and mutual codetermination he sought to reveal as the truth of reality. According to Adorno, Hegel's system replicates the selfsame violent relationship to the Other which it purports to overcome. Hegelianism becomes a form of imperialism over the object. Adorno rebels against Hegel's ontological identification of meaning and being as an imposed unity. Nonidentity denies that a concept is ever fully adequate to its object. Yet Adorno remains an immanent critic of Hegelianism.

By taking Adorno's Hegelianism seriously we can win back a degree of freedom within Adorno's own categories. Without keeping his Hegelianism in mind, it is all too easy to misinterpret Adorno's "philosophy of redemption" and his dialectic of reconciliation in such a way as to miss its ethical aspiration. If we consider Adorno's statement that "the idea of reconcilement forbids the positive positing of reconcilement as a concept"[3] within the context of his attempt to put Hegel's categories in motion from the inside, we can decipher what Adorno means and does not mean by that statement. As I have already suggested, Adorno argues that the Hegelian reconciliation of the dichotomies in a totalizing system turns against the mutual codetermination Hegel purports to show as the truth of all reality. In Hegel's *Logic,* the transcendental categories such as Being and Essence are unfolded in their reciprocal determinations against what they are not—to be something determinate is to be something in distinction to what it is not. The determinations of the categories ultimately are uncovered as reciprocally codetermined in the unfolding of the Absolute Idea. The deconstruction of the philosophy of substance and of constituted essences in the *Logic* shows us how the boundaries which give us the appearance of the existence of atomic entities yield to the reality of mutual codetermination, the dialectical permeation of purportedly opposite categories. The philosophy of substance which asserts that an entity can be understood on its own is exposed as a fallacy. Instead, the relata are shown to be internally interrelated, first negatively, in their contrastive relationship with that which yields their self-definition, and then "positively," as the "belonging together" in and through which the relata become what they are.

The gathering together of the multifold in the logos culminates in the self-recognition of Reason in Being. The awareness that the self-conscious subject comes home in and through the relationship to otherness is what Michael Theneuissen has called "communicative freedom." Communicative freedom is the truth of the belonging together of the relata. Communicative freedom, in other words, is the *coincidence* of love and freedom in which "one part experiences the other not as boundary but as the condition for its own realization."[4] Under the circumstances of communicative freedom "reality would have found its substantive 'truth' and thus become fully real . . . everything would be related to such an extent that the relata would not retain their separateness."[5] Under Theunissen's interpretation, which is also the one I adopt, the full integration of the relata is what Hegel means by Absolute Knowledge or "self-recognition in absolute otherness."

For Adorno, communicative freedom cannot be thought of as the unification of the relata into a comprehensive totality without violating the coincidence of love and freedom. The "belonging together" of the relata in conditions of freedom can only be realized if the difference from the Other is maintained in a dialectical interaction that does not yield to the ontological unity of meaning and being. Hegel's tendency to turn *Geist* into a deified subjectivity undermines the freedom to be in a relation of reciprocity to otherness because the status of the Other as

Other is ultimately denied. Yet "communicative freedom" is not simply rejected, it is redefined within Adorno's deconstruction of the truth of interrelatedness as the *Geist* that encompasses both self and other. For Adorno, Hegel's *Logic* exhibits a tension between his brilliantly executed deconstruction of the metaphysics of substances (a perspective marked by the indifference and unrelatedness of elements) and the metaphysics of constituted essences (a perspective marked by the subordination of elements to dominant categories), on the one hand, and his tendency to reintroduce substance in the form of a reified Spirit, the imposed unity of subject and object, on the other. As Adorno remarks, "The reconciled state would not be the philosophical imperialism of annexing the alien, if the proximity it is granted remains what is distant and beyond the heterogeneous and beyond that which is one's own."[6]

"Reconciliation," as I will use the term in this essay, is Adorno's redefinition of communicative freedom as the state beyond the heterogeneous as absolute otherness and beyond that which is captured by the Hegelian Concept. Reconciliation is the art of disunion that allows things to exist in their difference and in their affinity. Adorno, then, is a philosopher of reconciliation in a very specific sense. His defense of a reconciled state is presented in the name of the plural and of the different. Relations of reciprocal symmetry can only come into existence if the Other remains unassimilated. Once the unification of the relata into a comprehensive totality can no longer be conceptualized as the Concept returning to itself in an eternal present, the ideal of reconciliation can be shown or disclosed but not conceptualized.

The "philosophy of redemption" is the counterpole to Adorno's assertion that "the whole is false."[7] The "normative standard" of communicative freedom cannot be conceptualized as the truth of an already-achieved reality. The ideal's critical power lies precisely in its capacity to reveal the world as distorted and indigent in comparison with the reconciled state. It should be emphasized, however, that Adorno in *Negative Dialectics* denies that we can conceive of reconciliation; but this denial is not the same as Schopenhauer's insistence on the transcendental disjuncture between reality and utopia. That disjuncture renders the dream of reconciliation as an illusion of the desiring individual, an illusion that those who pierce the veil of Maya leave behind. Schopenhauer's message is clear: we can only find peace by forsaking the futile striving of those who seek to be at home in the world. Adorno's aspiration is the opposite. In his view it is only by developing perspectives which illuminate our state of homelessness that we can begin to glimpse through the cracks and the crevices what it would be to be at home in the world. These redemptive perspectives displace and estrange the world so that we are made aware that we are in exile. This exercise, however, is not intended simply to teach us to forsake the world. Through the development of redemptive perspectives we can resist "consummate negativity" without, on the other hand, perpetuating the myth of the ever-the-same, or, put in popular language, the myth that there is "nothing new under the sun." Determinate negation, in Adorno, becomes the form in which every claim to identity conceals its non-identity: the illusion of identity is destroyed, and with it the so-called realist perspective[8] which assumes that social life cannot be radically transformed. According to Adorno, in a corrupt world one can only teach the good life through immanent critique of the form of moralistic self-righteous subjectivity itself. Yet in his dedication to *Minima Moralia,* Adorno nevertheless justifies his reliance on aphorisms against Hegel's own dismissive gesture toward them precisely because aphorisms allow for the expression of subjectivity, even if that subjectivity takes on the voice of the isolated individual.

> In his relation to the subject Hegel does not respect the demand that he otherwise passionately upholds: to be in the matter and not always beyond it, or to penetrate into the innermost content of the matter. As today the subject is vanishing, aphorisms take upon themselves the duty to consider the evanescent itself as essential. They insist in opposition to Hegel's practice and yet in accordance with his thought on negativity: "the life of the mind only attains its truth when discovering itself in absolute desolation."[9]

The unalleviated consciousness of negativity holds fast to the possibility of a different future. As Adorno remarks, "What would happiness be that was not measured by the immeasurable grief at what is."[10] He is in earnest when he argues that his melancholy science should be placed in the region of philosophy devoted to the teaching of the good life.

I have already indicated that there are several ethical dimensions in Adorno's work. Each can be understood as an aspect of the critique of totality on which negative dialectics is premised. The first is the revelation of the "more-than-this" in nonidentity. The presentation of the "more-than-this" serves as a corrective to realist and conventionalist ethics with their shared impulse to enclose us in our form of life or language game. Adorno appeals to nonidentity to undermine what I call the ideology of lesser expectations. The second dimension lies in the redefinition of communicative freedom as the content of the utopian vision of reconciliation. The third is expressed in the critique of the Kantian subject of morality. For Adorno, a moral subject which does not know itself as a desiring, natural being will not recover the compassion for others that can serve as a non-repressive basis for moral intuition and, more specifically, of the goodwill. The critique of the Kantian subject of ethics emerges from the dialectic of natural history. To separate the dimensions of Adorno's message in the way I have just done is admittedly artificial, but it is necessary to decode his own ethical message.

The redefinition of communicative freedom, the dialectic of natural history, and the unleashing of difference in identity are ways of approaching Adorno's immanent critique of Hegel's *Logic*. They are, if you like, different emphases in the unfolding of the immanent critique, different ways of elaborating negative dialectics. My justification for artificially separating the dimensions is strategic; the separation helps us to distinguish Adorno's ethical message. Once we remark the ethical message of Adorno's negative dialectics, we can read his commentaries on the subject and on instrumental rationality, as well as his critique of common sense as tendering a powerful warning. This warning does not, however, degenerate into a harbinger of inevitable disaster; in other words, Adorno does not disparage the very idea of ethical mediation as simply more of the same. It should not be forgotten that for Adorno "he who dies in despair has lived his life in vain."[11]

The Reconstellation of Hegelian Categories

Nonidentity: The Critique of Totality

Adorno brushes aside the accusation that his negative dialectics is just one more replay of a tired and outdated left-Hegelianism with the following remark:

> The fact that history has rolled over certain positions will be respected as a verdict on their truth content only by those who agree with Schiller that "world history is the world tribunal." What has been cast aside but not absorbed theoretically will often yield its truth content only later.[12]

The unleashing of the "truth" of Hegelianism allows Adorno to show that the Hegelian "system was the source of Hegel's dialectics, not its measure."[13] Indeed, according to Adorno, the system turns against itself, choking off the freedom of dialectical movement by the self-containment of the Concept. Once freed from the circle of identification—the closed circle of the infinite—dialectics implies nonidentity between concept and thing. Nonidentity, in other words, is dialectics taken all the way down. For Adorno, Hegel's central error lies in his attempt to recuperate negativity in the Concept self-consciously returned to itself. This attempt leads Hegel to envelope otherness in an all-encompassing subjectivity in spite of himself. All his statements to the contrary notwithstanding, Hegel left the subject's primacy over the object unchallenged. It is disguised merely by the semi-theological "spirit" within its indelible memories of individual subjectivity.[14]

By reifying *Geist* into a deified subjectivity, Hegel's idealism involves an "imperialism" of the subject over the object, an imperialism which negates the very possibility of reconcilement that it purports to reveal.

> In Hegel there was a coincidence of identity and positivity; the inclusion of all-identical and objective things in a subjectivity expanded and exalted into an absolute spirit was to effect reconcilement. On the other hand, the force of the entirety that works in every definition is not simply its negation: that force is itself the negative, the untrue. The philosophy of the absolute and total subject is a particular one. The inherent reversibility of the identity thesis counteracts the principle of its spirit. If entity can be totally derived from that spirit, the spirit is doomed to resemble the mere entity it means to contradict; otherwise spirit and entity would not go together. It is precisely the insatiable identity principle that perpetuates antagonism by suppressing contradiction. What tolerates nothing that is not itself thwarts the reconcilement for which it mistakes itself.[15]

The attempt to achieve pure self-recognition in absolute otherness, in other words, violates the Other by denying its otherness to the Concept. Without the closure of the circle, the Concept can no longer fully incorporate objectivity as its own expression. The object, in other words, escapes ownership in its nonidentity with the Concept. This failure to achieve reconcilement becomes "the motor of disenchantment"—what Hegel called the "highway of despair"—which unleashes the dialectic previously rigidified in the frozen dance of the Concept returning to itself in an eternal present. Thought, confronted with its inability to achieve supremacy, turns against itself. The Hegelian system, according to Adorno, carries within it the seeds of its own destruction as system.

> By negating the concept of the limit and theoretically assuring itself that there always remains something outside, dynamics also tends to disarm its own product, the system.[16]

The "truth" is in the confrontation, in the nonidentity between concept and object. The "truth," in other words, is not to be found in the object, nor in the form of thought of the object, nor in the unity of subject and object in the Concept. The object can neither be grasped in its entirety by the Concept nor can it be known in its immediacy. Adorno took to heart the Hegelian insight into the inevitable conceptual mediation of immediacy. Yet, because of his refusal to complete experience in an infinite which totalizes its contents, he interjects a constitutive outside that is foreign to the Spirit of Hegel's absolute idealism. "The circle of identification—which in the end always identifies itself alone—was drawn by a thinking that tolerates nothing outside of it."[17]

The Hegelian system, as a result, is undermined by the very insight into the unfolding of negativity which is its hallmark. The nonidentity inherent in absolute identification turns against itself. Negativity is the escaped otherness, uncovered by "the logic of disintegration." The "truth" of negativity is "the negative reaction on the part of the knowledge that penetrates the object—in other words, extinguished the appearance of the object being directly as it is."[18] Adorno's materialism, with its recognition of the constitutive outside, reinstates the Hegelian category of essence not as "background world" but as the non-identity inherent in the limits of thought and the deconstruction of totality.

> [E]ssence passes into that which lies concealed beneath the facade of immediacy, of supposed facts, and which makes them as they are. It comes to be the law of doom. Thus far obeyed by history . . . it can be recognized only by the contradiction between what things are and what they claim to be.[19]

To deny essence altogether would be to side with appearance as if things were really what they are claimed to be within any current conventional system of definition. Siding with appearance would reinscribe identity thinking. The reality of the thing would be found to be fully expressed in its concept. For Adorno, essence is expressed as the concept of negativity that makes the world the way it is, but negativity expressed as "essence" can only be known indirectly through the nonidentity of subject and object; negativity is not to be hypostatized as absolute Other.

We can now summarize the difference between Adorno's and Hegel's understanding of negativity. For Hegel, negativity as a determining relation to the Other ultimately is explained as the inevitable incompleteness of brute entities. Negativity, in other words, is the expression of an infinite, in contradiction with the finite contents in and through which it is embodied. For Adorno, however, the dialectic proceeds by way of the critique of a totalizing infinite. Adorno takes seriously Hegel's insight that finite reality is not adequate to its concept. Indeed it is precisely the inadequacy of finitude to its concept that releases Adorno's negative dialectics. Whereas Hegel's dialectic in the *Logic* unfolds through the incompleteness of the categories such as Being and Essence until the progression culminates in the self-reflection of the Absolute Idea, Adorno's immanent critique cancels the privilege of "thinking" by its uncovering of difference in identity.

Nevertheless, negative dialectics is not true for all time. It is not another first principle. To make negative dialectics another first principle would be to hypostatize negativity in the exact way Adorno warns against. For Adorno, then, negative dialectics is not a method; nor is it simply material reality, as if material reality in its contradictoriness could be presented to us without mediation through concepts. Negative dialectics is instead the "truth" of an unreconciled reality, or antagonistic entirety, to be found in "the cogitative confrontation of concept and thing."

> To proceed dialectically means to think in contradictions, for the sake of the contradiction once experienced in the thing, and against that contradiction. A contradiction in reality is a contradiction against reality.[20]

The conditions in which negativity can be overcome are those of a reconciled world—a world which can be brought into being only if the antagonistic entirety is itself negated. Negative dialectics awaits its decline in a redeemed world.

> Regarding the concrete utopian possibility, dialectics is the ontology of the wrong state of things. The right state of things would be free of it.[21]

There is an ambivalence in Adorno's use of the expression "antagonistic entirety." Adorno seems to reintroduce the concept of totality as understood within a negative dialectic of history. Such a view of totality, however, takes a different shape from the absolute infinite that totalizes its contents. Robert Neville has succinctly summarized the form of totality in Hegel's negative dialectic of history:

> If *Geist* can be modeled on the negative dialectic of history, then we have a new opportunity to address the question of the determinateness of the totality. We may say that the transcending state is determinate with respect to the stage

it transcends precisely in those respects in which it negates the possibility of the transcended stage and carrying its bit along transformed by the determinate actuality of the later stage. The actuality of the moment then is determinate either with respect to a possibility that it excluded but with respect to a past actuality that it negates and subsumes. There may well be many elements in the moment which are not determinate either with respect to what is rational in the moment itself. But they might become determinate when the moment itself is totalized and negated by its own executioner.[22]

Totality, in the Hegelian dialectic of history, "has reason as a selective principle. Reason which proceeds with necessity distinguishes within a situation between the truly actual and the adventitious."[23] In Adorno's musings on Walter Benjamin's statement that "hope is only for the hopeless," however, it becomes clear that Adorno also rejects totality as a selection principle to distinguish what is crucial to the unfolding of Reason. Reason as a selection principle denies certain groups, peoples, and nations "actuality," on the grounds that they are incidental to the narrative of reason in history. By so doing it violates them, demonstrating once again that Hegel's unifying spirit is a coercive force. In its worst form, Hegel's unifying spirit becomes a "justification" for the imperialism of the West. The dialectic—so the story goes—proceeded in the way it did because it is only in the history of the West that Reason finds its adequate expression.[24] Adorno uses his deconstruction of the totality inherent in Hegel's dialectic of history to introduce *categorical* novelty and to expose the ethnocentricity of Hegel's own unfolding of the history of Reason. In the standard interpretation of Hegel, there is no categorical novelty, only categorical "improvement," of what has already been achieved. Adorno insists on the possibility of a future, a future in which the return of the negated would modulate the established categories allowing for the creation of what is truly new. The ephemeral nature of thought allows for the rising of the *new*, of that which was excluded from the grasp of the Concept or pushed out by the pressure of the Concept's progression. The eternal present is shattered on the bodies of those who were tossed aside in the Concept's development.

Why does Adorno proceed through negative dialectics to introduce the "truly" new and the possibility of categorical novelty from within the deconstruction of Hegel's own system? Adorno and Hegel both consider the philosophy of reflection philosophically false and ethically a distortion of relations of reciprocal symmetry. Adorno, in other words, forthrightly argues that he accepts the most lasting contribution of Hegel's *Logic*—the insight that identity is constituted in and through otherness. Otherness can no longer be understood as an external relation in which a self-identified subject stands over and against the object only to find itself reflected there.

The individual existence does not coincide with its cover concept of existence at large but neither is it impenetrable, another last thing against which cognition

> knocks its head in vain. The most enduring result of Hegelian logic is that the individual is not flatly for himself. In himself he is the otherness and linked with others.[25]

In the philosophy of reflection, on the other hand, the "I" sees itself reflected in the other but does not see the other looking back. The other is reduced to a mirror for oneself. Hegel's absolute knowledge, self-recognition in absolute otherness, is the overcoming of the mirror stage, the recognition of the reciprocity of self-consciousness. But for Adorno, the *experience* of interrelatedness in an antagonistic entirety is one of domination and not of communicative freedom. The "normative standard" of a reconciled condition awaits us; it has not been realized in the horizon of absolute knowledge. But, as already suggested, in Adorno the dialectic no longer defeats the philosophy of reflection through the identity of identity and nonidentity as it does in Hegel, but rather the dialectic proceeds through the "nonidentity" in identity. The shift denies that "the negation of the negation"—the "positive" reconstitution of an identity inclusive of otherness—is a possible occurrence within thought, even if it is accomplished in the name of Spirit, which is purportedly the revelation of the truth of the things themselves. It is precisely this identification of things and the Concept that Adorno denies as an accomplished "fact."

The positive, which Adorno understands in Hegel to ultimately overcome negation, has more than its name in common with the positivity Hegel fought in his youth. To equate the negation of the negation with positivity is the quintessence of the politics of identity for Adorno.[26] According to Adorno, Hegel's recuperation of the negative lends legitimacy to the current state of the world which it does not deserve. In this sense, the negation of the negation in Hegel serves as ideology.

> Against this, this seriousness of unswerving negation lies precisely in its refusal to level itself to sanctioning things as they are. To negate a negation does not bring about its reversal; it proves rather that the negation was not negative enough. . . . What is negated is negative until it has passed.[27]

Determinate negation, in other words, can no longer be thought of as a "positive" result of the negation of the negation but only as the self-canceling of the illusion of self-identity. Yet it would be a mistake to read Adorno's rejection of the "negation of the negation" as a retreat into "the predialectical stage: the serene demonstration of the fact that there are two sides to everything."[28] Instead, it leads beyond the circle of identification, to a different approach to the object.

The Metaphor of the Constellation

To quote Adorno:

> The unifying moment survives without a negation of negation, but also without delivering itself to abstraction as a supreme principle. It survives because there

is no step-by-step progression from the concepts to a more general cover concept. Instead the concepts enter into a constellation. The constellation illuminates the specific side of the object, the side which to a classifying procedure is either a matter of indifference or a burden.[29]

Because, according to Adorno, the thing's own "identity against its identifications" can never be grasped in its immediacy nor in its unity with the Concept, we can only approach the object through a constellation of concepts which attempts to bring into the light the specific aspects of the object left out by the classifying process. The constellation does not pretend to totality in the sense of fully expressing the sedimented potential of the object. What it does is unleash the fullest possible perspective on what the object has come to be in its particular context. Since an object only yields itself to us through the mediation of concept, the goal is not and cannot be the pure illumination of the object, beneath the Concept, even through the disclosure of its rightful name.[30] The sedimented history of the object revealed through its constellation cannot be separated from its entanglement with concepts. As a result, an object cannot be known except in its context. "Context" here is understood not merely as external relation but also as the internalized characteristics which make an object what is. The "substance" of the object is relational at the core.

Becoming aware of the constellation in which a thing stands is tantamount to deciphering the constellation which having come to be, it bears within it.[31]

A constellation, then, cannot merely be grasped as a conceptual apparatus imposed upon the object. Constellation should be understood as a metaphor for a process of decoding that can never once and for all come to an end in a philosophical system. To the degree that a constellation "succeeds" with the object it does so through a process of decipherment. One deciphers rather than "figures out" the object. The deciphering of the object involves mimetic capacity, a capacity "for those modes of behavior which are receptive, expressive and communicative in a sensuous fashion."[32] Mimesis, in other words, is the capacity to identify *with,* in sympathy and in appreciation, rather than the ability to identify *as,* as is characteristic of instrumental logic. In this sense, knowledge through constellation does not privilege the subject's purpose over the object's "right" to be what it has become. In Adorno, mimesis is connected with the attitude toward the other he associates with utopia. Mimesis lets the object be. By so doing, mimetic capacity foreshadows the nonviolative relationship to the other, beyond the heterogeneous and beyond what is one's own, that can only be fulfilled in a redeemed world.

Adorno's notion of "identifying with" is not a return to intuition or immediacy. The "emphatic idea" of reason can only be recovered by way of immanent critique of the Concept's own claim to identity. We can only form constellations if we have grasped the misrecognition inherent in identity-logical thinking. We cannot immediately see into the object; we can only approach it from different angles of contextual perspectives, knowing all the while that it is never truly recognized by our conceptual apparatus. The object ultimately remains outside, unassimilated in its entirety by thought. For Adorno, the re-experiencing of the object as nonidentical is the experience of misrecognition, in which the subject literally runs up against the limits of conceptualization and is opened to the Other as other, the unassimilated. Because Adorno rejects Hegel's move to totality, there is no context of all contexts. We can only know the object as it is in its different contexts, never immediately or as it is in its true reality. As Adorno explains:

> Cognition of the object in its constellation is cognition of the process stored in the object. As a constellation theoretical thought circles the concept it would like to unseal, hoping that it may fly open like the lock of a well-guarded safe deposit box; in response not to a single number but to a combination of numbers.[33]

Yet for Adorno, the relativity of the object to context, and the rejection of the context of all contexts, does not lead to skepticism. The "more-than-this" in the nonidentity of the real is in the object itself. As a result, such thinking does not turn the "object's indissolubility into a taboo for the subject."[34]

The Deconstruction of the Philosophy of Consciousness

Adorno holds that skepticism and relativism inhere in "the philosophy of consciousness." These philosophical positions not only "favor" the subject over the object but also understand the object as a mere derivative of the subject. As already suggested, Adorno reads Hegel as undermining the specular, monological view of the subject in which the subject sees itself mirrored in the other but does not see the other "looking" back. In Hegel, self-consciousness is constituted in and through otherness. Subjectivity is not substantial in and of itself; instead, the subject is correlative and codependent. The awakening of self-consciousness arises in and through entanglement with the other. The priority of interrelationship subverts the exclusive logic of identity; the other cannot be excluded from the internal processes of self-consciousness. The "I" comes to be only in the tissue of relations, in the interplay of "internality" and "externality." The "I" cannot achieve perfect self-containment, that is, the fullness of presence to itself. In other words, the "I" can no longer be grasped as a self-bounded substance prior to its predicates. Only within a metaphysics of constituted essence does Adorno believe it makes sense to privilege the subject's knowledge of itself over its knowledge of its others and to let such knowledge stand as the foundation for "certainty." Thus, for Adorno, the "antithesis" of the lie of the supposed unity of subject and object in the Concept is not to be understood as an essential structure of being. Such a misunderstanding would overlook the insight into the interrelatedness of all things that Adorno's critical reading of Hegel discloses. Adorno therefore warns us very carefully against hypostatizing the subject-object polarity. To do so would be once again to locate truth in the positive, this time in an undialectical structure in which all dialectics take place.

> If the dualism of subject and object were laid down as a basic principle it would, like the identity principle to which it refuses to conform, be another total monism. Absolute duality would be unit.[35]

Hegel opens us to the insight that the "substance" of all things is to be found in their interrelatedness and, as we have seen, Adorno accepts this insight as the lasting contribution of Hegel's *Logic*. For Adorno, that this interrelatedness is experienced as antagonism and not as "communicative freedom" because of the state of reality in an antagonistic society. Thus the "philosophy of consciousness" is both true and false: true, as the experience of the isolated subject blocked from coming to terms with the intersubjective constitution of the self in such a way as to yield a knowledge of the self as *other*, a knowledge that could assuage fear; false, as the firm foundation for an epistemology.

> The consciousness assumes a monadological shape, that the individual feels knowledge of himself *(Von Sich Selber)* is more immediate and certain than the same knowledge of all others—this is the correct appearance of a false world in which men are alien and uncertain to each other and every individual immediately related only to his particular interests but in which nevertheless universal essential laws are indeed realized.[36]

Cogitative self-reflection yields a knowledge of oneself as other, nonidentical, which in turn opens the self to the nearly suppressed mimetic capacity, the ability to identify with others through access to the other in oneself. Dallmayr explains the process of cognitive self-reflection as understood by Adorno as follows:

> Only insofar as it is non-ego, can the ego relate to the non-ego or alter ego, and can it perform an action, including an act of thought. By means of double reflection thought terminates its supremacy over non-thought, since it is itself shot through from the beginning with otherness.[37]

The Suffering Physical

Nonidentity, an idea Adorno derives from Hegel's own understanding of the constitution of self-consciousness in and through otherness, gives the lie to Hegel's subsequent, absolute identification of object and Concept; at the same time, it opens a breathing space for things which prevents them from being completely stifled by an imposed social totality. The disruption of totality gives us a glimpse of what things in their interrelatedness might become if they were allowed to rest in their affinity, rather than forever being stuffed into a new system of identification. The ethical significance of the disjuncture between meaning and being reminds us that reconciliation cannot be imposed. The oppressed thing—

the object itself, the suffering, physical individual—bears witness to the failure of history to realize itself in the unity of subject and object. The disruption of the circle of immanence does not allow history the pretense that it is "second nature." According to Adorno, Hegel's "natural history" bolsters this pretense:

> In the midst of history, Hegel sides with its immutable element, with the ever-same identity of the process whose totality is said to be salvation. Quite unmetaphorically he can be charged with mythologizing history. The words "spirit" and "reconcilement" are used to disguise the myth.[38]

Adorno's dialectic of natural history reminds us that neither history nor nature can be turned into a first principle.

> If the question of the relation of nature and history is to be seriously posed, then it only offers a solution, if it is possible to comprehend historic being in its most extreme historical determinacy, where it is most historical, as natural being, or if it were possible to comprehend nature as historical being where it seems to rest most deeply in itself as nature.[39]

The intertwinement, and yet disjuncture, between history and nature exposes Hegel's philosophy of history as a myth. Suffering is not merely recognized by Adorno as historical or natural necessity. Rather suffering, from the standpoint of the particular which endures it, is senseless. The only answer adequate to the suffering physical is the end to suffering, not a new version of the "meaning" of what it has undergone. Again, Adorno's disjoining of meaning and being takes on an ethical dimension. The anti-spiritual side of spirit is the promise of happiness that the desiring individual has been denied. In this sense, Adorno's shift to materialism carried within it a refusal of the continued denial of happiness.

> The smallest trace of senseless suffering in the empirical world belies all the identitarian philosophy that would talk us out of that suffering: "While there is a beggar, there is a myth," as Benjamin put it. This is why the philosophy of identity is the mythological form of thought. The physical moment tells our knowledge that the suffering is not to be, that things should be different. Woe speaks, "go." Hence the convergence of specific materialism with criticism, with social change in practice.[40]

The society "demanded" by the suffering physical is one in which a solidarity has been achieved "that is transparent to itself and all the living."[41] "The *telos* of such an organization of society would be to negate the physical suffering of even the least of its members, and to negate the internal unreflexive forms of that suffering."[42]

Adorno and Schopenhauer: The Reinterpretation of the Ethics of Pity

When put in the context of his dialectic of natural history, the "materialism," or indeed the sensualism of Adorno's philosophy of redemption, becomes evident.

By getting in touch with the "historicized nature" sedimented in the history of human suffering, we can potentially recapture the "mimetic" identification with otherness which has been pushed under in the subject's drive for self-preservation. The dialectic of natural history not only serves to expose the hardening of social formations into a "second nature"; the dialectic also potentially returns us to what has been "forgotten" within ourselves—our own physicality. The reminder that we, too, are the "suffering physical" marks the feeling of vulnerability that pushes further the knowledge necessary for controlling the Other; this effort to know the Other, and thus to control him, is done in the name of self-preservation. The awareness of our physical vulnerability is expressed in the quest for certainty and control over the Other, but the destructive "moment" inherent in the striving for self-preservation at the expense of otherness is made evident in Adorno's exposure of the basis of the identity logic.

The species "survives" through the domination of the "natural" by instrumental rationality, but it survives in this manner only by sacrificing "the sensual happiness" for which the suffering physical yearns. The subject's striving for self-preservation turns against itself by blocking the very reconciliation with otherness that would make happiness possible. For Adorno, to consciously *experience* our "unhappiness" is to remember the physical moment within ourselves and with it the "goal" of our longing, sensual ease.

> Conscious unhappiness is not a delusion of the mind's vanity, but something inherent in the end—the one authentic dignity it has received in its separation from the body. This dignity is the mind's negative reminder of its physical aspect; its capability of that aspect is the only source of whatever hope the mind can have.[43]

Put somewhat differently, the suffering physical "demands" its own redemption in a reconciled world, a world in which sensual ease is not blocked by the subject's striving for sovereignty. It is precisely this insistence that the experience of the suffering physical puts us in touch with the promise of happiness that separates Adorno from Schopenhauer. In other words, Schopenhauer's philosophy of despair is an expression of his identification of the truth of the real with the objectifications of the Will. Adorno contends that materialism controverts Schopenhauer's truth: according to the materialist, the world which includes the suffering physical cannot be reduced to or identified as the objectifications of the Will represented in the mind. The philosophy of redemption can be understood as Schopenhauer's philosophy of denial turned on its head. For Schopenhauer, a redeemed world is an illusion of the desiring Will. For Adorno, it is the promise that clings to the physicality of the particular. Thus, the Schopenhauerian elements in *Negative Dialectics* come to rest in a constellation which negates Schopenhauer's own philosophical conclusions.

In Schopenhauer, "the spell of subjectification" inheres in the *principium individuationis*. The endless spewing out of the expressions of the Will in the form of particular manifestations is utterly beyond our control. Reason cannot chain the Will because it is beyond the reach of its principles. The Will, in other words, is unfathomable, groundless, and free from the dictates of the principle of sufficient reason. The principle of sufficient reason is the universal form of every phenomenon of the Will, not of the Will itself. The expression of the Will in human willing is also subject to the dictates of the principle of sufficient reason but not the Will itself. The individual as a phenomenon of the Will is not free, in spite of the illusion of freedom that is created by the human ability to know the Will in oneself.

> The principle of sufficient reason is the universal form of every phenomenon, and man in his action, like every other phenomenon, must be subordinated to it. But because in self-consciousness the Will is known directly and in itself, there also lies in this consciousness the consciousness of freedom. But the fact is overlooked that the individual, the person, is not Will as thing-in-itself, but is the phenomenon of the Will, as such determined and has entered the form of the phenomenon, the principle of sufficient reason.[44]

Human freedom, then, is not to be found in the human capacity to act according to the dictates of reason nor in the effort to control the Will. Human beings cannot escape the necessity that is expressed in willing, but they can deny the will to live that inheres in individual phenomenon. Denial, for Schopenhauer, is the only freedom. This denial, of course, changes nothing; one still goes on as one must. To try to change one's fate is to live it out more completely. Our humanity, our unique capacity for reason, is evidenced in stoic denial. In this sense, the striving "self is what is inhuman."[45] By seeing individualism as form only, we can deny the egoism which is expressed in our mulish efforts at self-preservation. Reason lifts the veil of Maya and opens our eyes to the "truth" of individualism. Our individuality is epiphenomenon, the mere expression of the Will. In Schopenhauer, to grasp this truth is to be "humiliated." But the wound to our narcissism opens us to the only true "foundation" of morality—compassion for the suffering of others. Once the veil of Maya is lifted, the individual comes to understand that the sharp distinction between ego and other is an illusion. By penetrating the *principium individuationis,* we learn to identify with the other. We come to see the "true significance" of our own petty striving, its ultimate insignificance. What lingers after the denial of the Will is both the composure of one who knows and the pity of one who experiences the suffering of others as a shared human fate.

> If that veil of Maya, the *principium individuationis,* is lifted from the eyes of man to such an extent that he no longer makes the egotistical distinction between himself and the person of others, but takes as much interest in the sufferings of other individuals as his own, and thus is not only benevolent and charitable in the highest degree, but even ready to sacrifice his own individuality whenever several others can be saved thereby, then it follows automatically, that such a recognition in all beings, his true and innermost self, must also regard the

endless sufferings of all these lives as his own and taken upon himself the pain of the whole world. No suffering is any longer strange or foreign to him. All the miseries of others, which he sees and is so seldom able to alleviate, all the miseries of which he has indirect knowledge, and even those he recognizes merely as possible, affect his mind just as do his own. It is no longer the changing weal and woe of his person, that he has in view, as is the case with the man still involved in egoism, but as he sees through the *principium individuationis,* everything lies equally near to him. He knows the whole, comprehends its inner nature and finds it involved in a constant passing away, a vain striving, an inward conflict, and a continual suffering.[46]

Schopenhauer offers us an ethic of pity based on the identification of the "truth" of the human condition. His is the wisdom of disillusionment. The loss of innocence is the price we pay for the knowledge that can open us to the only true human freedom—denial of the Will. To know the world as Will and representation is to live beyond hope. The yearning for utopia is false consciousness, and one pays heavily for the mistake of hope. Hope enchains the utopian individual to the world he would deny. As Adorno explains: "For Schopenhauer any hope for the establishment of humanity was the fond delusion of a man who had nothing but misfortune to hope for."[47]

Adorno, on the other hand, considers the renunciation of hope to be an error of identity-logical thinking. In this sense, "despair is the last ideology."

The mistake in Schopenhauer's thinking is that the law which keeps immanence under its own spell is directly said to be that essence which immanence blocks, the essence that would not be conceivable as other than transcendent. But the world is better than hell because the absolute conclusiveness which Schopenhauer attributes to the world's course is borrowed in turn from the idealistic system. It is a pure identity principle and as deceptive as any identity principle. The world's course is not absolute conclusive nor is absolute despair; rather despair is its conclusiveness. However void every trace of otherness in it, however much all happiness is marred by revocability: in the breaks that belie identity, entity is still pervaded by the ever-broken pledges of that otherness.[48]

The materialist honors the pledge to otherness which idealism renounces. Adorno prefers "to read transcendence longingly rather than strike out."[49] The longing of the suffering physical is to be protected as a sign of what might be, what I would call the utopia of sensual ease. The confusion of the utopia of sensual ease, in which things are allowed to rest in affinity with death is itself due to the spell of subjectification in which otherness can only appear as the subject's mirror opposite—in this case obliteration. This confusion, for Adorno, was the central error in Wagner's sensualist recasting of Schopenhauer's insight. Schopenhauer even denies the status of otherness to obliteration, whereas Wagner thinks that obliteration is otherness. The hell of our mortal life lingers on in our death. This Schopenhauerian denial of the physical is echoed in Wagner in spite of himself. For Adorno, the spell of subjectification creates a false either/or: *either* the subject's endless, impotent striving *or* its longing for complete annihilation so as to be beyond this striving.

> As long as the world is as it is, all pictures of reconciliation, peace and quiet resemble the picture of death. The slightest difference between nothingness and coming to rest would be the haven of hope, the no man's land between the border posts of being and nothingness. Rather than overcome that zone, consciousness would have to extricate from it what is not in the power of the alternative.[50]

In a world in which the subject "survives" only through a frantic appropriation of otherness, sensual ease is recast as a death wish, as in Wagner's rendition of Schopenhauer.

The power of the alternatives between death and utopia lies in the individuality "signaled" in the noncaptured physical. Thus for Schopenhauer, the humiliated subject who relinquishes individualism must also relinquish desire for the end of suffering; whereas, for Adorno, the very suffering of the noncaptured physical gestures toward the coming into being of a multi-dimensional, desiring being. The subject, in its physicality, is something more than its categorization as subject over the object. To be in touch with this something more, one must reach out to the other in oneself that has been denied. To grasp the subject as constituted under the weight of a subjectivity that preserves itself at the expense of the suffering, longing, physical human being is to grasp the "truth" of Schopenhauer's vision of freedom through humiliation. In this sense, "the subject's dissolution presents at the same time the ephemeral and condemned picture of a possible subject."[51] To understand oneself as a "natural" subject is to retrieve in oneself a kind of innocence; denial is denied. The wisdom of disillusionment is exposed as the self-destructive impulse of idealism. The melancholy science is not one of defeat; to be melancholy is to experience deprivation as loss. This is itself a form of resistance in a world in which deprivation is justified as necessary. According to Adorno, to deny the desire of the natural Will is to subject oneself to the rule of the super-ego—a subjugation which is in league with the Kantian definition of freedom. The association of freedom in Kant with the postulation of a radically autonomous and completely unified ego contaminates freedom through its incorporation of aggression against the hapless, desiring self.

The Critique of the Kantian
Subject of Morality

Adorno maintains that freedom cannot be obtained from the heteronomous but only through it. The superego represents, in reified form, the subject's constitution in and through others. To be free from the superego is to render this intersubjectivity transparent to itself as a dialectical relation:

Instead of sanctioning the internalized and hardened authority of the superego, theory should carry out the dialectics of individual and species. The rigorism of the superego is nothing but the reflex response to the prevention of that dialectics by the antagonistic condition. The subject would be liberated only as an I reconciled with the non-I and thus it would also be above the freedom which is leagued with its counterpart repression.[52]

For Adorno, the paradox in Kant's definition of freedom as the constitution of causality by pure reason is that one is only free if one acts as one *must* as a rational being. One is free only if one obeys the law dictated by one's status as a rational noumenal Will. Adorno finds it no coincidence that "all the concepts whereby the Critique of Practical Reason proposes in honor of freedom, to fill the chasm between the Imperative and Mankind are repressive. A causality produced by freedom corrupts freedom into obedience."[53]

The repressive aspect of Kantian morality stems, in part, from the radical separation of reason and nature and can be overcome only through the dialectic of natural history in which the natural moment of reason itself is not denied.

> The prehistory of reason, that it is a moment of nature and yet something else, has become the immanent definition of reason. It is natural as the psychological force split off for purposes of self-preservation; once split off and contrasted with nature it also becomes nature's otherness. But if that dialectic irrepressibly turns reason into the absolute antithesis of nature, if the nature in reason itself is forgotten, reason will be self-preservation running wild and will regress to nature. It is only as reflection upon that self-preservation that reason would be above nature.[54]

The impulses of physical desire are part of the rational Will itself. The Will must be understood dialectically in its relation to the very desires it unifies and expresses.

> A Will without physical impulses, impulses that survive, weakened in imagination, would not be a Will. At the same time, however, the Will settles down as the centralizing unit of impulses as the authority that tames them and potentially negates them. This necessitates a dialectical definition of the Will. It is the force that enables consciousness to leave its domain and so change what merely exists; its recoil is resistance.[55]

Under a dialectical conception of the Will, there can be no absolute divide between the noumenal and the empirical subject, any more than there can be a transcendental gap between reason and desire. A person is never a completed unity as rational Will. Yet the independence of Will understood as the striving for the unity of the ego is also not denied. Here one hears the echo of Nietzsche. A self is not a given, it is a goal, an aesthetic achievement. "To become what one is" is an accomplishment, and one that is never completed as long as the desiring self continues to live.

As a result, the Will cannot be thoroughly objectified without losing itself as

Will. For the Will to be the Will it must retain the subjective moment that makes it irreducible to any categorical expression. As Adorno remarks: "We can as well talk of a Will that is independent and to that extent objective as we can talk of a strong ego or in the latter days of old character."[56] Kant's mistake was to make the noumenal subject into a totality. Only by so doing could he achieve the radical independence of the noumenal self. Adorno understands this move on Kant's part to be progressive as well as regressive:

> According to Kantian ethics the subject's totality predominates over the moments it lives by—moments which alone give life to the totality, although outside such a totality they would not make up a Will. The discovery was progressive . . . the subject becomes moral for itself; it cannot be weighed by standards that are inwardly and outwardly particular and alien to the subject. Once the rational unity of the Will is established as the sole moral authority, the subject is protected from the violence done to it by a hierarchical society— a society which (as still in Dante's sense) would judge a man's deeds without any previous acceptance of its law by his consciousness.[57]

There is a truth in "free Will" that Adorno does not want to deny. But once the transcendental divide between nature and reason is deconstructed, the notion of free Will takes on a new meaning. What Adorno rejects is the inescapable alternative inherent in the Kantian project: either the Will is free or it's unfree. According to Adorno, it is both:

> Each drastic thesis is false. In their innermost core, the theses of freedom and determinism coincide. Both proclaim identity. The reduction to pure spontaneity applies to the empirical subject the very same law which as an expanded casual category becomes determinism. Perhaps free men would be freed from the Will also; surely it is only in a free society that individuals would be free.[58]

Adorno sees as Hegel's great insight the understanding that concrete freedom is objective, not simply a state of the Will. Marx adds to this view the insistence that "objective" freedom always rests on the satisfaction of material needs. Freedom for the empirical subject cannot be had without the gratification of need. The very materiality of human existence demands a socially realized freedom in which want, in its extreme forms, has been eliminated. As already suggested, such a freedom can only be achieved intersubjectively because the "independent" self can only defeat its longing by alienating itself from the world, rather than by making the world a home. Satisfaction demands mutuality and adjustment. The atomic individual cannot lay hold of a world that yields to the need to negate suffering. However, freedom, in the form of the postulation of the radical autonomy of the rational Will, even if philosophically false, expresses a truth of social experience. We feel isolated from one another; our interdependence occurs behind our backs. Reified as social order and internalized as the superego, intersubjectivity is frozen into a context which determines us and appears beyond our control.

Individualism, as an imposed social form, turns against the aspiration to be free in the full, material sense precisely because realized freedom demands a "transparent solidarity" which individualism blocks. This view, of course, should not be taken to mean that Adorno rejects the association of freedom with individuality altogether. The relationship, however, is complex.

> The individual feels free insofar as he has opposed himself to society and can do something—though incomparably less than he believes—against society and other individuals. His freedom is primarily that of a man pursuing his own ends, ends that are not totally exhausted by social ends. In this sense freedom coincides with the principles of individuation. A freedom of this type has broken loose from punitive society; within an increasingly rational one, it has achieved a measure of reality. At the same time in the midst of bourgeois society freedom remains no less delusive than individuality itself.[59]

The delusion inherent in this kind of freedom is that it masks the necessity it imposes.

> The real necessity involved in the kind of freedom praised by radical individualism ideology—in a freedom which the free had to maintain and to enforce with their elbows—this necessity was an image designed to cover up the social necessity that compels an individual to be rugged if he wants to survive.[60]

Adorno ultimately endorses the view of individual freedom put forward in Hegel's *Phenomenology of Mind*. The individual as rational Will is not free of the heteronomous; (s)he comes to the concept of freedom only *against* it and in struggle with it. As material beings, we are beholden to one another and to the outside world more generally. The idea of freedom is entwined with the experience of unfreedom. In this sense, *individual* freedom is a moment, a historical mode, which resists what would deny it.

Freedom Rethought

> As perceived in Hegel's *Phenomenology*, it is only from that which has been divided from it, from that which is against it, that the subject acquires the concepts of freedom and unfreedom which it will then relate to its own structure.[61]

Freedom cannot be "positive" because, in the Hegelian sense, it is freedom against. The material moment of freedom can only be realized socially. But the inevitable social aspect of the conditions of freedom does not mean that freedom can be simply identified with what the collectivity defines freedom to be. Adorno's critique of Marx is that he, too, posited a positive notion of freedom, in which the tension between the "individual" and the "community" would collapse. Reconciliation demands that this tension be maintained, but not reified. A self-transparent solidarity would allow for much greater fluidity in relations between subjects, but it would not totally end the experience of the divide between the internal and external.

> In a state of freedom the individual would not be frantically guarding the old particularity—individuality is the produce of pressure as well as the energy center for resistance to this pressure—but neither would that state of freedom agree with the present concept of collectivity. The fact that collectivism is directly commanded in the countries which today monopolize the name of socialism, commanded as the individual's subordination to society, this fact belies the socialism of those countries, and solidifies antagonism.[62]

The recovery of "the natural" in reason itself rejects the idea of freedom as the notion of radical autonomy or sovereignty. There is no freedom except in and through otherness, and there is no freedom without an end to material deprivation. Adorno rejects completely the Schopenhauerian view of "freedom" as denial. Where Adorno agrees with Schopenhauer, however, is in his stress on sympathy for the other as the basis for moral intuition. Yet Adorno holds that it is compassion rather than pity which is the basis for sympathy for others. Pity reflects the helplessness inherent in Schopenhauer's idealism. The fate of the desiring individual is indeed pitiful in Schopenhauer. Compassion, for Adorno, is not rooted in the wisdom of disillusionment but in the recognition of the shared human plight which comes from the subject's reflection on his "natural side." The "mindfulness of nature," our grasp of our existence as the suffering physical allows us to be *soft*. Goodness, for Adorno, is a form of tenderness. To the degree that the Kantian "kingdom of ends" imagines something like a reconciled condition between human beings, it retains a utopian content. But the Adornian emphasis on the recovery of compassion, through the subject's reflection on her or his own otherness, breaks with the framework of de-ontological ethics.

In other words, Adorno wishes to preserve good will without repression or, more radically, to suggest that repression blocks good will. Adorno's moral subject that does not know itself as a "natural" desiring being will not recover the sympathy for others that can serve as a nonrepressive "basis" for moral intuition. Adorno's point, put starkly, is that an ethics separated categorically from what has been called the "natural" will be repressive.

"The mindfulness of nature" opens subjects to otherness in the recognition of their own nonidentity and, by so doing, allows us to appreciate ourselves and others as multidimensional beings. This openness to otherness is demonstrated in Adorno as a non-violative relation to the concrete which does not seek to appropriate or to remain indifferent. The "love" for otherness is blocked by a subject which can only see the Other as its own image or as its mirror opposite. Adorno's deconstruction, and yet incorporation, of Schopenhauer's ethic of pity in the dialectic of natural history helps us to think again about Herbert Marcuse's belief that the only foundation for our moral beliefs is the compassion for the suffering of others. The call to love things "both earnest and ironic" is not a call to focus merely on nature as an abstraction nor on things in their concrete individuality at the expense of relations between human beings. Such a shift in perspective is, if you like, the underpinning of a different unrepressed interrelatedness. To argue that there is something "there" that has been repressed, we need not rely on Freud's theory of the drives or on some other notion of an essential human nature. We must simply see the untruth of idealism, the identification of the real with its concept.

Negative Dialectics in Its Relation to Contemporary Trends in Philosophy

Following through Adorno's own insight into nonidentity allows us to reject Adorno's tendency to make negativity absolute. His emphasis, however, continues to provide us with an important reminder. For Adorno, what appears sensible is often that which has been imposed on us. Common sense too easily degenerates into the wisdom of rationalization. The significance of Adorno's warning against the complacent acceptance of common sense can best be brought out through a comparison with both Hans George Gadamer's appeal to tradition[63] and Richard Rorty's appeal to solidarity[64] as means by which we come to make sense of our ethical and political environment. Although they come to Hegel from very different beginnings, I understand both Gadamer and Rorty to be pragmatic Hegelians. While it would be unfair to Gadamer to suggest that his appeal to tradition does not allow for critique—the adherence to a tradition is a self-conscious appropriation of tradition, and such a self-conscious appropriation implies critique—there is nonetheless a quietism in his philosophy. Rarely does Gadamer reflect on *who* are the "we" who *share* a tradition. Rorty, likewise, appeals to "social practice" and "our shared conversation"; in a similar manner, he fails to come fully to terms with the ethical critique of "the conversation of mankind." In Hegelian terms, both Rorty and Gadamer fail to recognize the difference in identity. Adorno's negative dialectics reminds us again and again of the relations of domination and exclusion which are implicated in an abstract appeal to the "we" who *share*. The emphasis on the continuation of "the conversation of mankind" in the present is similarly undermined. An ethic which fails to incorporate the role not only of critique but also of the full disruptive power of the imagination[65] "condemns us to an unending commerce with the familiar objects of thought."[66] Adorno's negative dialectics disrupts this unending commerce at every turn. For Adorno, to gain insight into what is we must know it as other. To know it as other is to know it in the light of a redeemed world.

> Perspectives must be fashioned that displace and estrange the world, reveal it to be with its rights and crevices, as indigent and distorted as it will appear one day in the messianic light. To gain such perspectives without vulgarity or

> violence entirely from fleeting contact with its objects—this is the task of thought.[67]

Adorno's emphasis on the *unheimlich* need not be read as the denial of ethical mediation. Instead, Adorno should be understood as reminding us that we will not really find "our dwelling" in the world until we stop trying desperately to make a home out of our world by means of identity-logical thinking.

> In fear, bondage to nature is perpetuated by a thinking that identifies, that equalizes everything unequal. Thoughtless rationality is blinded to the point of madness by the sight of whatsoever will elude its rule. . . . Even the theory of alienation, the ferment of dialectics, confuses the need to approach the heteronomous and thus irrational world to be "at home everywhere" as Novalis put it—with the archaic barbarism that the loving subject cannot love what is alien and different, with the craving for incorporation and persecution. If the alien were no longer ostracized there hardly would be any more alienation.[68]

Adorno's melancholy science reminds us of the violence of intersubjectivity. He forces us to confront the content of the solidarity to which we appeal. And, of course, Adorno continually questions whether or not there can be a truly "self-transparent" solidarity within the frame of mass society. Adorno's suspicion, and indeed fear, of intersubjectivity when taken to its extremes can be understood as an expression of the very hostility to the alien he warns us against. Yet his suspicion does not result because he has no view of intersubjectivity, but rather because he adopts the strong Hegelian vision of self-consciousness as a social, interactive achievement. It is precisely his understanding of the intersubjective constitution of self-consciousness which leads him to question whether the conditions of mass society do not completely undermine the social conditions in which critical subjectivity can survive. Thus, Adorno emphasizes the vantage point of the exile for its value in preserving the remnants of critique. Who are the "we" who hear Adorno and why now? How does he speak to us? Why engage in the task of recovering "some freedom for history" within Adorno's own categories? What does it mean to take responsibility for Adorno's signature?

Conclusion

I begin my conclusion to this first chapter with an answer to my last question. In "taking responsibility for the signature of the other," we are tested in our own ability to exercise our openness to and tenderness toward otherness. To take responsibility for the signature of the other without violation demands that one seek to internalize the attitude toward otherness which shines through the cracks and the crevices of *Negative Dialectics*. It demands that we reflect on the ethical relation in general, the very relation to which Adorno directs our attention. What is at stake in such a project is less the following of rules than the open-minded spirit in which it is accomplished. In part, Adorno speaks to us now because his implicit ethical vision rests on expansiveness rather than on constriction. His is a gentle, directive message which does not demand the universalization of one particular behavioral mode of morality. The focus is less on doing what is right in accordance with one's duty than on the development of an attitude of tenderness toward otherness and gentleness toward oneself as a sensual creature. The dialectical richness of Adorno's deconstructive Hegelianism allows us to overcome the rigid divide between the serious business of ethics and the playfulness of the aesthetic realm. Adorno refuses the Kantian categorical divide between the ethical and the aesthetic. Yet if Adorno is to be rightly accused of "aestheticizing" the ethical, it is only in Charles Peirce's unique sense of aesthetics. For Peirce, the ethical is subordinate to the aesthetic. For Peirce, "esthetics is the science of ends, and the business of the esthetician is to say what is the state of things which is most admirable in itself regardless of any ulterior reason."[69] Adorno's pessimism about the effect of a "fallen world" on positive visions of the ultimate good led him to proceed by indication rather than by direct philosophical elaboration. In Adorno, the ultimate Good can only be *known* negatively. But without redemptive perspectives which, at the very least, indicate the ultimate good of communicative freedom, we would be unable to even glimpse the different way of belonging together which inheres in Adorno's critique of totality. The ultimate good, then, is present in Adorno in its negative force and as the force of the negative. The ultimate question whether Adorno's own formulation of his project degenerates into endless negativity depends, in part, on how seriously we take his attempt to develop constellations as a counter to determinate negation and, ultimately, on what we make of his critique of Hegel's move to totality. As I have suggested, Adorno took seriously the redefinition of "communicative freedom" as an essential aspect of a redemptive perspective. But the following question remains: is the rendering of communicative freedom in terms of a redemptive perspective appropriate enough, or must we, like Heidegger, attempt to think of "belonging together" differently or, like Peirce, develop a vision of "evolutionary love"? In other words, the question to Adorno remains as follows: Can we approach "diversity in unity" without thinking belonging together differently, or must we always fall back on an appeal to the whole, whether we call it Creativity or the Will? In spite of the perplexities which persist even after the most sympathetic reading of *Negative Dialectics,* Adorno remains a crucial voice for those of us who seek to aspire to the ethical relationship.

To see why Adorno's voice remains relevant, even if we need ultimately to surpass its limits through a more explicit, affirmative configuration of justice and its significance for legal interpretation, we will now return to his critique of the ideal of community. We will lay his critique alongside that offered by Jacques Derrida. We do so to indicate why, in spite of their suspicion of the reduction of the ethical relation to how it is defined by current conventional standards, they do not simplistically deny the ideal of community. And we will do so in order to begin the process of contrasting Adorno with the thinkers who have come to be labeled "postmodern." As we will see in the forthcoming chapters, for Derrida, unlike Adorno, the *right of philosophy* ultimately has important implications for the *philosophy of right* irreducible to a negative dialectics which can not directly address justice, let alone questions of legal interpretation. But first, we must turn to both the similarities and the differences in their philosophical relationship to the ideal of community.

2

The "Postmodern" Challenge
to the Ideal of Community

Introduction

In the twentieth century, a number of thinkers have become deeply skeptical of any appeal to the ideal of community. For example, Iris Young has argued that the very idea of community as a unit of ethical being in Hegel's sense must be rejected as philosophically wrong and normatively suspect.[1] Adorno is clearly one of the thinkers who have informed Young's position. As Young explains:

> I criticize the notion of community on both philosophical and practical grounds. I argue that the ideal of community participates in what Derrida calls the metaphysics of presence or Adorno calls the logic of identity, a metaphysics that denies difference. The ideal of community presumes subjects who are present to themselves and presumes subjects can understand [on] another as they understand themselves. It thus denies the difference between subjects. The desire for community relies on the same desire for social wholeness [an] identification that underlies racism and ethnic chauvinism, on the one hand, and political sectarianism on the other.[2]

In place of the ideal of the community, Young puts forward a vision of a nonrepressive city, which emphasizes difference. This skepticism, as we saw at the end of the last chapter, and as Young also points out, is based on the deep suspicion that lurking behind the ideal of community is a nostalgia for an integrated "organic wholeness" that inevitably excludes those who do not seem to fit into the community.

Philosophically and politically, twentieth-century experience has presumably taught us that the appeal to community ineluctably slides into an appeal to totality, closure, and exclusion. In his continuing influence on writers like Young, Adorno is one of the most significant initiators of this critique. Adorno, however, has now been joined, as we see in Young's quotation, with the "postmoderns." Jacques Derrida, for example, is also particularly incisive and illuminating on the multifarious ways in which community and convention can do violence to difference and particularity. (Although developed in different modulations, this line of criticism, as I suggested in the Introduction, bears a family resemblance to standard liberal skepticism of strong communitarian aspirations.)

Yet in spite of what seems at first to be a shared suspicion, I want to show that a more careful reading of Adorno and Derrida reveals that they do not totally reject the *aspiration* to the ideal of community. Indeed, the space that they keep open for difference and particularity would itself not make any sense unless we are sensitive to the seriousness with which they take the ideal of community. But before returning to this reading, we have to ask a further question that follows from Adorno's own critique of Hegel. If Hegel's "system" is rejected for once again re-inscribing the logic of identity, how does one approach the "ideal" of communicative freedom—which for Hegel had been realized at least on the level of the concept—in the modern state.[3] With the disruption of Hegel's system, at least as conventionally understood, we can no longer assume the actualization of communicative freedom in communal life. The ideal, in other words, can not be assumed to have been realized in the real, now understood as the conventions of social life of a particular community.

Thus, I separate my discussion of Derrida and Adorno's critique of social "order," either as *Sittlichkeit* or as a Rousseauian communal ideal, from their speculations on the problem of metaphysics and the chance of communicative freedom. This distinction between the perpetuation of order, and the dream of preserving or uncovering the truly ethical relationship as one of uncoerced affinity, becomes extremely important for Derrida, in his engagement with the work of Emmanuel Levinas. I will argue that Derrida does not simply reject the historical reality of community life, nor does he merely privilege the moment of "transgression" when the boundaries yield. He warns us against both the violence of identity that presents the community as a self-contained unit of *being* and the relegation of the other to a *phenomenological* relation of asymmetry in which the dance of sameness and difference is denied. It should not be forgotten that the general strategy of deconstruction is to disrupt the violent hierarchies of binary oppositions. Derrida is one of our sharpest critics of both sides of the myth of self-containment. Both Adorno and Derrida clearly guard against the violence of self-enclosed community. But is their message, then, that we must remain ever vigilant against the violence of the *ideal* of community? I suggest that the answer to this question is complex indeed.

My argument proceeds as follows: First, I discuss the early Hegel's critique of the elevation of civil society to absolute ethical life as this critique relates to Hegel's understanding of community, *das Gemeine*. Second, I return to how Adorno's negative dialectics, now played out against one understanding of communitarianism, and Derrida's writing (trace, *différance*, supplement) disrupt Hegel's move to enclose the community. This disruption, which proceeds through a recognition of the inevitability of a constructive outside, external to an all-encompassing spirit, radically undermines the right-wing Hegelians' appeal to the self-presence of a rigidly bounded *Sittlichkeit*. The graphic example of the constituted outside is death itself. To elaborate on Derrida's reminder of the violent moment in ethical life, I discuss the role of war in the consolidation of the Hegelian community.[4] To end, or to begin again, I speculate on the dream of communicative freedom.

Hegel's Critique of the Philosophy of Reflection: Law, Community, and Ethics

In his critique of natural law,[5] Hegel argues that an "idealized" state of nature, in which multiple, atomized individuals exist independently, is only a myth that confuses an *empirical* observation of the relations of indifference in civil society with a purportedly *natural* condition used to justify these relations of indifference.[6] Law, or indeed any ethical order, is, in the view criticized, that is, Kant and Fichte's, alien to the individual human being. Society is only accepted as the lesser evil to total destruction. Such a society does not unify the dispersed individuals. Ethical ordering remains a negative force which cannot realize freedom concretely through its embodiment in social institutions. According to Hegel, his predecessors in critical idealism, Kant and Fichte, could not overcome certain dilemmas in empirical natural law even though they purportedly rejected such theories. For Hegel, Kant's dilemma inheres in his absolute separation of the realm of necessity from the realm of freedom. Legality, and the institutional embodiments of ethical ordering more generally, is relegated to the heteronomous, the realm of necessity. Freedom of the moral will in Kant is freedom from necessity. As a result freedom can only be formally conceived.

As Gillian Rose explains Hegel's critique of Kant and Fichte:

> Transcendental or critical philosophy cannot conceive of the *content* of freedom but only of the *form* of freedom because it limits itself to justification of the kind of judgements made by a reason which is divided in two. Kant's notion of moral autonomy is formal, not only because it excludes natural desire and inclination from freedom, but because it classifies legality, the social realm, with the heteronomous hindrances to the formation of a free will. Fichte endorses Kant's distinction between morality and legality, but he argues, in his doctrine of natural law, that a community of free, rational beings is conceivable without any reference to the good will. Hence Fichte's natural law is also abstract and formal.[7]

According to Hegel, Kantian morality cannot overcome the dichotomous division between the realm of freedom and the realm of necessity. Thus, it can only provide us with a formal unity of the real and the ideal. This formal unity is not a true unity at all for Hegel but rather is the suppression of the "real," or the multiplicity.

Thus, in what is called practical reason, we can recognize only the *formal* Ideal of the identity of the real and the ideal, and in these systems of philosophy this Idea should be the absolute point of indifference. . . . This real is essentially posited outside reason, and practical reason resides only in its difference from it. The essence of this practical reason is understood as a causal relation to the many is an identity infected with a difference and does not go beyond appearance. This science of ethics, which talks of the absolute identity of ideal and real, belies its own words; its ethical reason is, in its essence and in truth, a non-identity of ideal and real.[8]

For Hegel, the sin of Kant's practical reason is that it can only dominate or suppress what is opposed to it because it sets itself up in opposition to the realm of necessity. Yet for Hegel, the lack of genuine identity of the realm of freedom and the realm of necessity expresses the real social relations of civil society in which domination is masked as relations of indifference. Hegel refers to the relations of civil society as relative ethical life. Again to quote Rose:

This ethical life is relative in two senses. In the first place, this sphere of life, the practical sphere of enjoyment, work and possession, is only part of the whole. It is a relative aspect of absolute ethical life, which natural law elevates into the unity of the whole, into the negative principle of the whole society. In the second place, bourgeois property relations are based on a lack of identity (relation). For they make people into competing, isolated, "moral," individuals who can only relate externally to one another, and are thus subjected to a real lack of identity. Bourgeois private property presupposes real inequality, for the law which guarantees abstract, formal property rights presupposes concrete inequality (lack of identity).[9]

Hegel does not deny the reality of civil society or suggest that the sphere of abstract right which grows out of it must be abolished. He insists however that these relations be mediated. The mistake lies not in the recognition of civil society as a separate sphere of the social, but instead in understanding it as the whole, as the community. As Hegel explains:

There is no question of denying this standpoint; on the contrary, it has been characterized above as the aspect of the relative identity of the being of the infinite in the finite. But this at least must be maintained, that it is not the absolute standpoint in which the relation has been demonstrated and proved to be only one aspect, and the isolation of the relation is likewise thus proved to be something one-sided.[10]

Civil society for Hegel is but one aspect of an encompassing *Sittlichkeit*. Civil society in other words is relative to the communal institutions of *Sittlichkeit* and can be circumscribed legitimately by them. For example, Hegel justifies taxation as a legitimate circumscription of civil society by the community seeking to redress the inequality brought about by the lack of identity inherent in the protection and enforcement of private property. For Hegel, the right of private property carries within it a contradiction. The right to possession is only guaranteed by the community. Yet the right is also a guarantee against community infringement. Without the guarantee of right, possession would be only possession, and not property. The very idea of property implies an established legal system. The right to property cannot be postulated as *a priori* with respect to society; for Hegel, the right is always relative to the universal, the community.

For Hegel, the community is not an external force that coerces the previously isolated individuals; rather, the community is internal to the individuals themselves, their own interrelatedness, which makes them who they are. Recognition *(Anerkennen)* is achieved between individuals when they understand community as their internal interrelatedness, "the we that is I and the I that is we." The community on this understanding is not an externality that uses the individual as a means in the name of redistributive justice. Again, I am referring to the example of a progressive taxation, which some conservatives have argued should be rejected precisely because such a measure uses the individual in the name of redistributive justice.[11] The community is internal to the constitution of self-conscious subjectivity itself. In Hegel, in other words, a good community is the condition of the flourishing of the individual. For Hegel the constitution of self-conscious subjectivity is the hallmark of modernity. The network of reciprocally constituted individuals is the ethical life premised on established relations with the others in and through which the self-consciousness of the individual develops. In one reading, Spirit in Hegel is the primordial relativity in which the boundaries yield to our fundamental interconnectedness and our corresponding understanding that we belong to our community and therefore cannot be separate objects to be used by it.

> Through ethical life and in it alone, intellectual intuition is real intuition, the eye of spirit and the loving eye coincide: according to nature man sees the flesh of his flesh in woman, according to ethical life he sees the spirit of his spirit in the ethical being and through the same.[12]

To see in the Other the spirit of oneself is also to recognize the other as different. The sameness that defines each one of us as an individual is not a composite of identifiable properties shared by all individuals. We are the same in that we are I's; but to be a subject, to be an I, is to be different. In the to and fro of mutual recognition we learn to see ourselves in what appears alien and experience the alien looking back at us, recognizing us as another self-consciousness. For Hegel, a true unity is brought about between universal and empirical consciousness only by rendering transparent the network of reciprocally interrelated selves. This unity demands reciprocal recognition. Only on that basis can the dilemmas of the philosophy of reflection be overcome. To summarize again the discussion from the last chapter, in the philosophy of reflection that Hegel associates with Fichte, the I sees itself reflected in the alien but does not experience the alien looking back. The philosophy of reflection is one-sided, the expression of individual domination. The other is reduced to a mirror for oneself. Absolute intuition, "self-recognition in absolute Otherness," is the overcoming of the mirror stage, the recognition of the reciprocity of self-consciousness.

The Hegelian Understanding of the Subject

The Hegelian understanding of community as the *internal* relations of a constituted intersubjectivity implies a view of the subject. For Hegel, to understand the subject itself as constituted in and through interactions in a pre-existing ethical life serves to expose the Kantian view of the autonomous will as an abstraction from ethical relationships. The isolated individual prior to society symbolized, for example, in the figure of Robinson Crusoe is criticized.[13] For Hegel, such a vision of the subject is inevitably implicated in the conservative outcome of measures such as progressive taxation.

The Hegelian view of the subject, then, at least as Hegel understood his own philosophical position, neither denies the self-consciousness of the individual nor privileges it as a *self-contained* entity existing prior to society. Self-consciousness is instead understood as an essential aspect of modern *Sittlichkeit,* which is made possible precisely because of the legal and moral achievements of modernity. In this sense, Hegel's understanding of the communitarian subject is uniquely modern in that it insists on the ethical significance of the protection of individuality. For Hegel, a modern reconciliation between the individual and the community must be a self-conscious reconciliation in which the individual recognizes that his or her individuality is achieved within a community that protects it. Reconciliation can only be achieved in a relationship in which individuals are able to recognize one another not as an externally imposed limit, but as the condition of self-realization. Hegel's critique of his predecessors was directed at the relations of domination he associated with the philosophy of reflection, which could not resolve the tension between the individual and the community, freedom and necessity.

The Critique of Hegel's Answer
to the Philosophy of Reflection

But does the Hegelian reconciliation of the individual with the community through a shared spirit in and through which individuals are constituted escape the relations of domination that he associates with his predecessors and that he so persuasively critiques? Both Adorno and Derrida suggest that Hegelian reconciliation does not achieve its stated goal and that it turns against the communicative freedom it purports to show as the truth of all reality. To summarize the central lesson of Adorno's negative dialectics, if communicative freedom is "thought" as the unification of the relata into a comprehensive unity understood— at least according to one reading of Hegel—as a deified subjectivity, *Geist,* then difference and individuality are again denied. In this sense, Hegel's conceptual dialectics turns against its own ambition, which is to overcome the dichotomy between the individual and the community, self and other, mind and matter. Hegel's move to finalize his critique in an all-encompassing system which is then embodied as the community has also been critiqued, for example, by Heidegger, who is in turn central to Derrida's thinking. The difference that makes a difference is whether "the matter of thinking is the idea as the absolute concept" or whether in a preliminary fashion "the matter of thinking is the difference *as* difference."[14]

For Heidegger, the matter of thinking is:

> Being with respect to beings having been thought in absolute thinking, and as absolute thinking. For us, the matter of thinking is the Same, and thus is Being—but Being with respect to its difference from beings.[15]

For Heidegger, we can only think of a belonging together in which difference is not eradicated if we step back[16] from the tradition of onto-theology Heidegger associates with the whole of Socratic and post-Socratic Western metaphysics. Heidegger agrees with Hegel that thinking and Being belong together but not within the horizon of Absolute Knowledge, at least not as Heidegger understands it.

> If we think of belonging *together* in the customary way, the meaning of belonging is determined by the word together, that is, by its unity. In that case, "to belong" means as much as: to be assigned and placed into the order of a "together," established in the unity of a manifold, combined into the unity of a system, mediated by the unifying center of an authoritative synthesis. . . .
>
> However, belonging together can also be thought of as *belonging* together. This means: the "together" is now determined by the belonging. Of course, we must still ask here what "belong" means in that case, and how its peculiar "together" is determined only in its terms. The answer to these questions is closer to us than we imagine, but it is not obvious. Enough for now that this reference makes us note the possibility of no longer representing belonging in terms of the unity of the together, but rather of experiencing this together in terms of belonging.[17]

Adorno shares with Heidegger the attempt to think "together" in terms of belonging rather than as an integration into a comprehensive system, although he does so in a manner very different from Heidegger's. As we saw in the first chapter, his negative dialectics still works within Hegel's *Logic*. Implicit in Adorno's attempt is the possibility that a deconstructive reading of Hegel, or as Derrida has put it, "agreeing with Hegel against himself,"[18] can potentially answer at least some of Heidegger's criticisms of Hegel's subjectivism. However, it should be noted that both Heidegger and Adorno read the Absolute Idea as the absolute subject which is the basis for the authoritative syntheses of Hegel's system (to borrow a phrase from Heidegger). On this reading, Hegel fails to overcome the relations of domination he criticized in his predecessors in critical philosophy,

Kant and Fichte, and indeed falls back into the very philosophy of reflection he set out to reject.

To summarize the last chapter, with the critique of communitarianism in mind reconciliation cannot be captured by an all-encompassing, totalizing reason conceived as deified subjectivity. In Hegel's supposed recovery of the difference and individuality of self in the identity of Spirit, *Geist* encompasses what stands opposed to it. In this sense, Hegel replicates the mistake of his predecessors by dominating the other, if this time through the other's subsumption into the Concept. Thus, in spite of the power of his critique, Hegel ultimately privileges the community over the individual and does not, as a result, solve the problem of freedom and necessity as he claims to do. This privileging, according to Adorno, is disguised by the semitheological "spirit," with its indelible memories of individual subjectivity.

Negative dialectics, on the other hand, exposes the violence of Hegel's "authoritative synthesis." Derrida makes a similar critique of Hegel's *Aufhebung* of the divide between the realms of necessity and freedom and the individual and the community. To quote Derrida:

> The Hegelian *Aufhebung* is produced entirely from within discourse, from within the system or the work of signification. A determination is negated and conserved in another determination which reveals the truth of the former. From infinite indetermination one passes to infinite determination, and this transition, produced by the anxiety of the infinite, continuously links meaning up to itself. The *Aufhebung* is included *within* the circle of absolute knowledge, never exceeds its closure, never suspends the totality of discourse, work, meaning, law, etc. Since it never dispels the veiling form of absolute knowledge, even by maintaining this form, the Hegelian *Aufhebung* in all its parts belongs to what Bataille calls "the world of work." . . . The Hegelian *Aufhebung* thus belongs to restricted economy, and is the form of the passage from one prohibition to another, the *circulation* of prohibitions, history as the truth of the prohibition.[19]

Repression in this sense lies at the core of the Hegelian unification of Mind and Being in *Geist* which is, in turn, the basis for Hegel's reconciliation of the realm of necessity with the realm of freedom. Spirit then, does not truly overcome the binary oppositions of subject/object, particularity/universality, individual/ community. This failure, for both Adorno and Derrida, has implications for the way in which the community is conceived in Hegel and how such a view should be critiqued or deconstructed. More specifically, we see the affinity with liberalism, because their concern is with the concrete individual and the protection of individuality.

Individuality Rethought against Hegel

For Adorno, Hegel's deified, purportedly collective subjectivity does not unite the individual with the community because world Spirit is what counts as the true substance of the individual, even if that substance be the self-reflective subjectivity of *Geist*. Since what "counts" as the true *substance* of the individual is the collective, the concrete individual is erased. As Adorno remarks,

> Even to Hegel, after all, subjectivity is the universal and the total identity. He deifies it. But he accomplishes the opposite as well: an insight into the subject as a self-manifesting objectivity. There is an abysmal duality in his construction of the subject-object. He not only falsifies the object ideologically, calling it a free act of the absolute subject; he also recognizes in the subject a self-representing objectivity, thus anti-ideologically restricting the subject. Subjectivity as an existing reality of substance did claim precedence, but as an "existing," alienated subject it would be both objective and phenomenal.[20]

As we saw in the last chapter, the subject as spirit, the substratum of freedom, is detached from the concrete subjectivity of the embodied, living human being. According to Adorno, Hegel's subjugation of the concrete subject in the name of an imposed unity of the individual and the community in *Geist* is demonstrated in Hegel's philosophy of law.[21] "As the state, the fatherland makes out a community of existence; as man's subjective volition submits to the laws, the antithesis of freedom and necessity that Hegel critiqued in Kant and Fichte supposedly disappears."[22]

Law is not external to the self-conscious subject who understands her oneness with the community. Obedience to the rules is correct consciousness. Those who don't obey the laws don't know who they really are. Thus, Hegel undermines the sphere of private conscience he purportedly protects. This undermining of the sphere of private conscience in turn has implications for the way in which the relationship of law and morality is understood. For example, in Hegel, the separation of conscience and legal norms expressed in civil disobedience is ultimately a form of false consciousness. The danger here is that

> [t]he reigning consensus puts the universal in the right because of the mere form of its universality. Universality, itself a concept, comes thus to be conceptless and inimical to reflection; for the mind to perceive and to name that side of it is the first condition of resistance and a modest beginning of practice.[23]

It is important to remember that Adorno's critique of Hegel's subsumption of the concrete individual in objective spirit does not lead him to reject "the central insight of Hegel's *Logic*,"[24] the reciprocal codetermination of purportedly individual entities. In Adorno, however, individuality is defined in relation to what it is against, and is against it, the social leveling of mass society. Our self-definition is completely contaminated, for Adorno, by the consumer, which makes each one of us a target for products. We may think we are being free when we choose the latest product that will allow us to be who we are, but in reality we are simply following the advertiser. As a result of his critique of mass society, Adorno wants to give a different and indeed frightening interpretation of Hegel's insight that "society is essentially the substance of the individual."[25] According to Adorno, what parades as the reconciliation of the individual and the community, the particular and the universal in the later Hegel, is the annihilation of individual difference and, more specifically, the end of the dissenter. We can approach this point from a slightly different angle using Hegel's own insight to undermine his conclusions; the recognition of the universal *form* of subjectivity undermines the very subject it was meant to give expression to and to protect.

As a result,

> [i]n the hundred and fifty years since Hegel's conception was formed, some of the force of protest has reverted to the individual. Compared to the patriarchal meagerness that characterizes his treatment in Hegel, the individual has gained as much in richness, differentiation and vigour as, on the other hand, the socialization of society has enfeebled and undermined him. . . . In face of the totalitarian unison with which the eradication of difference is proclaimed as a purpose in itself, even part of the social force of liberation may have temporarily withdrawn to the individual sphere.[26]

In other words, Hegel's siding with the universal in the form of deified subjectivity cuts off the very dialectical reciprocity he wanted to present as the truth of all reality.

According to Adorno, as we saw in the last chapter, the recognition of the nonidentical relation of thought to reality, Being and the Concept, unleashes the dialectic that has been contained in the Hegelian attempt to complete experience, including ethical, political, and legal experience in the philosophical ascension to absolute knowledge. Adorno's materialism is the reverse side of his critique of Hegelian totality. Once we understand Adorno's materialism we can see the relationship between his suspicion of the Hegelian community and his affirmation of singular individuals irreducible to their definitions within a pre-existing ethical life.

Death, War, and Individuality

The trace of the constitutive outside, that which cannot be encompassed in *Geist,* presents itself most starkly as death. Hegel himself attempts to reconcile us with death as the inevitable falling away of the finite so that the infinite can be. But death also plays a political role in Hegel. War is the ultimate expression of the collective subjectivity of the people, an action against the other which consolidates the reciprocally related network of individuals into a unit, a self-conscious people.

> In absolute ethical life, infinity—or form as the absolutely negative—is nothing other than subjugating . . . taken up into its absolute concept. There it relates not to single specific matters, but to their entire actuality and possibility, that is, to life itself. Thus matter equals infinite form, but in such a way that its positive element is the absolutely ethical element (i.e., membership in a people);

the individual proves his unity with the people unmistakably through the danger of death alone. Through the absolute identity of the infinite, or of the aspect of relation, with the positive, ethical totalities, such as peoples, take form and constitute themselves as individuals. . . . Just as the blowing of the winds preserves the sea from the foulness which would result from a continual calm, so also corruption would result for peoples under continual or indeed "perpetual" peace.[27]

Here, Hegel gives us a graphic image of the violent opening of ethics necessary for the people to establish their image of themselves as a consolidated subjectivity. (The Other must go under for the people to become one.) The tragedy of the individual who dies is wiped out in the march of world spirit. The individual's biological destruction is given meaning in the larger ethical life of the people. For all of the poetic language about the honor of death, those of us who have lived through the horrors of the twentieth century find it easy to agree with Adorno:

What is decisive is the absorption of biological destruction by conscious social will. Only a humanity to whom death has become as indifferent as its members, that has itself died, can inflict it administratively on innumerable people. Rilke's prayer for "one's own death" is a piteous attempt to conceal the fact that nowadays people merely snuff out.[28]

Derrida's Exposure of the Violence Inherent in Rousseau's Dream of Community

We now need to return to the more subtle forms of violence inherent in the idealization of communalism. Adorno clearly reminds us that the ideal of a universal, transparent, thoroughly rationalized humanity, the society of rational wills, carries within it a violent attitude toward the nonconformist who can always be labeled irrational. But in addition, the very idea of a fully rationalized mankind—and I am using that word deliberately—carries within it the repression of what is other to any particular ideal of a rationalized community, including aspects of ourselves as creatures of the flesh. In Derrida's words:

Man *calls himself* man only by drawing limits excluding his other from the play of supplementarity: the purity of nature, of animality, primitivism, childhood, madness, divinity. The approach to these limits is at once feared as a threat of death, and desired as access to a life without *différance*. The history of man *calling himself* man is the articulation of *all* these limits among themselves.[29]

We turn now to Derrida's engagement with Rousseau. Rousseau has been memorialized for his attempt to reconcile romantic conceptions of community with democracy. But, for Derrida, even Rousseau's democratic dream of community—certainly more democratic than the one offered by Hegel—that emphasizes self-government still carries within it the dilemmas Adorno criticized in Hegel. Therefore, Derrida's critique of Rousseau becomes relevant to our discussion of the ideal of community.

Derrida uncovers in the Rousseauist vision of equals forming themselves into a community in the burst of life of the festival, a festival of joy and sensuality, the dream of life without *différance* and indeed of life without mediation. In the dream, the participants are fully present to one another in a *direct* meeting of equals. The dream is also of an originary instant of coming together without a trace of what has gone before.[30] The festival is an originary ritual which allows for a nonviolent opening of ethics. It is also a festival, not a debate between rational men. In the dream people drink, dance, sing, and celebrate as they come together to form the community. The Dionysiac moment in the forming of the community is thus not denied. The Rousseauist community, originating in the festival and based on direct, unmediated face-to-face relations, expresses Rousseau's dream of nonopposition between human beings and nature, the individual and the community, the desiring, willful subject of the flesh and the public role of the citizen. Rousseau privileges the living voice, speech as the vehicle for co-equals who are literally present to one another as they codetermine their government and indeed their destiny. The goal of full presence is precisely to help us escape fate by redefining our destiny together.

But according to Derrida, what one finds in Rousseau is not the fulfillment of the dream of nonoppositional relation but the replication of the violent hierarchies that inhere in the principle of identity.

> What are the two contradictory possibilities that Rousseau wishes to retain simultaneously? And how does he do it? He wishes on the one hand to *affirm*, by giving it a positive value, everything of which articulation is the principle or everything with which it constructs a system (passion, language, society, man, etc.). But he intends to affirm simultaneously all that is cancelled by articulation (accent, life, energy, passion yet again, and so on). The supplement being the articulated structure of these two possibilities, Rousseau can only decompose them and dissociate them into two simple units, logically contradictory yet allowing an intact purity to both the negative and the positive. And yet Rousseau, caught, like the logic of identity, *within* the graphic of supplementarity, says what he does not wish to say, describes what he does not wish to conclude: that the positive (is) the negative, life (is) death, presence (is) absence and that this repetitive supplementarity is not comprised in any dialectic, at least if that concept is governed, as it always has been, by a horizon of presence.[31]

In political terms, Rousseau's vision of egalitarian community life perpetuates the social inequalities that inhere in the violent oppositional hierarchies that Rousseau hoped to overcome. Using Adorno's terminology, Derrida undermines the logic of identity by uncovering the difference in the identity of Rousseau's idealized community. Thus, for example, he shows us how Rousseau's originary myth of full speech assumes a linguistic system already in place in which the members come to language. Speech implies "writing." Against Rousseau, and the latter-day Rousseauian Claude Lévi-Strauss, Derrida argues that there is no innocent community initially free of writing which is then corrupted by the unintentional imperialism of the anthropologist. Indeed, the myth of natural innocence which Derrida associates with the belief in a community free from writing, is exposed by Derrida as itself a version of ethnocentrism. By writing, Derrida means the system of representation that makes communication possible, not just what we normally mean by writing, a system of graphic signs with something like a recognizable alphabet. As Derrida explains, "[t]he genealogical relation and social classification are the stitched seam of arche-writing."[32] Arche-writing is standing in here for the structure of supplementarity, *différance*, "the chance of interruption" of the Hegelian *Aufhebung*.

To back his assertion that there is no community without writing, Derrida argues that the bestowal of the proper name, which no society can avoid, signifies writing in the sense that it implies a system of classification by which people recognize one another. The proper name carries within it the trace of institutional history. In other words, the identity of speech is contaminated by its other, writing. Yet Derrida's rejection of Rousseau's myth of original innocence does not lead him to reject what he understands to be the central insight of both Lévi-Strauss and Rousseau—the association of writing with violence. Writing and other forms of "representational" systems, whether they be kinship systems or political institutions, are an attempt to defend against human violence. But to the degree that the establishment of systems for ethical and political "representation" identifies the norm and rigidly circumscribes the definition of right behavior, such establishments carry within them their own violence. The very power to name is for Derrida "the originary violence of language which consists in inscribing within a difference, in classifying. . . . To think the unique *within* the system, to inscribe it there, such is the gesture of arche-writing: arche-violence."[33] For Derrida, Rousseau's ethic of speech is a "delusion of presence mastered," a delusion that is dangerous because it conceals or effaces the violence of language's classifying power.

> There is no ethics without the presence *of the other* but also, and consequently, without absence, dissimulation, detour, *différance*, writing. The arche-writing is the origin of morality as of immorality. The nonethical opening of ethics. A violent opening. As in the case of the vulgar concept of writing, the ethical instance of violence must be rigorously suspended in order to repeat the genealogy of morals.[34]

Speech and the speaking subject cannot achieve full presence because speech is embedded in an already-given linguistic system, independent of any empirical subject. As a result, linguistic meaning cannot be reduced to the intent of the speaking subject. The very iterability of a system of signs, the iterability that makes a system of signs a language, is paradoxically what allows for the spiriting away of the message of the sender. Language cannot be *owned* by the subject as her own expression. The inability to achieve full self-transparency or community transparency can be understood as "the Law" of human finitude, as well as the result of the community's basis in language.

The disruption of identity of the individual or community by difference, including the in-place linguistic system through which the individual and the community have been constituted, is not overcome in a "new" identity inclusive of difference, as Derrida believes it is in the Hegelian system. Derrida's objection is not only philosophical, the objection is clearly ethical. For Derrida, as for Adorno, Hegel's *Aufhebung* is another guise of assimilation. The other is consumed by Spirit, so that the difference of the Other is erased. Hegelian metaphysics is the myth of full presence in its most sophisticated form. Derrida connects Rousseau's dream (in spite of its obvious differences from Hegel) to Hegel because of a shared implicit reliance on the myth of full presence. As Derrida explains:

> Moreover, Rousseau is not alone in being caught in the graphic of supplementarity. All meaning and therefore all discourse is caught there, particularly and by a singular turn, the discourse of the metaphysics within which Rousseau's concepts move. And when Hegel will proclaim the unity of absence and presence, of nonbeing and being, dialectics or history will continue to be, at least on the level of discourse that we have called Rousseau's wishing-to-say, a movement of mediation between two full presences. Eschatological parousia is also the presence of the full speech, bringing together all its differences and its articulations within the consciousness (of) self of the logos. Consequently, before asking the necessary questions about the historical situation of Rousseau's text, we must locate all the signs of its appurtenance to the metaphysics of presence, from Plato to Hegel, rhythmed by the articulation of presence upon self-presence.[35]

Here again we are returned to Hegel's *Geist,* the subject in and for itself, and thus completely self-transparent. Derrida's problematization of the myth of full presence and, more specifically, of the dependency of Hegel's understanding of community on the myth of self-presence, can be interpreted as a reading of Hegel against himself. On this reading, Hegel's vision of the primordially communal subject is not rejected, it is instead rendered consistent with Hegel's own "deconstruction" of the metaphysics of constituted essences.

> [S]upplementarity, which *is nothing,* neither a presence nor an absence, is neither a substance nor an essence of man. It is . . . that [which] no metaphysical or ontological concept can comprehend. Therefore this property . . . of man is not a property of man: it is the very dislocation of the proper in general.[36]

What is the ethical and legal significance of this dislocation of the proper? The personhood of the individual can no longer be conceived as the initial form of property as Hegel, under one reading, makes it in the *Philosophy of Right.* The decentered subject is relational to the core. The subject can no longer be thought of as a self-identical, self-present entity, a self-bounded substance, but it can also not simply be conceived as *one* with the collectivity.

The Relationship of Derrida's Deconstruction
of the Myth of Full Presence
to His Reading of Levinas

The deconstruction of the subject as an irreducible substance takes the critique of constituted essences in Hegel's *Logic* to its conclusion. Such an admittedly Hegelian and indeed communal interpretation of Derrida's deconstruction of the proper is consistent with Derrida's deeply sympathetic encounter with Emmanuel Levinas' attempt to move beyond metaphysics in the portrayal of the face-to-face as a relation "prior" to the established unity of the community.[37] As Bernasconi has succinctly explained:

> For Levinas the face to face "relation" is immediate. This serves as an additional ground for excluding the possibility that it can be thought or presented from outside by a third party. In the perspective of the third the face to face is totalized, reduced to a unity for which he is the mediator.[38]

The insistence on the face-to-face as a relation non-encompassable by the Spirit of the community expresses Levinas' rejection of the Hegelian dialectic of recognition and even of Heidegger's *Miteinandersein,* the collectivity of the "with." Levinas rejects the reciprocal constitution of subjectivities in and through the *Mitte.* The Other as "absolute Other" cannot be reduced to a relationship to me. The alterity of the Other is displayed in her separateness or asymmetry in her stance toward me. She is the stranger; yet as the orphan, the widow, and the hungry, she is also the one who judges me on the basis of my responsibility to her. In Levinas, responsibility does not await reciprocity, and therefore the relationship to the other is necessarily asymmetrical. As Levinas himself explains:

> One of the fundamental themes of *Totality and Infinity* . . . is that the intersubjective relation is a non-symmetrical relation. In this sense I am responsible to the Other without waiting for reciprocity, were I to die for it. Reciprocity is his affair.[39]

Yet at times, Levinas goes beyond his own assertion that reciprocity is the Other's affair. His anti-Hegelianism is expressed in his rendering the "absolute Other" as master. The recognition of the other as master—as she who cannot be recognized in Hegel's sense of *Anerkennen*—lies at the very heart of the ethical relationship, or what Levinas speaks of as religion: "The interlocutor is not a Thou, he is a You; he reveals himself in his lordship. Thus exteriority coincides with a mastery. My freedom is thus challenged by a Master who can invest it."[40]

Derrida's critique of Levinas' anti-Hegelianism has both an ethical and a philosophical dimension. Derrida asks who is the "absolute Other" in Levinas or, perhaps more precisely, is there an "absolute Other" that is not, ironically enough, absolutely identical? Here Derrida explicitly reminds us of the Hegelian lesson that the hypostatization of difference—alterity is absolute—reinstates absolute identity. As Hegel tells us again and again, difference from the Other is an internal relation to the other. Derrida has clearly heard Hegel and heeds his message when he challenges Levinas' infinite Other.

> Does not Levinas treat the expression *alter ego* as if *alter* were the epithet of a real subject (on a pre-eidetic level)? As an ephithetical [sic], accidental modification of my real (empirical) identity? Now, the transcendental syntax of the expression *alter ego* tolerates no relationship of substantive to adjective, of absolute to epithet, in one sense or the other. This is its strangeness. A necessity due to the finitude of meaning: the other is "absolute Other" only if he is an ego, that is, in a certain way, if he is the same as I. Inversely, the other as *res* is simultaneously less other (not absolutely other) and less "the same" than I. Simultaneously more and less other, which means, once more, that the absolute of alterity is the same.[41]

Derrida uncovers in Levinas a "strange symmetry" in that "I am also essentially the other's other and that I know I am."[42] The other is an other who can open herself to me precisely because she is an other "in my economy." Without this strange symmetry, or the introduction of a positive notion of infinity in which the encounter with the infinite Other is an encounter with God, Levinas' insistence on the *phenomenological* as well as the ethical asymmetry of the Other would degenerate into the worst sort of violence.

> This is why God alone keeps Levinas's world from being a world of the pure and worst violence, a world of immorality itself. The structures of living and naked experience described by Levinas are the very structures of a world in which war would rage—strange conditional—if the infinitely other were not infinity, if there were, by chance, one naked man, finite and alone.[43]

For as Derrida only too well understands, the *phenomenological* asymmetry between finite human beings is itself a form of violence. One example of the violence of *phenomenological* asymmetry to which Derrida has been very attentive is the asymmetrical relationship between Man and Woman. What has been protected in the asymmetrical relationship is not the mystery of difference but the reality of domination. I will return to a more elaborate discussion of Derrida's understanding of phenomenological symmetry in the next chapter.

The Critique of Levinas

For now, let me emphasize that Derrida argues that the relegation of the Other to pure externality is itself a form of self-containment. To be self-enclosed, to deny the "trace" of the Other in oneself, is to be impenetrable, safe from the contamination of the "outside." *"Différance* is difference under erasure," not the glorification of phenomenological asymmetry. Derrida's specific intervention into Levinas is to argue instead that ethical asymmetry, if it is to be ethical, now defined as respectful of the otherness of the Other, must be based on phenomenological symmetry. The strangeness of the Other is that the Other is an "I." But, as an "I," the Other is the same as "me." Without this moment of universality the otherness of the Other can be only too easily reduced to mythical projection. The example of men and women is only one example. Even so, we can remember here Simone de Beauvoir's account of how Woman's definition as Man's Other does not recognize her otherness at all.[44] Derrida is also extremely sensitive to the exclusionism and prejudice that marks the arrogance of Western imperialism. Derrida's concern can be translated into an attempt to dream the dance of sameness and difference beyond the demonstration of shared substantive properties and its counterpart, the denial of all phenomenological symmetry.

Levinas ultimately cannot help us in dreaming this dream precisely because of his re-inscription of a positive vision of infinity. As Derrida explains:

> The positive Infinity (God)—if these words are meaningful—cannot be infinitely Other. If one thinks, as Levinas does, that positive Infinity tolerates, or even requires, infinite alterity, then one must renounce all language, and first of all the words *infinite* and *other*. Infinity cannot be understood as Other except as the form of the infinite.[45]

Yet, as we have also seen, for Derrida the ultimate attempt to think the infinite, Hegel's *Logic,* re-inscribes the very metaphysics of constituted essences to which the *Logic* aims its fire. According to Derrida, if we are to convey a sense of relation in which the relation is prior to the whole, we must begin with Heidegger's distinction between the belonging together, which is a unity, and the togetherness of belonging. Derrida traces Levinas' misguided rejection of Heidegger to a misunderstanding. As Derrida explains:

> If to understand Being is to be able to let be (that is, to respect Being in essence and existence, and to be responsible for one's respect), then the understanding of Being always concerns alterity, and par excellence the alterity of the Other in all its originality: one can have to let be only that which one is not. If Being is always to be let be, and if to think is to let Being be, then Being is indeed the other of thought.[46]

To think the Being of the Other in this way is to think the Other as a being of phenomenological symmetry, and thus as both same and different.

The Thinking of Finitude

For Derrida, the original finitude that disrupts Hegel's *Aufhebung*—called, according to context, writing, *différance,* the structure of supplementarity—is graphically apparent in its effects in death. Death is the constitutive outside par excellence as it is shared by all of us as mortal beings. Death belies the myth of full presence, and foils our human attempts ultimately to control our fate. Yet the death we know is not our own death but the death of the desired other. As Freud has so beautifully demonstrated, the fear of death is the fear of object loss;[47] it is the fear of being helpless before our own grief and of being powerless to bring the Other back. To love the mutable is to risk this loss, to experience inevitably the absence of the one we have loved. The desire to draw rigid boundaries, to achieve satisfaction purely in oneself—clinically referred to as narcissism—is an attempted defense against both the risk and the loss of love. The fear of death is the fear of the Other we cannot enclose. It is no coincidence that grief over the death of a lost one and grief over the desertion of a lover are both experienced as grief, as the longing for the one who is absent. To be with *différance* is to be with the mutable.

Derrida and Adorno, in their recognition of the constitutive outside, are materialists. *Geist* cannot encircle itself, protecting us from that reality of finitude. The Other always escapes the subject's attempt to make it its own. We cannot make up in the "reassuring *other* surface of the positive"[48] all we have lost. The risk of love for the mutable is not an investment in the ascension to absolute knowledge. For Derrida and Adorno, Hegel's system was to free us from the risk of love for the Other; their message is not only that we cannot be safe from the risk of the love of the mutable, it is also a warning against the hubris of the myth of safety, if understood as protection against otherness, maintained by the illusion of self-containment.

The Ideal of Communicative Freedom

Does this warning mean that we reject the *ideal* of community as the hope for a nonviolent ethical relationship to the other? I think the answer is no. But first we must distinguish between the effects of Adorno and Derrida's deconstruction of the logic of identity, as these shift both our understanding of the actuality of concrete ethics, *Sittlichkeit,* and the "ideal," or the chance of communicative freedom which is often blurred with acceptance of participation in an already established community life. If anything is clear, as we have seen, it is that Derrida and Adorno reject the identification of ethics with the perpetuation of order per se or with the current order, even if conceived of as a "conversation of mankind."[49] The disruption of the force of the Other and otherness turns against the appeal to a self-enclosed tradition.

According to Derrida, there can be no self-enclosed tradition, ethical or otherwise, which will not show the effects of the economy of *différance*. Remember, for example, Derrida's demonstration of how Rousseau's community of self-presence denied the disruptive force of language. The historical horizon of understanding which gives body to our ethical precepts is not denied, it is instead shown to be open-ended, precisely because such precepts cannot be separated from language's power to define the ethical, but only as linguistic formations which can never be firmly rooted in reality. As a result, the conventions of a community cannot be shown to be a closed totality. The ethical message in both Derrida and Adorno reminds us to care for difference, the difference we can only glimpse as beyond contradiction and appropriation. The care for difference needs a generosity that does not attempt to grasp what is other as one's own. The danger of certainty is that it turns against the generous impulse to open oneself up to the Other, and to truly listen, to risk the chance that we might be wrong. The move to nonclosure, then, can and should be understood ethically.

Derrida has eloquently elaborated the significance of this move to nonclosure by playing off the beginning and the end of the *Phaedrus*.[50] The deconstruction of the myth of origin leaves the question "from whence do I hail" with no definitive answer. Without an answer to that question, and without an ability to know and thus possess the Good once and for all, there can be no confident taking the other by the hand, and saying "Let us go." For Derrida, the "community" that has learned the humility and the pain of the lesson of finitude cannot steer with confidence, driving the misguided who do not see it their way out of their path.

> A community of the question, therefore, within that fragile moment when the question is not yet determined enough for the hypocrisy of an answer to have already initiated itself beneath the mask of the question, and not yet determined enough for its voice to have been already and fraudulently articulated within the very syntax of the question. A community of decision, of initiative, of absolute initiality, but also a threatened community, in which the question has not yet found the language it has decided to seek, is not yet sure of its own possibility within the community. A community of the question about the possibility of the question.[51]

And what is the question about the possibility of the question, if not the dream of communicative freedom, in which this dream of reconciliation is no longer conceived as a unity? If the Other is assimilated as one's own, then we have fallen back into the philosophy of reflection Hegel eloquently critiqued. To put it as strongly as possible, the protection and care of difference is not carried out to the detriment of the possibility of mutual self-recognition, if understood in the sense of the recognition of *phenomenological* symmetry, but in its name. Adorno put it this way: "The reconciled condition would not be the philosophical imperialism of annexing the alien. Instead, its happiness would lie in the fact that the alien, in the proximity it is granted, remains what is distant . . . and beyond that which is one's own."[52]

Adorno's philosophy of redemption is the counterpole to his assertion against Hegel: "all knowledge is false."[53] The normative standard of communicative freedom cannot be thought as an already-achieved reality. Its critical power lies precisely in that it shows the world as distorted and indigent in comparison with the reconciled state. Adorno openly embraces an apocalyptic tone.

The only philosophy which can be responsibly practiced in face of despair is the attempt to contemplate all things as they would present themselves from the standpoint of redemption. Knowledge has no light but that shed on the world by redemption: all else is reconstruction, mere technique. Perspectives must be fashioned that displace and estrange the world, reveal it to be, with its rifts and crevices, as indigent and distorted as it will appear one day in the messianic light.[54]

Derrida's Warning against Adorno's Philosophy of Redemption

Derrida warns us against the apocalyptic tone while expressing his deep sympathy with it. For as Derrida himself realizes, when one speaks of such a tone one inevitably speaks with it. Yet Derrida also warns that such a tone seeks to soar above the lessons of finitude. Derrida mimics that apocalyptic tone in its defense of sectarianism:

We are all going to die, we are going to disappear. And this death sentence, this stopping of death . . . can only judge us. We are going to die, you and I, the others too, the goyim, the gentiles, and all the others, all those who do not share this secret with us, but they do not know it. . . . We are the only ones in the world. I am the only one able to reveal to you the truth or the destination. . . . We shall be a sect; we shall form a species, a sex or gender, a race . . . by ourselves alone; we shall give ourselves a name.[55]

Derrida, in other words, warns us also against the sin of the Semites, which, in spite of the best intentions, replicates a form of domination. But does he completely reject the dream of communicative freedom? Does he turn away from the dream of relations beyond indifference and domination that Hegel tried to show as the truth of his *Logic* and Heidegger dared to approach again, understanding that his approach would take him beyond the reaches of Western metaphysics? "The economy of *différance*" can convincingly be interpreted to belie and disrupt even Adorno's appeal to redemptive perspectives. As Derrida himself explains: "Thus, *différance* is the name we might give to the 'active,' moving discord of different forces, and of differences of forces, that Nietzsche sets up against the entire system of metaphysical grammar, wherever this system governs culture, philosophy, and science."[56]

Différance names the deferral in time and space of the closure of the circle of immanence in Hegel's absolute knowledge. That much is clear. But the attempt to think difference as a conceptual counter to Hegel's absolute knowledge is also rejected. As Derrida knows only too well, the attempt to disprove Hegel proves Hegel right at the very moment of rejection. Derrida's own moves to disrupt the Hegelian system have been characteristically cautious. As Derrida explains:

Elsewhere, in a reading of Bataille, I have attempted to indicate what might come of a rigorous and, in a new sense, "scientific" *relating* of the "restricted economy" that takes no part in expenditure without reserve, death, opening itself to nonmeaning, etc., to a general economy that *takes into account* the nonreserve, that keeps in reserve the nonreserve, if it can be put thus. I am speaking of a relationship between a *différance* that can make a profit on its investment and a *différance* that misses its profit, the *investiture* of a presence that is pure and without loss here being confused with absolute loss, with death.[57]

But how much does this tell us beyond the suggestion made earlier that we cannot self-satisfiedly make an appeal to a self-enclosed *Sittlichkeit?* Is *différance* the constant reminder of the limits of philosophy or more than that, is it the lie to all redemptive visions?

I would suggest that Derrida's ambivalence toward giving voice to "redemptive" perspectives does not just express the reluctance to "represent" divine aspiration. This reluctance, for example, is not found in all of his texts. In his essay on Walter Benjamin's "The Task of the Translator,"[58] Derrida appeals to the promise of reconciliation in a messianic tongue as the promise of translations. Yet Derrida insists it is a *promise* of reconciliation and not an achieved reality. But he reminds us, "[a] promise is not nothing," and indeed he suggests that without this promise the task of the translator would be impossible. Derrida is surprisingly sympathetic to Benjamin's assertion that translation is a "redemptive" task, because it inevitably appeals to the promise of reconciliation in a messianic tongue.

Derrida also is only too well aware of the danger of a retreat into pre-Hegelian metaphysics, in which we are left again with the irreconcilable dichotomies. He would, I believe, agree with Adorno's warning against the reversion "to the pre-dialectical stage: the serene demonstration of the fact that there are two sides to everything."[59] Deconstruction dedicates itself to the disruption of dualistic hierarchy, not to its acceptance.

And as I have already suggested, Derrida and Adorno associate hierarchical dualism with the imperious subject of logocentrism, *Geist*. But does the disruption of dualistic hierarchy and the dislocation of the centered, sovereign subject lead to the embrace of communalism? Certainly, not in the Hegelian sense of encompassing the individual and the community. But as we have also seen, both Adorno and Derrida understand individuality relationally, even if it is a relation against the social leveling of mass society. In a thoughtful essay, Charles Levin suggests that Derrida stops short of communalism, precisely because of its Hegelian overtones, replacing community with "networks of reciprocally constituted subjects."

If hierarchy is the foundation of an imperious subject, the network is the *unilateral construct* of a subject, albeit a self-effacing subject, a subject that orients and displaces itself at will. Only the community *challenges* with its unpredictable heterogeneity, for the community cannot be broken down in a sequential play of discrete encounters riveted on a uniform coefficient; and only the community can be challenged. . . . Derridean deconstruction is another gambit in the old philosophical game of deferring the danger of the world.[60]

But the philosophy of the limit, as I have renamed deconstruction, can also be understood as deferring the danger of communities that insist on full presence. The power of communalism as a dream lies in the chance of uncovering or having revealed to us a different way of belonging together, which does not revert to classic individualism and which is also not just the identification of the individual with the community in mass society. Derrida hesitantly steps forward into the haze of the dream of communicative freedom. We cannot with certainty point toward the good life and say "Let us go," but we can beckon:

"Come" [*Viens*] beyond being—this comes from beyond being and calls beyond being, engaging, starting perhaps in the place where *Ereignis* (no longer can this be translated by event) and *Enteignis* unfold the movement of propriation. If "Come" does not try to lead or conduct, if it no doubt is anagogic, it can always be led back higher than itself, anagogically, toward the conductive violence, toward the authoritarian "duction." This risk is unavoidable; it threatens the tone as its double. . . . "Come" does not address itself, does not appeal, to an identity determinable in advance. It is a drift . . . underivable from the identity of a determination. "Come" is *only* derivable, absolutely derivable, but only from the other, from nothing that may be an origin or a verifiable, decidable, presentable, appropriate identity. . . .[61]

Derrida does not simply refuse the apocalyptic tone of many of the writers he most admires, he warns them against their own violence. He hesitantly recognizes the dream of communicative freedom, the ideal of community or communalism understood as belonging together without violence, because he understands so clearly the horror of the distortion of that dream. And yet, without it, we cannot recognize the phenomenological symmetry of the Other, which demands the affirmation of our sameness as well as our difference. Communalism, in this sense, as an *ideal,* expresses the recognition of the sameness that marks each one of us as an individual and thus as both different and the same. It is in this recognition of the connection between sameness and difference that allows us to understand belonging together without some overriding spirit in and through which we are connected. If this is just a dream in our world of antagonism and violence, it does not mean that it is not a dream worth dreaming. Nor does the language of the dream mean that it is absolutely impossible. To quote Derrida, "Does the dream itself not prove that what is dreamt of must be there in order for it to provide the dream?"[62] Perhaps there is no answer to that question except that some of us continue to dream.

But if we are to understand more fully the ethical and political significance of this "dream," we must return again to the relationship between Derrida's deconstructive exercises, the ethical relation, and the law. Otherwise, at least on one interpretation of deconstruction, we are left with the "politics of suspicion." The role of the deconstructionist is reduced to the exposure of the marginalized, the excluded, from any community. Deconstruction, in other words, exposes how the very logic of the establishment of community draws boundaries that by necessity leave some out. Alasdair MacIntyre has gone so far as to argue that the "postmodern" and, more specifically, the French "postmodern" suspicion of any and every tradition exemplifies what Emile Durkheim referred to as social pathology.[63] On this reading, the political role of the deconstructionist can only be to disrupt, not to participate.[64] To answer MacIntyre we have to examine more carefully the intersection between Derrida's deconstructive intervention into the works of Hegel, Levinas, and Lacan because, as we will see, it is precisely the rereading of this intersection that yields a "new" ethical configuration irreducible to the politics of "suspicion."

3

The Ethical Significance
of the *Chiffonnier*

Let us descend a little lower and consider one of those mysterious creatures who live, as it were, off the leavings (*déjections*) of the big city . . . . Here we have a man whose task is to gather the day's rubbish in the capital. Everything that the big city has cast off, everything it lost, everything it disdained, everything it broke, he catalogues and collects. He combs through the archives of debauchery, the stockpile of waste. He sorts things out and makes intelligent choices; like a miser assembling his treasure, he gathers the trash that, after being regurgitated by the goddess of Industry, will assume the shape of useful or gratifying objects.

—Walter Benjamin

Introduction

How are we to begin to present the intersection of a deconstructive intervention into the works of Hegel, Levinas, and Lacan as an ethical configuration? As I hope to show, the figure of the *Chiffonnier* may help to bring into focus what is unique about the ethical positioning of the philosophy of the limit. To understand why I have chosen the figure of the *Chiffonnier,* we need to focus again on the rebellion against Hegelianism. In this chapter, I want to give a different emphasis to the ethical impulse behind the rebellion against Hegelianism, beyond the positioning vis-à-vis the ideal of community we discussed in the last chapter.

Indeed, I will suggest that the entire project of the philosophy of the limit is driven by an ethical desire to enact the ethical relation. Again, by the ethical relation I mean to indicate the aspiration to a nonviolent relationship to the Other, and to otherness more generally, that assumes responsibility to guard the Other against the appropriation that would deny her difference and singularity. I am deliberately using a broad brush in defining the ethical relation, so as to include a number of thinkers who share the aspiration to heed the call to responsibility for the Other, but who would otherwise disagree on the philosophical underpinnings of the ethical relation and on its precise definition. I am, then, defining the ethical relation more broadly than the thinker Emmanuel Levinas, with whom the phrase is usually associated.[1] I will, however, return again and again to Levinas' specific formulation of the ethical relation as the "beyond" to ontology,[2] because, as we began to see in the last chapter, it is Levinas' own understanding of the ethical relation that Derrida interrogates. I will attempt to make explicit the ethical desire of the philosophy of the limit by further examining Derrida's engagement with Levinas' ethical philosophy of alterity.

But, as we also saw in the last chapter, we cannot fully understand Derrida's encounter with Levinas without also engaging with his deconstruction of Hegelianism. When we confront our desire to "escape" from Hegel, to put him to rest once and for all, we need to ask why we are trying to get out from under his shadow; or, more precisely, in the name of what do we make our escape. One answer, of course, is that the deconstruction of Hegel simply puts into operation "the truth" that speculative reason will always turn against its own pretenses if it cannot come home to itself in Absolute Knowledge. On this reading, the motor of deconstruction is speculative reason, even if now turned against itself.

But there is, as I have suggested, an alternative reading that locates the drive behind deconstruction in an ethical desire. On the ethical reading I offer here, we ask ourselves the opening question of Derrida's *Glas*[3]—a kind of wake for Hegel, with all the implications of both death and salvation that a wake implies— "what, after all, of the remain(s), today, for us, here, now, of a Hegel?"[4] in the name of the elusive residuum left over once the relentless machinery of the Hegelian dialectic has finished its work. The subtle phrasing of Derrida's opening question acknowledges that we cannot separate the question of what remains of Hegel from the question of the remains of Hegelianism. What of the rest that has been pushed out of the system? To ask the question is already a kind of tribute to the forgotten Other, whose remains have been scattered. *Glas* attempts the only salvation of the rest that remains possible through the work of mourning itself, but the project is still one of "salvation" and not just disruption. Indeed, for Derrida, it is only through the work of mourning that we can remember the remains because there has never been, nor can there be, a gathering of the rest that makes fully present what has been shut out: For what has been shut out is literally not there for us. Even so, the work of mourning the remains demands the mimetic persistence to scrape through the debris left over from Hegel's system at the same time that we recognize that " '[t]he rest, the remain(s), is unsayable.' "[5] *Glas* does rather than says. Derrida may well be our best salvage man, our ultimate *Chiffonnier*.

Even if, however, Derrida practices Walter Benjamin's redemptive criticism only through parody and irony, that is still the way he practices redemptive criticism.[6] It is precisely the silence before the name of the prescriptive or ethical force heeded in the philosophy of the limit that has misled many readers to argue that what has been called deconstruction has to do with the radical indeterminacy of meaning and, therefore, with the impossibility of ethical judgment. But the purpose of this chapter is to show that this silence should not be confused with the complete rejection of the ethical relation, nor, as we will see in the following chapters, does this silence implicitly reject the need, within specific contexts, of ethical and legal judgments. Instead I want to argue that Derrida theoretically clears the space for the elaboration of the nonviolent relationship to otherness that Levinas describes as proximity,[7] a relation that is prior to the subject and to contractual consent and yet not encompassed within a unity. Derrida, however, is always careful to preserve the distance that respect for the otherness of the Other implies—which is not to contrast Derrida with Levinas necessarily, because Levinas' conception of proximity is based on the temporal distance that inheres in the precedence of the Other to me. Deconstruction practices Nietzsche's action at a distance in the name of responsibility to the Other.[8] As we will see, a crucial aspect of this "action at a distance" is the recognition of the question of sexual difference as crucial to the aspiration to enact the ethical relationship. As such, the engagement with Levinas cannot be separated from a deconstructive intervention into the psychoanalytic theory of Jacques Lacan.

Derrida is often mistakenly understood to criticize Levinas for his inevitable fall back into the language of ontology. Derrida recognizes, however, that Levinas himself understands that he can only disrupt metaphysics from within the tradition. I will suggest that Derrida *does* show the inevitable dependence of Levinas' project on the language of ontology, but not, however, to resist Levinas' conception of the ethical relation; rather, to salvage it from potential degeneration into the very violence toward otherness that the philosophy of alterity attempts to guard against. In other words, Derrida's deconstruction of Levinas can itself be read ethically. Instead of simply preferring one to the other, we need to read Derrida and Levinas together to heed the call to responsibility and to enact a nonviolent relation to otherness.

The Ethical Significance for Levinas of the Relationship between Being and Nothingness in Hegel

But let me turn now, first to Levinas' rejection of Hegelianism for its replication of the logic of identity, and then return again to Derrida's interrogation of both Levinas and Hegel. By the logic of identity, as we have already seen, I mean to indicate the unity of Meaning and Being that is disclosed in Hegel's *Logic*,[9] as the "truth" of the actual. To understand the ethical interrogation of the logic of identity, then, we must once again move within the circle of Hegel's *Logic*, this time with an emphasis on the relationship between the categories of Being and Nothingness. What I offer here is a conventional reconstruction of the *Logic* that does not attempt to defend a reading of the *Logic* that might meet the opposition of Hegel's poststructuralist or "postmodern" challengers.

In Hegel, the category of Being is the necessary starting point of all thought. Things manifest themselves in and through Being. Reality appears to the thinking subject as an object of thought only because first and foremost things "are." Without the category of Being there would literally be no reality; we would instead be immersed in "the night in which cows are all black." Being is both the necessary starting point of all thought and the minimal determination of things. Being is, thus, the most universal ontological category. And yet Being as a category is both abstract and empty. Certainly Being is "nothing," not just *a* being, because a thing presupposes many determinations other than its mere being. Being "is" only in and through opposition to nothingness. We know "Being" only by what it is not: nothing. The copula affirms the inevitability of the is, the category of Being, yet at the same time, Being can be conceived neither as a predicate nor as a subject of the sentence. As copula, Being exists as something other to itself in which it is united to the diversity of determinations. It includes, therefore, that which is not: nonbeing. Of course, nonbeing is also not able to be what it *is,* nonbeing, unless it relies on its opposite, of which it is the inseparable complement. Hegel's opening moves in the *Logic* show that Being and nonbeing cannot be what they are unless they pass continuously into one another as Becoming. The unity of Being and non-being is their ceaseless changing into their opposite, an endless movement of becoming which is the ontological core of all movement and materiality. The interplay of Being and nonbeing signals the presence of the Absolute as the very movement of the interpenetration of oppositional categories. Nothing is, unless it comes to be in and through the circle of Absolute Knowledge. Hegel's *Logic* culminates in the demonstration that thought and Being are the two opposite names of the Concept or Idea. The thinking which achieves Absolute Knowledge realizes that the self-movement of the Concept or Idea is its own essence, and grasps the full actualization of the structure of the logos in thought and reality itself. The unity of Meaning and Being within the circle of the Absolute yields full knowledge of the truth of the essence of the actual. We come home to ourselves through the recognition of identity in nonidentity, of thought in Being. There is no remainder, no outside. Otherness is recaptured, and completely so, in the circle of the Absolute. Nothing escapes, for nothing is, only as nonbeing,[10] the dialectic opposite of Being.

Within Hegel's *Philosophy of Right,*[11] as we saw in the last chapter, the realization of the truth of the actual yields the complete transparency of the determinations of *Sittlichkeit,* the collective ethics of modernity. For Hegel, as a result, we can know the truth of the ideal of the community.[12] Although we need again to be reminded that if Hegel himself retained the tension between any existing state of affairs and what the actualized concept of democracy demands— and, therefore, his account of *Sittlichkeit* cannot be simplistically condemned, as it often is by Hegel's "liberal" critics,[13] as merely an apology for the current social order—he did identify ethics with the actual. As a result, the dilemma of legal interpretation we are so troubled by today was resolved by the Hegelian identification of truth with history. The meaning of life in the strongest possible sense of meaning is revealed in the circle of the Absolute. The self-conscious recognition of the "we that is I and the I that is we,"[14] the coming home to oneself through the Other, is not only a description, but also a normative practice embodied in the institutions of right in a modern legal system.[15]

For Emmanuel Levinas, Hegel's political philosophy exemplifies the thinking of totality he associates with ontology. The thinking of totality, for Levinas, carries within it the danger of totalitarianism because such a thinking would deny "actuality" to the Other "excluded" from the system. We are again reminded, here, of Hegel's infamous statement that there is no place for Siberia in the philosophy of history.[16] Siberia becomes the symbol of the otherness that has been squeezed out through the operation of the Hegelian dialectic. That which is left out and thus denied actuality does not count. Levinas' ethical subject called by the Other "dispenses with the idealizing subjectivity of [Hegelian] ontology, which reduces everything to itself."[17] So far we would seem to only be going over the familiar territory of the last chapter, but we need to explore in more depth the significance of Levinas' own conception of infinity, which is to counter Hegel's infinite.

According to Levinas, relations of mutual recognition in Hegel's Absolute Knowledge are the example par excellence of the reduction of the Other to the synchronization of self and other that denies the otherness of the other. There is always a trace of otherness that cannot be captured by my "*identifying*" with the Other in relations of mutual recognition. The Other cannot be reduced in relation to me, by which I grasp her essence in the "we that is I and the I that is we." The basis of ethics is not *identification with* those whom we recognize as like ourselves, instead the ethical relation inheres in the encounter with the Other, the stranger, whose face beckons us to heed the call to responsibility. The precedence of the Other means that my relationship to her is necessarily asymmetrical. Reciprocity is, at the very most, the affair of the Other.[18]

In the asymmetrical and yet face-to-face relation with the Other, the stranger who calls to me, the subject first experiences the resistance to encapsulation of the "beyond." In the face-to-face relation we run into the infinity that disrupts totality. Levinas' account of the face to face is still a phenomenology, however, precisely because it is in and through our proximity to the Other in the interface that we experience the resistance of otherness. We encounter God as the transcendence inherent in the ethical relation itself. Transcendence in Levinas is temporal, not spatial. He does not point us to a "beyond" that is "there," a someplace where we are not. Nor can infinity be reduced to the mere Other, to the totality of what is, although there is a reading of Levinas on which infinity is completely "beyond" history, a reading founded in the ambiguity of Levinas' own text. There is, however, clearly another reading, which understands Levinas to seek to displace the traditional oppositions of the inside and the outside, the immanent and the transcendent. The beyond, on this reading, is within totality as its very disruption, but not just as its negation. As Levinas himself explains, "This 'beyond' to the totality and objective experience is, however, not to be described in a purely negative fashion. It is reflected *within* the totality and history, *within* experience."[19] Yet on either reading, infinity cannot be reduced to actuality.

According to Hegel, on the other hand, infinity must be infinite, and thus embodied in the actuality of what is. Otherwise, the finite would be the limit of the infinite.[20] Differentiation into the finite then is the necessary condition for the infinite to be. Exteriority, therefore, is the inevitable result of the *presence* of the Absolute. The necessary estrangement of the infinite from its self is overcome through the self-conscious recognition of exteriority as the manifestation of the Absolute. Nature, in this sense, is conceived as spirit. In Hegel, matter is purportedly redeemed, by being uplifted into the Hegelian system. Here, we have Hegel, symbolized as the eagle who struggles to lift "the stone," the dead weight of the remains, through the help of the machinery of the dialectic. For Derrida, Hegel's name gives the real nature of his enterprise away.

> His name is so strange. From the eagle it draws imperial or historic power. Those who still pronounce his name like the French (there are some) are ludicrous only up to a certain point: the restitution (semantically infallible for those who have read him a little—but only a little) of magisterial coldness and imperturbable seriousness, the eagle caught in ice and frost, glass and gel.[21]

What of the remains of Hegel then? In Hegel everything that counts, counts as part of a greater whole. Only the whole is actual. Truth is the whole, and once we have finished the *Logic,* we have the whole truth. We think God's thoughts.

The Relationship between Infinity and Materiality in Levinas

For Levinas, the blasphemy that identifies God with the actual and therefore denies God's otherness, cannot be separated from the violation of the *heteros* more generally. For according to Levinas, the "redemption" of otherness purportedly achieved by the Hegelian system is ironically the refusal of the Other, or put somewhat differently, the condemnation of the Other to the remains, the refuse, that which does not count.

On any reading we give to Hegel, then, we are always returned to Derrida's opening question in *Glas,* what of the remains of Hegel? The system gives us the truth of the actual. The full presence of Being to itself in Absolute Knowledge denies actuality to what is left over. Of course, in Hegel, otherness remains Other to the Absolute, there is no simple "identity" between Meaning and Being in Hegel. And yet, *ultimately,* otherness is reduced to the *Other of the Absolute,* or it does not *count.* The complete apprehension of the *truth* of Being denies its otherness to thought. By rendering the truth of Being fully present in thought, Hegel ironically forgets the "is" of the copula. According to Heidegger, the forgetfulness of Being, which forgets what is forgotten, is Hegel's great sin.[22] For Heidegger, the Other of thought cannot be reduced, then, to thought's Other. And yet how does one think Being if it is truly Other to thought? How does one pay tribute to the Other, which can only be known as the difference from beings and from thought itself? For Derrida, the "prior" forgotten "is" cannot be revealed as an original anteriority to the dialectic. We can only "think" of Being through its absence, which is why Derrida has been so engaged with Heidegger's later work.[23] One then cannot remember the "is" as a primordial gathering precedent to representational thought. As Derrida explains, "[t]*here is* does not mean (to say) *exists, remain(s)* does not mean (to say) *is*. The objection belongs to ontology and is unanswerable. But you can always let-fall-(to the tomb)."[24]

But how, then, does one remember the Other, pay tribute to the rest, if the remains are beyond thought, beyond remembrance, and beyond what is there for us? How does one recover the "matter" that has been left out of the system? Levinas continually grapples with this question. The "*il y a*" is Levinas' name for the *irreducible* being of exteriority. The "*il y a*" is not an object for the thinking subject, and therefore it cannot be conceptualized as the Other to spirit. The "*il y a*" resists the imposition of meaning by any representational or conceptual scheme. We run up against the "*il y a*" as the outward clash. It is this experience of resistance that indicates the irreducible trace of radical otherness that remains in any given conceptual system. The "*il y a*" then, is within our experience, not simply the "outside" to it. Levinas, however, also does not reduce the "*il y a*" to our experience of resistance, for that would once again deny the independence of the exterior.[25]

We cannot "know" the "*il y a*" because we can only know things from within a system of representation. Knowledge, at least in the sense of representation of exteriority, is always a violation of otherness. For Levinas, representation is suppression in this sense. Levinas brings us up against the limits of representation. We cannot know the "outside," the "beyond," of any system of objectification, for the world that appears to us is the world represented to an objectifying consciousness. As a result, there is nothing that can be said about the "*il y a*." Levinas himself relies on poetic evocation of the anonymous, faceless, "beingness" out of which things manifest themselves. We are in awe of the "*il y a*" and more than a bit frightened by the stirrings and rumblings from the "beyond" which we cannot understand and which is beyond our grasp. We are reminded of the world of horror movies, "the Blob," for example, in which we run up against the dead weight of an indifferent "matter" that takes no heed of our puny humanity. The "*il y a*" resists Hegel's attempt to lift "matter" into the system.

Derrida's Critique of Levinas' Conception of Infinity and Matter

Derrida is only too well aware that there is nothing to be said of the "*il y a*," as the "matter" which remains Other to all our systems of representation, because to speak of the "matter" would again be an act of appropriation which would deny the existence of the remains, as remains, as that which is left over, as that which is beyond what has ever been there for us. As already suggested, Derrida resists, as well, the temptation to speak of the "*il y a*" as an original anteriority, as a primordial gathering of Being before the dialectic. As he remarks,

There never existed (there will never have existed) any older or more original "third term" that we would have to recall, toward which we would be called to recall *under* the aporetic disjunction. This is why what resists the non-dialectizable opposition, what "precedes" it in some way, will still bear the name of one of the terms and will maintain a *rhetorical* relation with the opposition. It will be figured, figurable.[26]

Derrida also rejects the dualism that Levinas' own formulation tempts. I use the word temptation deliberately. As I have suggested, we can also read Levinas to displace the traditional dialectical oppositions, exterior and interior, outside and inside, mind and matter. Yet Derrida rightfully points us to a tension that is never completely resolved in Levinas' own text. There is the temptation in Levinas to turn the excess within history and within totality into the absolutely Other to totality. Derrida highlights this tendency. Yet for all of his care to remind us that there can be no rupture with metaphysics except from within the tradition, for all of his insistence that the excess, the remains, are there only as the absence of what has never been present within the system, Derrida still recognizes *the absence,* so defined by the system, that is the excess to totality. Derrida, then, is by no means simply denying Levinas' aspiration to heed the beyond, the remains.

What I want to emphasize here, however, is the ethical impulse implicit in Derrida's deconstruction of Levinas. Levinas' objection to Hegel is that infinity cannot be found in nature, because infinity "is" within totality in another way than "being." Due to Levinas' anti-Hegelianism, however, the "*il y a*" can potentially be reduced to the unredeemable Other of the infinite; that which the infinite is not. Matter comes close to being condemned as unholy.[27] Derrida understands that because of his temptation to dualism, Levinas risks being swept back into the Hegelian system by postulating "dead" matter as the Other to the infinite. More importantly, Levinas risks betraying his own project of a "pure heterology" which faithfully heeds the call of otherness. Levinas' fidelity to Infinity as Absolute Other, in other words, carries within it its own potential violence to things, to the remains. Ironically, this potential violence toward the remains can also be understood as violence to Infinity itself as Other. For as Derrida reminds us, either we turn Infinity into Absolute Other, which would reduce Infinity to absolute Identity, or we recognize that we do not confront the Infinite other than as the remains. We cannot tell the difference between otherness as the highest and as the lowest. We do not look for God other than in the remains. The trace of the beyond lingers as what remains, and only "there." But what remains beyond of course, was never and is not now present to us, for then it would not mark the trace of radical otherness. For Derrida, in other words, Levinas' "messianism" is inevitably an allegory. Moreover, unless we read Levinas allegorically, his philosophy of ethical alterity runs the risk of the very violence towards the otherness of the remains it abhors.

For Derrida, we confront the "matter," the remain(s), the "beyond," only through *différance;* the trace of what differs from representational systems and defers indefinitely the achievement of totality. When we attempt to think "exteriority," whether as Infinity or as "matter," we are always walking on a tightrope and risking the fall into another mechanism of appropriation. Derrida reminds us of exactly what is risked in the fall.

> Of the remains(s), after all, there are, always, overlapping each other, two functions.

> The first assures, guards, assimilates, interiorizes, idealizes, relieves the fall [*chute*] into the momument. There the fall maintains, embalms, and mummifies itself, monumemorizes and names itself—falls (to the tomb (stone)) [*tombe*]. Therefore, but as a fall, it erects itself there.

> The other—lets the remain(s) fall. Running the risk of coming down to the same. Falls (to the tomb (stone))—two times the columns, the waterspouts [*trombes*]—remain(s).[28]

The remains then, are what cannot be said. Again to quote Derrida, further on, at the penultimate sentence of the book, "The rest, the remain(s), is unsayable."[29]

Of course, Levinas is not only aware of the risk of the fall in the attempt to speak of the beyond to metaphysics; he knows it to be inevitable. For Levinas there is always a difference between my exposure without reserve to the Other which is Saying and to the exposition of the statement of the said in which I thematize my relation to the Other.

We cannot escape representational schemes. Yet, at the same time, we must recognize their inevitable infidelity to radical otherness. The Saying cancels itself as soon as it is said. Any theoretical conception of the Saying, then, necessarily fails. Levinas understands that the resolution of his call for the synchronization of the affirmation of the Saying and its cancellation in the said can only yield an aporia. Yet he insists that even so we must philosophically both affirm the Saying and negate the Saying in the said. For Derrida, what we confront in the aporia presented by Levinas is *différance,* the inevitable difference between the Saying and the said that can only indicate the beyond allegorically. In other words, one can only "speak" of the Saying in the language of ontology.

Why Derrida's Critique of Levinas is Not Nihilistic

But it would be a mistake to read Derrida's encounter with Levinas as simply the return of the skeptical critic, the perpetual disrupter.[30] Certainly Derrida does not refuse the affirmation of the "Saying" as the stand-in for the indication of the excess, the "beyond" more generally, just because the Saying cannot be said other than in the language of ontology. Derrida constantly warns us against "the sinister ineptitude of the accusation—that of 'nihilism.' "[31] To run into an aporia, to reach the *limit* of philosophy, is not necessarily to be paralyzed. We are only paralyzed if we think that to reach the limit of philosophy is to be silenced.[32] If we, in other words, conclude that because we can only *ironically* sign for our promise to the remains, we should not sign at all. Derrida's irony does not stop him from signing for his promise to the remain(s). To read "messianism" allegorically is not at all to deny its force. The dead end of the aporia, the impasse to which it takes us, promises through its prohibition the way out it seems to deny. To promise through prohibition is the "action" of allegory. Aporecity, in other words, evokes precisely through its prohibition. What Derrida says of Paul de Man's use of the word aporia, equally applies to his own deconstructive exercises.

> The word "aporia" recurs often in Paul de Man's last texts. I believe that we would misunderstand it if we tried to hold it to its most literal meaning: an absence of path, a paralysis before roadblocks, the immobilization of thinking, the impossibility of advancing, a barrier blocking the future. On the contrary, it seems to me that the experience of the aporia, such as de Man deciphers it, gives or promises the thinking of the path, provokes the thinking of the very possibility of what still remains unthinkable or unthought, indeed, impossible. The figures of rationality are profiled and outlined in the madness of the aporetic.[33]

Derrida's difference from Levinas then cannot be reduced to skepticism or to nihilistic refusal. The philosophy of the limit does not leave us to wander in circles before the limit we have reached at the "end of metaphysics." The limit challenges us to reopen the question—to think again. In this sense Derrida affirms that the "end of metaphysics"[34] returns us, again and again, to the central philosophical questions. Thus, it is not quite as Levinas would have it that the deconstruction of metaphysics yields for Derrida an irredeemable crisis rather than a golden opportunity.

The reaching of aporia for Derrida is precisely what provides us with the golden opportunity. The difference between the two thinkers has to do with their approach to the beyond, the excess, the remain(s). As we will see, Derrida does recognize the excess to established reality but only as the absence that brings us to mourning. And, as I have also indicated, depending on how we read Levinas' understanding of infinity, it is possible to bring Derrida and Levinas very close together. Yet, that being said, Derrida still questions more radically than does Levinas the ability of traditional philosophical discourse to evoke the aporia of the beyond through the Saying of what cannot ever be said.[35] For Derrida, messianism is also an allegory because we are left only with the promise implicit in the aporia itself. As Derrida himself explains: "The promise prohibits the gathering of Being in presence, being even its condition. The condition of the possibility and impossibility of eschatology, the ironic allegory of messianism."[36] But, "a promise is not nothing."[37]

The recovery of the excess, the remain(s), then, is both "impossible" and necessary; impossible, and yet necessary—for to fail to pay tribute to the remains would be another violation of the *heteros*. We would once again deny that which cannot be represented. We would refuse it, or more precisely, turn it into refuse whose existence does not and cannot count. This refusal reinstates the subject-centered system that fails to heed the call of otherness. Derrida remains a material-ist in spite of his recognition that there is no adequate metaphysical representation of the "matter" he is evoking, and in spite of his awareness of the inadequacy of dualistic formulations. Again in speaking of Paul de Man, Derrida relates the significance of the word materiality to the philosophy of the limit.

> There is a theme of "materiality," indeed an original materialism in de Man.
> It concerns a "matter" which does not fit the classical philosophical definitions
> of metaphysical materialism any more than the sensible representations or the
> images of matter defined by the opposition between the sensible and the
> intelligible. Matter, a matter without presence and without substance, is what
> resists these oppositions.[38]

This resistance is what shatters the subject's illusion of sovereignty. Thus Derrida can say "[w]e might have associated it yesterday with death and with that allusion to 'true "mourning" ' which makes a distinction between pseudo-historicity and 'the materiality of actual history.' "[39] For death, too, shatters the subject's illusion that he is the meaning-giving center and puts him in touch with "the materiality of actual history." We confront the materiality of actual history not so much through the confrontation with our own death which always remains beyond us, but instead through the death of Other. The starkness of losing one you love to death throws us against "irreducible exteriority."

The Call to Mourning

Yet it is not death itself that is real to us as the presence of the "outside"—we do not directly know the death of the Other. We only know the Other's absence. The Other's death, in other words, is only there for us as *her* absence. This is why Derrida says that death does not *literally* exist, *for us,* only mourning exists. It is precisely because we cannot know the death of the Other except as his absence, and as our loss, that we are always in danger of violating otherness. For it is our loss that we mourn as we remember the name of the Other.

> Upon the death of the other we are given to memory, and thus to interiorization,
> since the other, outside us, is now nothing. And with the dark light of this
> nothing, we learn that the other resists the closure of our interiorizing memory.
> With the nothing of this irrevocable absence, the other appears *as* other, and
> as other for us, upon his death or at least in the anticipated possibility of a
> death, since death constitutes and makes manifest the limits of a me or an us
> who are obliged to harbor something that is greater and other than them;
> something *outside of them within them.*[40]

We run into the limit of our narcissism, however, as we realize that, will what we might, we cannot rewrite the other back into life, remaking history so that she is still with us. She is gone. In her very absence we feel the pull of otherness.

> The materiality of actual history is thus that which resists historical, historicizing resistance. De Man continues: "True 'mourning' is less deluded. The most *it* can do is to allow for non-comprehension and enumerate non-anthropomorphic, non-elegiac, non-celebratory, non-lyrical, non-poetic, that is to say prosaic, or, better, *historical* modes of language power." Matter of this sort, "older" than the metaphysical oppositions in which the concept of matter and materialist theories are generally inscribed, is, we might say, "in memory" of what precedes these oppositions.[41]

The irrevocable absence of the Other resists our rewriting of history. We can remember her, but we cannot recall her. When we speak her name there is no answer. We are left only with the memory of her. Yet it is the Other as Other that leaves the "trace" of herself within us, within our remembrance of her. There is no "within me" without this experience of loss. As Derrida explains, for Freud successful mourning involves mimetic interiorization in which the Other lives on "in us." But for Derrida, this process of mimetic interiorization will always fail, precisely because the Other's absence, which puts the memory in us, cannot be revoked. The precedence of the Other whose mark continues to be felt in his absence, aborts interiorization. Ironically, it is only through this failure to fully recollect the Other that we "succeed" in mourning the Other as Other. As Derrida remarks, "an aborted interiorization is at the same time a respect for the other as other, a sort of tender rejection, a movement of renunciation which leaves the other alone, outside, over there, in his death, outside of us."[42]

For Derrida, then, the "*il y a*," the rest, the excess, is only "there" for us as the loss that calls us to mourning. But as a "loss," the remains are not there for us. There is always an allegorical dimension to mourning. And, therefore, "true" mourning is itself impossible. Yet the trace of the Other remains in the act of mourning. It is in mourning, then, that we remember the remains. But ironically, it is the very failure of mourning as mimetic interiorization that allows us to attempt fidelity to the remains. The inevitable failure of memory to enclose the Other, opens us to the "beyond."

> It is the other as other, the non-totalizable trace which is in-adequate to itself and to the same. This trace is interiorized *in* mourning *as* that which can no longer be interiorized, as impossible *Erinnerung*, in and beyond mournful memory—constituting it, traversing it, exceeding it, defying all reappropriation, even in a coded rhetoric or conventional system of tropes, in the *exercises* of prosopopeia, allegory, or elegiac and grieving metonymy.[43]

The remembrance of the "remains" then can best take place in a wake. Thus *Glas* engages us in the impossible task of mourning to which we are called by otherness. Hegel's philosophy of history in which everything that is to count as Spirit is re-collected into the system is disrupted by the Other that cannot be fully interiorized. There is an otherness beyond Spirit which cannot be reduced to Spirit's Other. And it is precisely the trace of otherness that cannot be recouped that is the defective cornerstone of the entire Hegelian system. It is this defective cornerstone that both de Man and Derrida understand as allegory. Hegel's philosophy then, reread as allegory, "re-read from the most deficient and efficient cornerstone, is said to be—over its dead body—an allegory of disjunction."⁴⁴ Such an allegory of disjunction has as its object not the whole, Hegel's object, but the morsel, which has been disjoined from the system. "The object of the present work, and its style too, is the *morsel*."⁴⁵ In place of the book that tells us the whole truth and the truth of the whole, we have the text that testifies to what has been spat out, the morsel.

> The object of the present piece of work (*ouvrage*) (code of the dressmaker) is what remains of a bite, a sure death [*une morsure*], in the throat [*gorge*]; the bit [*mors*].
> Insofar as it cannot, naturally, bind (band) itself (erect).
> Graft itself at the very most, that it can still do.
> The graft that sews itself [*se coud*], the substitution of the supplementary *sewing*, "constitutes" the text. Its necessary heterogeneity, its interminable network of listening lines *en allo*, in hello, that compels reckoning with the insert, the patch.⁴⁶

Derrida's graft or patchwork bears a family resemblance to Benjamin's and Adorno's uncovering of constellations. The singularity of the scraps pieced together in the patchwork is preserved in the outline of the act of grafting, or sewing; "Sewing [*couture*] then *betrays,* exhibits what it should hide, dissimulacras what it signals."⁴⁷ The part is not lost in the whole. The remain(s) are not grasped as simply the expression of a greater system. Yet the remain(s) cannot be known in and of themselves. There can be no direct "perception" of exteriority or of singularity. The very word, remain(s), or morsel, implies a greater configuration from which it has been left over or bitten off. As Walter Benjamin would acknowledge, things do not go straight to heaven.

And yet in the wake for the dissolution of the Hegelian system, we also find the *promise* of the resurrection of the remain(s); for resurrection is the promise of a wake. For Derrida the promise of the future inherent in the allegory of messianism is only "there" as the trace of otherness that marks the impossibility of true mourning. Yet we also encounter the impossibility of "true mourning" only in our remembrance of the remains. As we remember we also resurrect.

> Memory stays with traces, in order to "preserve" them, but traces of a past that has never been present, traces which themselves never occupy the form of presence and always remain, as it were, to come—come from the future, from the *to come*. Resurrection, which is always the formal element of "truth," a

recurrent difference between a present and its presence, does not resuscitate a past which had been present; it engages the future.[48]

The future, the beyond, is revealed in the remembrance of the remains; the chance for the future, in other words, is preserved in the work of mourning which ironically remembers the remains through the experience of the limit of interiorization, through the very finitude of memory that makes "true" mourning impossible, and yet so necessary. "This work of mourning *is called—glas*."[49]

The Significance of the Figure of Woman
and Its Relation to the Figure of the Chiffonnier

And whose work is it to mourn? In *Glas* Antigone stands in as the very figure called to mourning by the law of singularity and by her responsibility to the remain(s). It is the Woman who mourns.

> The two functions of (the) burial (place) relieve the dead man of his death, spare him from being destroyed—eaten—by matter, nature, the spirit's being-outside-self, but also by the probably cannibal violence of the survivors' unconscious desires. That is, essentially, the women's, since they, as guardians of (the) burial (place) and the family, are always in a situation of survival. The law of singularity (divine, feminine, family, natural, nocturnal) protects itself as it were from itself, against itself. And in the same stroke [*du même coup*] against the other law, the human (virile, political, spiritual, diurnal) law.[50]

Derrida joins Woman in her work of mourning. The very work of mourning demands her rebellion against Hegelian *Aufhebung* that would deny the remains. Derrida follows her law. Derrida remembers that the mother comes first. He is constituted by her. The subject only follows the Other. Derrida does not say of himself "I am" (*je suis*), he says instead "I follow" (*je suis*). If there is a masculine certainty it lies in that knowledge, in that act of remembrance that marks the precedence of the Other; I follow.

> I am (following) the mother. The text. The mother is behind—all that I follow, am, do, seem—the mother follows. As she follows absolutely, she always survives—a future that will never have been presentable—what she will have engendered, attending, impassive, fascinating and provoking; she survives the interring of the one whose death she has foreseen.[51]

The Mother gently gathers the remain(s) together, insists that they be protected. Here we are reminded of another great figure of Woman, offered to us in *Finnegans Wake*,[52] Anna Livia Plurabelle ("ALP"). ALP is also devoted to salvaging the remains. As she stitches and patches together the scraps she has salvaged she is "sewing her dream together." The Mother, ALP, feminizes the figure of the *Chiffonnier*. Like the ragpicker, she spends her time sorting through the refuse. She is always turned toward the sewer. But unlike Benjamin's ragpicker she has little about her of the destructive character[53] (although Derrida himself is always careful to remind us of the fearsome aspects of the phallic mother). She gets on with her daily project of salvation not just for the sake of clearing away the false positivity of the bourgeois world. She is a different kind of gravedigger. She scrapes through the debris and pieces together the remains as an act of care. She is tireless and fearless in her effort to be faithful to the remains. She gives her tribute to singularity through her persistence in mourning.

Derrida gently mimics ALP's hen-like scraping through the debris. He writes, "And I scrape [*racle*] the bottom, hook onto stones and algae there that I lift up in order to set them down on the ground while the water quickly falls back from the mouth. And I begin again to scrape [*racler*], to scratch, to dredge the bottom of the sea, the mother [*mer*]."[54] Derrida sews together his "reading effect"— which is how Derrida refers to *Glas*—as a gift to her, to open up another way of reading—Woman. Not, however, so he can give us that reading, but instead so that Woman can finally be heard when she speaks for herself and in her own name. By opening up another way of reading Woman, Derrida wants to make it clear that he is not trying to establish her proper place.

> Such recognition should not make of either the truth value or femininity an object of knowledge (at stake are the norms of knowledge and knowledge as norm); still less should it make of them a place to inhabit, a home. It should rather permit the invention of an other inscription, one very old and very new, a displacement of bodies and places that is quite different.[55]

Derrida, in other words, is faithful to Woman in his remembrance of her as more than just the successful interiorization of the Other in himself. Derrida does not simply conjure her up, instead, he heeds her call. "I call myself my mother who calls herself (in) me."[56] It is the Other that leaves within us the trace that we recall. Here again, Derrida is emphasizing the precedence of the Other to the subject. The subject only comes to himself by recalling Her. Subjectivity is not constituted in the present, nor does the subject exist as a presence in and for itself. Instead the subject recollects himself in the act of remembrance of the Other in himself; an Other, however, that is beyond his memory, since she remains other. In spite of the limit of memory, the remembrance of things past is the story of the subject, the only one he can tell.[57] For Derrida, the subject only becomes a self in and through the possibility of mourning.

> We know, we knew, *we remember*—before the death of the loved one—that being-in-me or being-in-us is constituted out of the possibility of mourning. We are only ourselves from the perspective of this knowledge that is older than ourselves; and this is why I say that we begin by *recalling* this to ourselves: we come to ourselves through the memory of *possible* mourning.[58]

Through the act of remembrance of the Other in himself, Derrida refuses to forget the mother's name. And what is the mother's name or more precisely her name(s) that Derrida inscribes in the text of *Glas?* "The mother's name would be—commonly—the name of a plant or flower. . . ."[59]

In *Glas,* she is inscribed in the name of Jean Genêt, the blossoming flower.[60] Alongside Hegel's sanctimonious statements about the place of Woman in his system, we have in the second column pieces of Genêt's texts which pull apart the very erection of feminine identity that Hegel tries so patiently to secure. Hélène Cixous and Catherine Clément explain the feminine power of Genêt's texts.

> Thus what is inscribed under Jean Genêt's name, in the movement of a text that divides itself, pulls itself to pieces, dismembers itself, regroups, remembers itself, is a proliferating, maternal femininity. A phantasmic meld of men, males, gentlemen, monarchs, princes, orphans, flowers, mothers, breasts, gravitates about a wonderful "sun of energy"—love,—that bombards and disintegrates these ephemeral amorous anomalies so that they can be recomposed in other bodies for new passions.[61]

The "double klang" effect of the two columns in *Glas* makes us distance ourselves, as we read one column from the side of the other. As we read *Glas,* we practice, with Derrida, action at a distance. Derrida, however, takes sides. He views Hegel from the side of Genêt, the name of the "feminine." Perhaps there has never been a more careful deconstruction of Hegel's phallogocentrism than that given to us in Derrida's *Glas.* Derrida painstakingly shows us that Woman in Hegel is simply man's Other, her distance reduced, so that she can be grasped as an object in the man's field of vision. She is lost to herself in the name of the system. She is classified, given her proper place. We see her from the perspective of the man only. Derrida refocuses our attention on the mother, on Woman. His, however, is the "auratic gaze"[62] that preserves her otherness by respecting her distance, and that by so doing conjures up the "memory" of a different world, in which she is not seen by man as merely his Other, mirrored in his eyes. The auratic gaze defies the organization of looking as a form of mastery. Derrida does not attempt to see through her in order to classify her. The Other is allowed to be in her distance precisely so that she can look back.[63] The mother's distance from man is temporal. She both comes before and remains after. (Not literally, although she well might, but in the sense that she symbolizes the site of regeneration.) As Derrida reminds us, "Remain(s)—the mother.[64] The distance of the mother opens up the diachronic experience of time, the difference that triggers memory and calls us to mourn with her the remains she guards. Of course, this story of the mother is itself an allegory.

The Parody of Dialogism
and the Refusal of Castration

But to proceed with the allegory, to speak from the side of the mother is also to speak from the side of the more (*mère, mehr*). There may be no other "voice" that comes so close to echoing the call of the remains. To take on the name of the Other, to recall the trace of the Other in one's self, to be dialogical, is to refuse castration, the rigid erection of sexual difference in the unconscious that Jacques Lacan refers to as *Ça*.[65] Through the practice of writing two texts at once, Derrida skirts being labeled either this or that. He defies castration in the name of Genêt.

> If I write two texts at once, you will not be able to castrate me. If I delinearize, I erect. But at the same time I divide my act and my desire. I—mark(s) the division, and always escaping you, I simulate unceasingly and take my pleasure nowhere. I castrate myself—I remain(s) myself thus—and I "play at coming" [*je "joue à jouir"*].
> Finally almost.[66]

By writing two texts, Derrida is always talking to the Other in himself. But his dialogism is itself a parody because the Other he speaks to is never "there." The subject of *Glas* mourns for himself as he mourns for the one who has made him what he is, the one who is before him, the one whose passing leaves its mark. The subject is "there" for himself only in and through the dialogue with the Other who is never fully present and, yet, who calls him to mourning by her very absence. Derrida's parody of dialogism, however, exposes the lie of *Ça* and *Sa*, Derrida's phrase for Hegel's Absolute Knowledge, that would reduce the Other to one's own thoughts, or to what is absolutely exterior to the self-constituted subject. "*Sa* loves *Ça*" in that each sets Woman's place in stone through an appeal to an unshakable system and to the truth of the whole.[67] Yet the refusal of castration as an unshakable truth, at least in the system of gender hierarchy described by Lacan, should not be understood as the turning away from the social reality that perpetuates the gender hierarchy through castration. Such a rejection would deny the violation to Woman that has been done in order to secure her place. What is denied is the "there is" that refuses the remain(s) to the rigid system of gender identity. "There is" no initial erection of gender that can effectively and once and for all block the chance for a new choreography of sexual difference. The possibility of a choreography other than the one practiced in our current system of gender identity cannot, then, be wiped out. The dream of a different choreography is "there" in the deconstruction of the "there is" implicit in the erection of the *Ça*.

> That does not mean (to say) that there is no castration, but that this *there* does not take place. There is that one cannot cut through to a decision between the two contrary and recognized functions of the fetish, any more than between the thing itself and its supplement. Any more than between the sexes.[68]

The fall of Hegel, which is also the fall of the remain(s) from the eagle's talons, is not just cause for mourning, but for celebration (particularly if one is a woman). Hegel's "fall" cannot be separated from the fall of the erection of the *Ça*.

Je/tombe, I/fall(s), I/tomb. The play of the anth-erection by which I waken
to, embark on [*nais à*], my name supposes that, in more than one stroke [*coup*],
I crush [*foule*] some flowers and clear [*fraye*] the virgin thicket of erianthus
toward the primitive scene, that I falsify and reap [*fauche*] the genealogy. . . .
. . . the Father's dwelling.[69]

The clamor of the fall of *Ça/Sa* unleashes the many voices that have been
silenced by the law which identifies proper speech with the name of the father.
Glas does not try to suppress the noise. The phallus falls and with its fall goes
its claim that its turgidity elects it as the transcendental signifier. Here we find
the ultimate embarrassment to the sovereign subject, for as he falls, he finds that
he's not as in control as he likes to think.[70]

The Problem with Walter Benjamin's Conception of Mimesis

By evoking the figure of the *Chiffonnier,* I am suggesting that Derrida is deeply
sympathetic with Walter Benjamin's "infinite task" of salvaging the remains
through the work of mourning that practices mimetic persistence and the auratic
gaze. And, indeed, I am suggesting that such a sympathy exists. Yet, in spite of
his sympathy, Derrida is obviously wary of spelling out a conception of mimesis,
as either Benjamin or Adorno does, as a non-violative approach to the remains.
Derrida does not so much tell us about mimesis and the auratic gaze as he
"practices" them; and there is no better example of his practice than his deconstruction of Hegel's phallogocentrism from the side of the mother. "I do what I do not
say, almost, I never say what I do."[71]

And yet how do we account for his wariness of mimesis? In Walter Benjamin
the mimetic capacity signals the ability of human beings to respond to patterns
of similarity in nature and to produce such similarities in return.[72] Benjamin
traces the imitation of nature to the recognition of nature's greater force as the
constitutive Other. Mimesis does not aim to control nature, but rather seeks to
imitate the patterns of similarity in nature as a form of paying tribute to her. For
Benjamin, as for Adorno, mimesis yields a form of knowledge that differs from
what we usually think of as knowledge of the object.[73] As I argued in the first
chapter, for Adorno the object of mimesis is not just there for the subject. Mimetic
capacity does not attempt to identify the object as comprehensible through the
supposition of this or that classification. The human being who exercises her
mimetic ability is not acting as a meaning-giving center; she is responding to
what is given to her. In constellations, Adorno preserves what is valued in the
object-realism—the realization that the object remains beyond its conceptualiza-
tions without demanding some conception of *direct* access to the object.

For Benjamin, this mimetic capacity, exercised through constellations, has
almost been eclipsed by the rise of calculative thinking or what Adorno referred
to as "instrumental rationality."[74] But Benjamin adds an analysis of how the

mimetic capacity itself carries within its own potential danger for decay precisely because it is open to otherness and therefore to transformation as it mimics its environment. But in spite of the potential for its own eclipse, mimesis still promises a form of knowledge different from the one offered to us by the logic of identity whose sole business is to identify and to classify. The mimetic capacity, as we saw in the first chapter, is emphatic. Mimesis identifies *with*, rather than identifies *as*. Derrida does not simply reject Benjamin's understanding of mimesis, but he does give it a new twist.

For Derrida, mimesis is a parodic strategy. Indeed, *Glas* is certainly one of the great satiric parodies of the humanist tradition, and it continually "mimics" mimesis. The problem for Derrida with even the Benjaminian understanding of mimesis is that, in spite of its promise of a different kind of knowledge, the very notion of mimesis as a theoretical capacity still relies on the traditional, dualistic oppositions between mind and matter, and more importantly on the presence of a nature that is just "there." Mimesis, in other words, lives dangerously close in its recognition of the "there is" to the inevitable perpetuation of myth. (Benjamin himself was very aware of this danger.) As Derrida explains:

> There, account taken of the bit and the sublingual slaver, of caesura and agglutination, there is no sign, no tongue, no name, and above all no "primitive word" in the Cratylean sense; nor any more some transcendental privilege for an elementary couple where the analytical regression should finally stop, nor even, since no being [*étant*] or sense is represented there, a mim(s)eme [*mi-même*]. Remains that: the problem of *mimesis* must be re-elaborated here, beyond the opposition of nature and law, of the motivated and the arbitrary, all the ontological couples that have rendered it, with the *Cratylus*, illegible.[75]

Yet Derrida respects the attitude toward things that lets things address us rather than the other way around. "I don't believe it at all, but if I were to believe that a proposition acquired its pertinence by miming its subject matter and letting the thing speak (and the thing here is Francis Ponge), I would justify my attack in the name of *mimesis*."[76]

The problem, of course, with any attempt to let the thing speak directly in its language is that it is always blocked by the imposition of our language, our meaning. We are always translating, but without the assurance of the presence of the messianic language that makes translation possible. Yet Derrida continually explores strategies that try to displace the subject who imposes his meaning on the world around him. What obsesses Derrida is not what he says, but what can be said, given our inevitable placement in language and into pregiven representational systems. His strategies are a promise to the thing, to the remains, to otherness, he knows he can't fulfill—the promise to let the thing speak. And yet he promises, and attempts fidelity to otherness through the constant displacement of representational systems that attempt the capture of the Other. "Here again I do nothing other, can do nothing other, than cite, as perhaps you have just seen:

only to displace the syntactic arrangement around a real or sham physical wound that draws attention to and makes the other be forgotten."[77]

The Ethics of "Deconstruction" as a Practice of Reading

I must begin this section with a reminder of the Introduction. I put "deconstruction" in quotation marks to indicate that I do not accept this designation of Derrida's work and that, because of my disagreement, I have relabeled "deconstruction" the philosophy of the limit. Even so, I do not eliminate the word from this section altogether because "deconstruction" has come to have an historical, institutionalized meaning that identifies a certain group of literary critics. But let me turn to how "deconstruction," by its practitioners, has interpreted the ethical significance of reading. Even in this practice, the very work of "deconstruction," as a practice of reading, embodies the promise—even if only promised ironically—to be faithful to otherness. Deconstruction does not impose itself upon the text it reads. In this sense, "deconstruction" is not criticism. Derrida is suggestive, if only suggestive, on the relationship between "deconstruction" and the text:

> As we have seen, the very condition of a deconstruction may be at work, in the work, *within* the system to be deconstructed; it may *already* be located there, already at work, not at the center but in an excentric center, in a corner whose eccentricity assures the solid concentration of the system, participating in the construction of what it at the same time threatens to deconstruct. One might then be inclined to reach this conclusion: deconstruction is not an operation that supervenes *afterwards,* from the outside, one fine day. . . .[78]

For all of Derrida's hesitancy here—he leaves how he stands on this interpretation open—it is only too clear that "deconstruction" does not leave the subject free to do with the text what he would. Interpretation is not simply the individual, or for that matter the community, playing with itself. It is a serious error, then, to read "deconstruction," as its meaning has been institutionalized, as advocating the position that there is no text that guides us or more strongly commands us in our readings. Of course, a precise statement of the "thereness" of the text remains problematical in "deconstruction" because of the dilemma inherent in speaking of "thereness" more generally. What is heeded in the text, as J. Hillis Miller has pointed out, is not the "thereness" of the text nor just what the text "actually" says. Yet when one is reading, one is reading "some-thing." For "deconstruction," however, "the thing" that one is reading is the "heart of the matter" allegorized in the text. The word "thing," here, echoes the Heideggerian usage. As Miller explains:

> The thing is what James calls, in two story titles, "the real thing" or "the right real thing" or what he hailed at the moment of his death as "the distinguished thing at last." Heidegger in "Das Ding" and Derrida in *Signéponge/Signsponge* have sought to define the elusive residuum we name "the thing." To " 'put'

things" is, it may be, to enter into a transaction with that real thing behind the human things narrated and to respond to an obscure demand for narration made by that "real thing." The "thing" demands that it be respected by being put in words, so becoming a doing which may do other "things" in its turn, as James says.[79]

The ethics of reading practiced by "deconstruction" commands us to heed "things" in the sense defined by Miller.

Nor is the word command being used capriciously. Again to quote Miller:

> The ethical moment in the act of reading, then, if there is one, faces in two directions. On the one hand it is a response to something, responsible to it, responsive to it, respectful of it. In any ethical moment there is an imperative, some "I must" or *Ich kann nicht anders. I must* do this. I cannot do otherwise. If the response is not one of necessity, grounded in some "must," if it is a freedom to do what one likes, for example to make a literary text mean what one likes, then it is not ethical, as when we say, "That isn't ethical." On the other hand, the ethical moment in reading leads to an act. It enters into the social, institutional, political realms, for example in what the teacher says to the class or in what the critic writes.[80]

We can now see how the very practice of deconstruction, conceived as a practice of reading, can be interpreted as an exercise of responsibility to otherness. Derrida is obviously profoundly concerned with the institutional structures in which academic discourse takes place. He distinguishes his own philosophical position from other forms of critique because it is committed to the examination of political institutions as well as of texts. But alongside his interest in the politics of interpretation he has also shown an "individual" ethical commitment to take responsibility both for the Other and for his own signature as he engages with and signs for the Other. Derrida, in other words, understands both directions of the ethical moment of reading. He signs for the role he has played in reading the Other. The very recognition of the precedence of the Other, also means that the Other is dependent on me. Derrida takes responsibility for who he makes the Other become when he reads her.

His call to responsibility, then, should not be reduced to an idiosyncratic commitment that might well be in conflict with his larger philosophical project which I have renamed the philosophy of the limit. The reading of the philosophy of the limit that denies or at the very least downplays its ethical desire more often than not stems from an interpretation of the relationship between Heidegger and Derrida. On that reading the deconstruction of the metaphysics of humanism begun by Heidegger and taken to its radical conclusion by Derrida effaces the ethical even as I have defined it as the aspiration to a nonviolent relationship to otherness. Of course, the question of Heidegger and ethics is itself very complex and much debated.[81] But I want to continue to focus on the relationship of the philosophy of the limit to the ethical by returning to Derrida's remarkable essay on Levinas' philosophy of alterity.

The Return to Ethical Significance
of Derrida's Interpretation of Levinas

As I have already suggested, Derrida's essay *Violence and Metaphysics*[82] should not be read as a fundamental disagreement with Levinas' project because Derrida demonstrates that one cannot speak of the ethical as the beyond to metaphysics other than in the language of ontology. Derrida, in other words, does not refuse Levinas' project because he recognizes that it is a logical "impossibility." He knows that Levinas recognizes that the trace of the Other, the "beyond," is the unthinkable. Indeed, he explicitly acknowledges Levinas' own awareness of the impossibility of his project.

> It is true that Ethics, in Levinas' sense, is an Ethics without law and without concept, which maintains its non-violent purity only before being determined as concepts and laws. This is not an objection: let us not forget that Levinas does not seek to propose laws or moral rules, does not seek to determine a morality, but rather the essence of the ethical relation in general.[83]

Instead of just as a critique, I read Derrida's essay also as an interpretation of Levinas that preserves the ethical relationship without reducing it to the mere Other of Ontology, and therefore as identical, by demonstrating that the ethical relation can only be preserved as Other if it is left as the unsayable. The affirmation of Levinas' project, in other words, demands that we mark the ethical relationship as the limit of the possible and, therefore, as the Saying rather than as the said. The possibility of the ethical lies in its impossibility; otherwise, the ethical would be reduced to the actual, to the totality of what is. This paradoxical formulation, in other words, is necessary if we are to respect the otherness of the Other.

In this insistence on the disjuncture between the ethical and the actual, we are again returned to the "break" with Hegel. In Hegel, as we have seen, ethics is possible because the ethical relationship of mutual recognition has been realized in the actual. For Hegel, if the ethical had not been realized in the actual, the aspiration to ethics would always be a source of dissatisfaction in that the ethical would be sought after and yet unrealizable. Of course, Levinas recognizes that to render the ethical beyond the actual is to leave us with the dissatisfaction that led Hegel to reject Kantian morality. We can never meet our responsibility to the Other. Our responsibility to the Other is absolute. But for Levinas, this inevitable dissatisfaction is sublime. As Levinas explains:

> I can never have enough in my relation to God, for he always exceeds my measure, remains incommensurate with my desire. In this sense, our desire for God is without end or term: it is interminable and infinite because God reveals himself as absence rather than presence. Love is the society of God and man, but man is happier, for he has God as company whereas God has man! Furthermore, when we say that God cannot satisfy man's desire, we must add that the nonsatisfaction is itself sublime![84]

Derrida is both "suspicious" of Levinas' acceptance of the inevitability of dissatisfaction and of the right-wing Hegelian's complacency that reduces the ethical to the actual and, therefore, at least on the conventional reading of Hegel, to the perpetuation of order. On Derrida's reading, the Saying of the ethical as the beyond to metaphysics can only be indicated as the difference that disrupts Hegelian totality. But by the impossible we should not understand an absolute barrier, for to erect such a barrier would be again to mistakenly attempt closure. Nor should the impossible simply be understood as the not possible, a formulation that would also reduce the ethical to the mere Other of the same. As Derrida reminds us, the impossible occurs at every moment. "There is" disruption of totality. The Other cannot be completely eliminated in any given representational system. The Other survives. In this sense, the ethical is a necessity as well as an impossibility—a necessity in that the remain(s) cannot totally be evaded even if they need not be heeded. The Other remain(s). The call to responsibility is prior to our subjectivity, prior to our choice. We may not answer, but we are not free to simply silence the call.

Robert Bernasconi has offered a reading of Derrida's essay on Levinas similar to the one I have given here.

> Though the ethical relation as described by Levinas is thought both by logic and by deconstruction to be impossible, logic dismisses this "original ethics," while deconstruction maintains it by insisting on its impossibility. Deconstruction can—and to a certain extent does in "Violence and Metaphysics"—give a rigorous reading of Levinas which preserves the ethical relation without reducing it to the order of ontology. But the insistence that a [conception] of the ethical relation is impossible—unthinkable—unsayable might be said to preserve the *thought* of the ethical relation (a thought which is not yet also practice) rather than the ethical relation itself.[85]

Bernasconi goes on to say that "[t]he issue . . . is whether deconstruction enacts the ethical relation."[86] I agree with Bernasconi that this is the issue. The purpose of this chapter is to show how one can give an affirmative answer to the question of whether or not the philosophy of the limit *aspires* to enact the ethical relationship because, of course, the ethical relation cannot be enacted in the sense of actualized but only adhered to as an aspiration. By making the claim that the philosophy of the limit does aspire to enact the ethical relation, I am going beyond Derrida who, in spite of his brilliant salvaging of Levinas' project, remains wary of the very word "ethical." I would trace Derrida's wariness to Heidegger and Nietzsche; to Heidegger, as we have seen, because the question of ethics remains entrapped in the metaphysics of humanism, and to Nietzsche because the morality as positive system of rules that prescribe human beings circumscribes the possibilities of aesthetic re-creation. Yet in spite of Derrida's own wariness, I would read his engagement with Levinas as in the service of the ethical relation. The philosophy of the limit clearly guards the trace of otherness that resists assimilation and reduction to the selfsame while deconstructing Levinas' *specific* formulation of the ethical as the beyond to metaphysics and therefore as a radical rejection of Heidegger. Indeed, I read Derrida to warn Levinas against the potential violence to otherness inherent in his own understanding of the ethical, a warning that itself can be understood to be inspired by an ethical desire, as much as it can be read to embody the "truth" that there is no beyond-the-undecidable. As Derrida explains: "*There is no* beyond-the-undecidable, but this beyond nevertheless remains to be thought from this 'somewhat more reliable point of "reference" '; and one can only be involved there in a promise, giving one's word on the subject, even if one denies it by signing ironically."[87]

We can approach Derrida's warning to Levinas from two directions. First, Derrida shows us that there can and should not be an absolute priority of Levinas' Infinity over and against Heidegger's Being. Levinas' ethical philosophy cannot, in other words, just displace Heidegger's ontological project. We saw why in the last chapter. To respect the Other as other and, therefore, as phenomenologically symmetrical to me is to respect the being of the Other. Even a "transcendental" ethics presupposes respect for the phenomena of the "being" of the Other. Derrida shows us that Levinas' ethical philosophy works within rather than just against phenomenology. As Derrida explains: "For without the phenomenon of other as other no respect would be possible. The phenomenon of respect supposes the respect of phenomenality. And ethics, phenomenology."[88]

In speaking of Husserl's project, Derrida suggests that it is this move to recognize the Other as ego, this strange symmetry, that prevents Levinas' project from degenerating into the worst kind of violence.

> If the other were not recognized as a transcendental alter *ego*, it would be entirely in the world and not, as ego, the origin of the world. To refuse to see in it an ego in this sense is, within the ethical order, the very gesture of all violence. If the other was not recognized as ego, its entire alterity would collapse.[89]

Ethical asymmetry, then, must operate within phenomenological "symmetry" if it is to be ethical.

The Feminist Critique of Levinas and Its
Relationship to Derrida's Intervention into Lacan

We can now understand the full significance of the intersection between Derrida's deconstructive intervention into Levinas, particularly in his insistence on the recognition of *phenomenological symmetry* of the Other as ego, and the undermining of the rigid gender hierarchy as described in the writing of Jacques Lacan. In Lacan's analysis, women, as individual egos, are erased in the "psychical fantasy of Woman."[90] The "psychical fantasy of Woman" indicates the process by which Woman is not only culturally devalorized under patriarchy, but is also projected into two types, the good and the bad. The idealization of the one is the flip side of the denigration of the other. For Lacan, the "psychical fantasy of Woman" is the very condition for the masculine ego, which depends on the Woman mirroring him back to himself so he can achieve the illusion of consolidated identity. Masculine ego identity thus turns on the gender hierarchy, which relegates Woman to this projected fantasy. Yet, as we have seen, it is precisely the inevitability of gender hierarchy that Derrida deconstructs. Derrida reinterprets Lacan's insight into what is perceived as the inability to separate the truth of Woman from the "psychical fantasy of Woman," which is a fiction. Lacan teaches us that any concept of gender identity, which is what determines sex and sexuality and not vice versa, cannot be separated from what shifts in language, what he calls *signifiance*. *Signifiance* is a technical term to describe his position that gender identity is given to us by linguistic and cultural structures and as a result can never come to rest in an accurate depiction of sex. The slippage of language that Lacan recognizes prevents gender identity from ever being guaranteed in an outside referent. But for Lacan, the semantic structures of gender are frozen in, or even are, the unconscious and, therefore, are self-replicating.

Against Lacan, Derrida shows us that what shifts in language, including the semantic code of gender identity, cannot be definitively stabilized. Nor is this destabilization to be feared as a threat to sanity.[91] The argument that this destabilization of gender hierarchy would threaten insanity rests on a particular concept of ego, which in turn argues that the refusal of castration—castration in Lacan's sense of acceptance of the loss of an imagined symbiotic unity with the Mother—brings with it psychosis and the loss of individuation. Derrida's allegory of the mother we read earlier should then be read as an answer to Lacan's political conclusions as if they could be based on Lacan's analysis. Why? Derrida's answer suggests that violence toward women implied in the "psychical" fantasy of Woman is itself a threat to the ethical relation. Thus, I would argue that Derrida's answer to Lacan is that the gender hierarchy is unethical. But he also suggests that Lacan's political pessimism rests on a misunderstanding of his own insight into the construction of the gender hierarchy through a semantic code. The "psychical" fantasy of Woman demands the denial of women's phenomenological symmetry. That is why there can be no aspiration of the ethical relation within the gender hierarchy.

Thus phenomenological symmetry demands the specific recognition of the symmetry of Woman as another being, ego, which ironically demands the dismantling of the conditions of ego-identity as understood within gender hierarchy. It is precisely in his own perpetuation of Woman as the Other to Man, that Levinas fails in his own ethical aspiration. Luce Irigaray has criticized Levinas, arguing:

> Is there otherness outside of sexual difference? The feminine, as it is characterized by Levinas, is not other than himself. Defined by "modesty," a mode of being which consists in shunning the light (see *Time and the Other*), the feminine appears as the underside or reverse side of man's aspiration toward

the light, as its negative. The feminine is apprehended not in relation to itself, but from the point of view of man, and through a purely erotic strategy, a strategy moreover which is dictated by masculine pleasure (*jouissance*), even if man does not recognize to what limited degree his own erotic intentions and gestures are ethical.[92]

As we saw in the last chapter, Simone de Beauvoir, in her preface to *The Second Sex*,[93] was the first feminist to criticize Levinas for perpetuating the definition of Woman as Man's Other, a relational concept, which is Hegelian to the core. Irigaray has developed her criticism. Irigaray explains the way Levinas' conception of religion as the inevitably unfulfilled relation to the Other rests on a conception of fault in the sense of the failure of the fulfillment of the ideal. For Irigaray, this ideal is love. But in her distinction between two interpretations of fault in Levinas she shows us how the failure of the ideal and the failure of fulfillment is often read as the failure to live up to the ideal of the man's genus, even if conceived as the ethical subject. In crass language, the fault is that the man is not the perfect "man" for himself, rather than the failure to be a good lover for the other genre.

> The other sex, then, would represent the possible locus of the definition of the fault, of imperfection, of the unheard, of the unfulfilled, etc. But this fault cannot be named except by my other or its substitute. More precisely, there are at least two interpretations of the fault: that which corresponds to the failed fulfillment (*défaut de l'accomplissement*) of my sex, to the failure to become the ideal of my genus (*genre*), and that which is defined in relation to the ideal of the other genus. These faults are not the same. For centuries, one has been cruelly masked by the other. This puts society permanently in the position of being ethically at fault, a position which often has the backing of religion.[94]

Her question, very simply put, is, Why is fault defined as it is as the failure of the ethical subject to an unknown other? Why not the "known" other? In Levinas it is literally an unknown other. The second question Irigaray investigates is, Why is communion between lovers not stressed? Levinas' first answer would be of course, that the very ideal of communion has Hegelian overtones. But, for Irigaray, communion need not carry the Hegelian message. Her idea of communion demands that we embrace the Other as Other rather than encompassing her in a pregiven unity. In accordance with the second chapter, I would argue further that the recognition that communion is possible demands that women be recognized as in a situation of phenomenological symmetry. Irigaray would not write in these terms. Even so, I would argue that for Irigaray, the mystery of the Other as other, not just as other to the man's self, as his imaginary projection, is necessary if there ever is to be such communion. In Levinas, on the other hand, woman is not recognized in her phenomenological symmetry, because the psychical fantasy of Woman is replicated in his own symbolization of woman. Woman is indeed symbolized in Levinas, but not as the lover who promises, if not satisfaction, both comfort and pleasure. The burden of responsibility is evoked in Levinas through the figure of the pregnant woman. For Levinas, the pregnant woman completely turns her body over to the Other, but not for her own enjoyment. In addition, the feminine is sentimentalized as the "good mother" of her son. The mother/son relation is for the son. Furthermore, at least according to Irigaray, the relation between the lovers is neglected in Levinas because the caress in Levinas is man's touching of woman, not the embrace that can bring the two together. Thus, for Irigaray, his view of sexuality is both controlled and controlling. The failure to speak of the embrace becomes the symbol of the failure to speak of the power of love as other to the patriarchal gender hierarchy. In order to correct Levinas' sentimentalization of woman, we need, then, to confront the conditions in which phenomenological symmetry of actual women would not be blocked by the masculine imaginary. Only then would love as communion be possible. Thus, the insistence on the moment of universality takes on a particular meaning in the case of the feminine and in the hope of a love irreducible to sadomasochism. (It is not a coincidence that Irigaray's interrogation of Levinas is entitled "The Divinity of Love.") Without the recognition of phenomenological symmetry, Levinas' ethical relation inevitably degenerates into violation. His writing on Woman as Man's Other is an example of this degeneration, inseparable from Lacan's own analysis of how the process of projection of Woman proceeds. As a result, a deconstructive intervention into Lacan and Levinas is necessary if we are even to attempt fidelity to the ethical relationship, let alone if we are to aspire to live Irigaray's dream of love.

We can now see a similar suspicion in Irigaray and in Derrida to Levinas' insistence on the lack of fulfillment in the ethical relationship. Although it is beyond the scope of my discussion here, it is necessary to note that Derrida is not as optimistic as Irigaray about communion[95] through a love that as a love *becomes divine*. Yet with this caveat we can still trace both Derrida's and Irigaray's interrogation of Levinas to a Nietzschean suspicion of the unhappiness potentially generated by an eschatology without hope for the "fulfillment" of the individual. Although Derrida himself does not interrogate Levinas from a Nietzschean position, the account I offer here reflects his deep sympathy for Nietzsche and his suspicion of the ethical more generally. In Levinas, we must constantly remind ourselves of our inevitable failure to fulfill our responsibility. We must constantly seek to do more for the Other. We can never do enough. We do not have much fun in "the ethical relation." In Irigaray, more specifically, Levinas' emphasis on the inevitable lack of fulfillment of the individual allows the source of dissatisfaction of women to be ignored. No woman finds enjoyment in her *reduction* to either the good wife or the bad mistress. Concentration on the failure to the stranger diverts attention from the failure that is closer to "home." For Derrida and Irigaray, in other words, nonsatisfaction may well not be "sublime." In Irigaray, it may be explicitly "sexist."

In his later writings, Levinas recognizes that an emphasis on the Good as the beyond to Being can be found within the philosophical "tradition" itself, starting with Plato. But certainly this tradition, as Nietzsche so brilliantly demonstrates, carries within it its own tremendous violence. We might put it this way: absolute responsibility to the Other demands that we suppress the Other in ourselves.

For Levinas, to seek happiness in communion is to fall from the sublime of nonsatisfaction into the profane. Levinas' "messianism" then—by which he means to indicate our "lack of peace" before our responsibility to the Other— seems to be at odds with the striving for happiness. Yet as Benjamin has argued, even though the profane striving for happiness *does* work in the opposite direction of messianic intensity, such striving can be understood to *assist* the coming of the messianic kingdom. As Benjamin notes: "For in happiness all that is earthly seeks its downfall, and only in good fortune is its downfall destined to find it."[96] Those of us, then, who have been hopelessly profaned because we cannot deny our longing to be happy may still cheer ourselves with the knowledge that our refusal of nonsatisfaction may itself serve to clear the way for salvation.

But we can now see another danger in the example of Levinas—a danger of which Derrida is only too well aware—inherent in the very effort to name or symbolize what difference is, particularly feminine sexual difference. To risk the name of the law of allegory in action is to potentially reinstate myth. The danger of myth, of course, is the very erection of the "there is" that cannot be challenged, including the "there is" (*Ça*) of the gender hierarchy. Derrida consistently deconstructs the "there is." We have seen how Levinas' symbolization of the burdened subject as the mother perpetuates a myth of feminine identity, and by so doing reinscribes the rigid sexual difference of Lacan's *Ça*. We can, then, read Derrida's hesitancy to name the ethical law or impulse of deconstruction as itself an enactment of the ethical relationship which seeks to deconstruct the "there is" implicit in the myth for the sake of letting otherness be Other.

Levinas' response to Derrida

Yet as Levinas has remarked, this hesitancy takes its toll. Without the risk of the name, the ethical impulse of deconstruction can easily go unnoticed. Even so, just as it would be a serious mistake to read Derrida as if he simply rejected Levinas' project, it would be an error to deny his *affirmation* of responsibility. Yet unlike Levinas, he hesitates to name the prescriptive force that prompts his call. Derrida, in other words, leaves us with the paradox that the Saying can never be said, and yet we must at the same time wordlessly attempt the thematization of the Saying if we are to heed the call to responsibility. For Levinas, on the other hand, we must philosophically attempt to *synchronize* the affirmation of the Saying with its negation in the said. Such a *synchronization* for Levinas yields a positive, philosophical statement of the significance of the negation of the present and of representation. It is in this attempt at synchronization that Levinas endeavors to move beyond the philosophy of the limit. As Levinas explains:

Infinity is beyond the scope of the unity of transcendental apperception, cannot be assembled into a present, and refuses being recollected. This negation of the present and of representation finds its positive form in proximity, responsibility and substitution. This makes it different from the propositions of negative theology. The refusal of presence is converted into my presence as present, that is, as a hostage delivered over as a gift to the other.[97]

Very simply put, for Levinas the practice of allegory may not be enough in this troubled age. By attempting to *say* what Derrida *does* I am also naming the ethical force of the philosophy of the limit. To my mind, this attempt at naming is still true to the paradox that I have just described as inherent in the philosophy of the limit. In that sense, the arguments I have made take us beyond Derrida's own relative silence, before the name of the ethical aspiration enacted by "deconstruction." Humility before the paradox undermines the self-righteousness that Nietzsche so despised, through the recognition that we can never fully meet the promise of fidelity to otherness inherent in the ethical relation to which we aspire.

4

The Good, the Right
and the Possibility of
Legal Interpretation

Introduction

In the last chapter I discussed why what has been called "deconstruction" should be understood to aspire to enact the ethical relation. Indeed, I suggested that Derrida's deconstructive intervention into Levinas gives witness to the ethical relationship by uncovering how Levinas' project turns against itself without the recognition of a "strange symmetry." As we saw, the danger in Levinas' own evocation of the asymmetry of the ethical relationship was made evident in his writing on Woman as the Other and, more specifically, in his use of the pregnant woman as the very symbol of a subject constituted by its burden of responsibility to the Other. I also suggested that Derrida's deconstructive intervention into the theory of Jacques Lacan is necessary if we are to think through how the psychical fantasy of Woman blocks the recognition of women's phenomenological symmetry.

In this chapter, I want to discuss how the ethical configuration provided by the intersection of Derrida, Levinas, and Lacan, can help us rethink the question of legal interpretation. But let me begin with a quote from Blanchot which elaborates the three different realms that must be given notice for an adequate account of legal interpretation.

> Laws—prosaic laws—free us, perhaps, from the Law by substituting for the invisible majesty of time the constraints of space. Similarly, rules suppress, in the term "law," what power—ever primary—evokes. Rules also suppress the rights which go along with the notion of law, and establish the reign of pure procedure which—a manifestation of technical competence, of sheer knowledge—invests everything, controls everything, submits every gesture to its administration, so that there is no longer any possibility of liberation, for one can no longer speak of oppression. Kafka's trial can be interpreted as a tangle of three different realms, (the Law, law, rules).[1]

My purpose is to tell three different stories to show what the tangle of the three realms to which Blanchot refers means for understanding the recent debates in

American jurisprudence over the question of legal interpretation. The three realms as I interpret them from Blanchot's quote are: (1) the Good, or the Law of Law; (2) the Right, or the moral Law of the self-legislating subject; and (3) the principles inherent in an existing legal system. There are two senses in which I refer to the Good. First, the Good should be understood in the strong sense, the universal, as Levinas uses the word. Levinas, as we saw in the previous two chapters, understands the Good as an irremissible necessity for all subjects. Second, the good should be conceived as the universals within a given legal system conceptualized as an indeterminate *nomos*. These three realms, the Good, the Right, and the good embodied in the legal principles, are not reducible to categories of the mind, because they describe codes of a legal system of human interaction.

To tell the first story I will once again return to Hegel, but with yet another emphasis. In Hegel's *Philosophy of Right,* the three realms are shown to be a part of the system which ultimately gives each realm its meaning. Hegel, of course, recognizes the interplay between the three realms, but even so, their true meaning is only given to us in Absolute Knowledge, in which the Good is fully revealed.

Hegel, then, rejects de-ontological theories of the Right as the sole basis for a modern legal system. In other words, Hegel reminds us that we are inevitably caught in the tangle of the three realms; the Law of Law, or the Good, the Law of the self-legislating subject, the Right, and the legal principles which embody the concrete good of the *nomos*. For the strong neo-Kantian, on the other hand, the Law of Law or the Good is replaced by the Law of the self-legislating, free subject. It is precisely the realm of the Good that the strong neo-Kantian morality argues is inconsistent with modernity. As we saw in the Introduction, much of the recent writing in liberal analytic jurisprudence has implicitly rejected the rigid distinction between the Good and the Right. Even so, it continues to inform many of the debates between the new communitarians and one of the main strands of critical social theory presented in the work of Jürgen Habermas.[2] As a result, we must keep in mind the traditional terms of the debate between Kant and Hegel over the relationship between the Right and the Good. For Hegel, we cannot escape the *Law* of Law understood as a conception of the Good, because theories of *right* can only be normatively grounded through an implicit reference to the Good. It is precisely this insistence on the inevitable interplay of the three realms that also distinguishes the "postmodern" stories I will tell from neo-Kantianism. As we will see, what is rejected is not the ideals of modernity, and certainly not the "gains" of a modern legal system, but instead the illusion that a normative conception of modernity can be so self-grounding that the realm of the Good is at best irrelevant and at worst a regression to the premodern. Hegel always reminds us that the very ideal of law as the *nomos* of a community implies a story of the good life. This fundamental insight is recast but not rejected in the so-called "postmodern" stories I offer.

The "postmodern" story has at least two distinct versions. But let me begin with the shared assumptions evidenced in the two stories. Both versions of the "postmodern" story reveal the inevitable diremption of the Hegelian reconciliation of the three realms once the Hegelian system has been unraveled. Both versions also agree that there can be no *foundationalist* grounding of any given system of legal rules and norms in the Law of Law. Furthermore, both versions not only reject the illusion of the normative *self-grounding* of the Right in transcendental subjectivity, they also reject the positivist solution to *Grundlosigkeit*—the loss of an independent foundation for Law—which finds the Law of Law within the mechanism of validation internally generated by an existing legal system. For the legal positivist, the Law of Law of a modern legal system can only find its grounding in its own positivity.[3] But in order for the Law of Law to be reduced to the mechanism of the perpetuation of legal rules, as we will see in the next chapter, the legal positivist must postulate a self-enclosed system. The philosophy of the limit, on the other hand, persistently exposes the philosophical fallacy of legal positivism by showing us the moment of ethical alternity inherent in any purportedly self-enclosed system, legal or otherwise.

But how is the moment of ethical alternity "presented" in the philosophy of the limit and in other versions of "postmodern" discourse as it is relevant to an account of legal interpretation? We now come to the difference between the two versions of the "postmodern" story. In the first version of the story, the Law of Law is only "present" in its absolute absence. The "never has been" of an unrecoverable past is understood as the lack of origin "presentable" *only* as absence. The Law of Law, in other words, is the figure of an initial fragmentation, the loss of the Good. But this absence is inescapable because the lack of origin in which the Good could be rooted is an inescapable, fundamental truth. In this story, a distinction is not made between the Good in the strong sense of the Law of Law and the good embodied in the legal principles of any given legal system. As a result, the "definition" of the Law as Law as absolute is taken to imply that there is also no horizon of the Good, projected out of the principles embodied in the nomos, to which one can appeal to for guidance in evaluating competing legal interpretations of a case or a statute. This version of the "postmodern" story has often been received as the "truth" of "deconstruction" in American literary as well as legal circles. As we will see, I will reject this version of the story.

The second version was introduced in the last chapter. In Levinas' conception of the Good and, as I also argued, in Derrida's critical intervention into Levinas, the Good remains as the disruption of ontology that continually reopens the way beyond what "is." As the call to responsibility for the Other, the Law of Law is irreducible to negative theology, or to the allegory of an "initial" fragmentation that can only be indicated as absence.

As I also hope to show, it is precisely the projection of a horizon of the good within the *nomos* of any given legal system, even if reconceived, that is essential to the possibility of legal interpretation. But if all we do is reinterpret the *nomos* from within its own terms without understanding its limit, we would not be faithful to the Good in Levinas' strong sense of the term. (In the next chapter we will see how Levinas' messianic conception of justice is inseparable from the Good as he understands "it.") It is only once we grasp the complex relationship between the de-limitation of ontology and the recognition of its inevitable rein-statement through linguistic stabilization of systems of representation that we can understand why the Good in both senses I have described remains crucial for the possibility of legal interpretation. The call of the Good in Levinas' sense commits us to the not yet of what has never been present, cannot be fully recalled, and therefore cannot be adequately projected in an all-encompassing *positive* description of the Good or of Justice. We are called to the commitment to the impossible, the full realization of the Good, and to the need to defy the impossible by projecting a horizon of the good embodied in the *nomos,* even if in the form of the classical modern emancipatory ideals within any given legal system. Both Levinas and Derrida leave us with this paradox. I will argue further that Derrida's double gesture can only be understood as a response to this paradox, which recognizes that it would be unethical ultimately to resolve it. As we will see, any ultimate resolution would once again collapse prescription into description, and would, as a result, be unfaithful to either the Good or to Justice. The significance for legal interpretation of the Derridean double gesture can only be understood once we understand the double gesture not as cynical duplicity, but as an aspiration to pay witness to the otherness of the Good with respect to established convention.

At stake in the recent debates in American jurisprudence over the possibility of legal interpretation is the answer to the most fundamental question: Can we escape from the Penal Colony in a "modern/postmodern" legal system?[4] If law is reduced to the positive legitimation of institutional power through established legal procedure, we will only know the meaning of a legal proposition as it is engraved on our backs. Robert Cover has rightfully insisted that we must remem-ber that the legal sentence takes on meaning "in a field of pain and death."[5] Law has only too much power to enforce its meaning. It is for this reason that the central error of the "irrationalists" in the Conference of Critical Legal Studies has tragic potential. The central error is to confuse *Grundlosigkeit* (loss of an independent foundation for law) with *Unsinnlosigkeit* (complete loss of meaning or sense), a confusion that is repeatedly made in the tirades against "deconstruc-tion" as well as by its friends in the Conference. If legal sentences can have no ethical meaning, not even institutionalized meaning, then the machine is free to make us feel its meaning nevertheless. The machine needs no justification to keep on running. The hope for transformation, however, is precisely in the impossibility of such a machine. The machine of Kafka's parable literally runs amok once it is no longer seen by the one who runs it as an instrument of the Good.

The central message of this chapter is that we cannot escape the appeal to the Good as we interpret legal sentences. Therefore, the possibility of escape from the Penal Colony can never be foreclosed, as we condemn the machine in the name of the Good. The significance of this assertion is that the recent debates on legal interpretation which have predominantly turned on linguistic intelligibility have focused on the wrong question.[6] The issue is not whether or not there is intelligibility, but rather what figure the Good can take on after the deconstruction of foundationalist philosophy. If I am right, then I have potentially answered Robert Cover's concern that the interpretive turn in American jurisprudence is ideologically dangerous because it masks the inherent violence of the legal sentence.

Hegel Resummarized

But let me now briefly turn to the Hegelian reconciliation of the three realms, which we have already discussed in earlier chapters. As we saw in chapters 2 and 3, the Good in Hegel is translated into the legal sphere as the realized ideal of the relations of reciprocal symmetry between persons.[7] Taking this as the realized Ideal or the Good, Hegel provides us with a rational limiting principle by which we can judge competing interpretations. This limiting principle, it may be noted, is by no means a matter of linguistic convention. This diremption is purposeful. The point is that the act of interpretation cannot be separated from an appeal to the Good because legal interpretation *is* justification through the appeal to the Ideal, and this appeal cannot be limited to the establishment of accepted conventional meaning because it is precisely this meaning that must be justified.[8] In Hegel, this process of justification can come full circle so that there is no distinction between the Real of conventional meaning and the Ideal because the Good has been realized in history. As a result, the problem of the grounding of actual legal principles in the Law of Law is solved.

For Hegel, the ideal of relations of reciprocal symmetry between persons is the crowning achievement of a modern legal system. This ideal is embodied in the breakdown of legally recognized hierarchies. We are now equals at least as legal persons. The legal person is an abstract definition of the self in which the individual is understood as irreducible to her concrete social situation. It is precisely the realized good of relations of reciprocal symmetry that gives content to existing legal rights established by law. As a result, Hegel always leaves open the possibility that a tension will exist between the Law of Law as the Good and any system of legal rules. The "real is rational" only to the extent that it embodies the Good, the Law of Law. Legal rules are given meaning by reference to the Good; the uniqueness of modernity is that the realized ethical *Good* now encompasses the sphere of private right and the principle of subjectivity.

The full recognition of the principle of subjectivity requires the protection of the sphere of private conscience or the *law* of self-legislating subjectivity, as well as the sphere of private right. But in Hegel, *Moralität* cannot be self-sustaining.

Hegel argued that Kant's own categorical imperative is saved from vacuity only by smuggling in the substantive Christian maxim, "Do unto others as you would have them do unto you." The problem of the vacuity of the categorical imperative can be solved only if the private morality of the individual is given content in a shared ethical reality. Otherwise, the moral imperative is not only vacuous, it is an abstract "ought to be" that cannot be lived.[9] For Hegel, as we saw in chapter 1, the only solution to the vacuousness of the categorical imperative and the reconciliation of the realm of freedom, the free subject of morality, with the realm of necessity, the subject of law, is the realization of the Good in an actual community.

Levinas Reviewed

For Emmanuel Levinas, as we have already discussed, the Hegelian conception of the Good, which unifies subject and substance in *Geist*, is the example par excellence of the violence to the Other, to Infinity, which is perpetuated by Western metaphysics. The otherness of the Good is reduced to the order of the Same in the metaphysical move to establish the philosophical system as a totality. Hegel's solution to the problem of how the Good is to be reconciled with what "is" so as to provide a knowable basis for legal interpretation cannot, then, be separated from the violence entailed in totalization. *Geist*, or cosmic subjectivity, is self-constituting not only of itself as subject, but of all that purportedly stands against it as the objective world. This process of the self-constitution of *Geist* in Hegel, as Levinas understands it, is not the simple identification of self with the Other. And yet as Levinas explains,

> [T]he identification of the same in the I is not produced as a monotonous tautology: "I am I." The originality of identification, irreducible to the A is A formalism, would thus escape attention. It is not to be fixed by reflecting on the abstract representation of self by self; it is necessary to begin with the concrete relationship between an I and a world. The world, foreign and hostile, should, in good logic, alter the I. But the true and primordial relation between them, and that in which the I is revealed precisely as preeminently the same, is produced as a sojourn [*séjour*] in the world. The way of the I against the "Other" of the world consists in *sojourning*, in *identifying oneself* by existing here *at home with oneself* [*chez soi*]. . . . Everything is here, everything belongs to me; everything is caught up in advance with the primordial occupying of a site, everything is comprehended. The possibility of possessing, that is, of suspending the very alterity of what is only at first other, and other relative to me, is the *way* of the same.[10]

For Levinas, the rhetoric of ontology which proclaims the Being of what is as the truth of the whole, and even in Hegel, as the realized Ideal of the Good, constitutive of the actual, is a declaration of war on all that attempts escape from the "objective" order.

> We do not need obscure fragments of Heraclitus to prove that being reveals itself as war to philosophical thought, that war does not only affect it as the most patent fact, but as the very patency, or the truth, of the real. In war reality rends the words and images that dissimulate it, to obtrude in its nudity and in its harshness. Harsh reality (this sounds like a pleonasm!), harsh object-lesson, at the very moment of its fulguration when the drapings of illusion burn war is produced as the pure experience of pure being. The ontological event that takes form in this black light is a casting into movement of beings hitherto anchored in their identity, a mobilization of absolutes, by an objective order from which there is no escape. The trial by force is the test of the real.[11]

Ironically, the violence of what Levinas calls ontology is also the basis for legal positivism—a solution to the problem of legal interpretation seemingly at odds with Hegelianism—which, too, must exclude the exterior, in order to fulfill its claim that the meaning of the legal system is only to be found in itself. Positivism attempts to fill the legal universe. The individual subject gobbled up in the system has significance only as a cog through which the legal machine works. For Levinas, the mobilization of war expresses the erasure of the individual by the system most graphically. If a war is legally declared, then it is "good" to kill, and the individual must follow his legal duty. The commandment "Do not murder me" is ignored. The system's ontological force breaks down attempted resistance in the name of the commandment.

> The visage of being that shows itself in war is fixed in the concept of totality, which dominates Western philosophy. Individuals are reduced to being bearers of forces that command them unbeknown to themselves. The meaning of individuals (invisible outside of this totality) is derived from the totality.[12]

Levinas shares with Adorno the ethical critique that Hegel's closed circle of the Absolute is a prison for the individual, because there can be no transcendence of the system. The system establishes an order from which no one can keep her distance; nothing henceforth is exterior. Ontology enforces the status quo in the name of a tired, cynical realism: "This is all there is."

In this sense, the condemnation of the "myth of full presence" should be understood to have self-evident ethical, legal, and political ramifications. The individual should not, and indeed, cannot be reduced to a container of the "here and now" of any system. The trace of otherness cannot be obliterated, even if the Other can be physically killed by the "war machine."

> The Other who can sovereignly say *no* to me is exposed to the point of the sword or the revolver's bullet, and the whole unshakable firmness of his "for itself" with that intransigent *no* he opposes is obliterated because the sword or the bullet has touched the ventricles or auricles of his heart. In the contexture

of the world he is a quasi-nothing. But he can oppose to me a struggle, that is, oppose to the force that strikes him not a force of resistance, but the very *unforeseeableness* of his reaction. He thus opposes to me not a greater force, an energy assessable and consequently presenting itself as though it were part of a whole, but the very transcendence of his being by relation to the whole; not some superlative of power, but precisely the infinity of his transcendence. This infinity, stronger than murder, already resists us in his face, is his face, is the primordial *expression,* is the first word: "you shall not commit murder."[13]

The trace marks what "is" through the "anterior/posterior." The trace "constitutes" the order of the system, whether of language or in law, because for Levinas all language, and therefore the very possibility of meaning, presupposes the command of the Other, "You shall not murder me." The Other is first on the scene, and we encounter her through this command. The subject endures a latent birth from this encounter which carries within it the burden of responsibility.

Signification as proximity is thus the latent birth of the subject. Latent birth, for prior to an origin, an initiative, a present designatable and assumable, even if by memory. It is an anarchronous birth, prior to its own present, a nonbeginning, an anarchy. As latent birth, it is never a presence, excluding the present of coinciding with oneself, for it is *in contact,* in sensibility, in vulnerability, in exposure to the outrages of the other.[14]

The subject, then, is not born or constituted in an act of self-conscious assertion. He instead comes to himself in his proximity to Her. This proximity "is" "there" as the unavoidable contact with the Other to whom we are fated to be exposed, and who in turn is fated to be exposed to us. But the trace also points us toward the future as a prescriptive command: "Do not murder me," not now, not ever. (As we will see in the next chapter, the prescriptive command "Be just" calls us not only in the particular case before us, it calls us to judge again and to live up to the command in each new case.)

But the trace, in Levinas, of the Other that remains in proximity cannot be understood, as in Hegel, as the establishment of a fully present relationship between the three realms, the Law of Law, the Law of the self-legislating subject, and legal rules and principles that can be comprehended as the Good of the relations of reciprocal symmetry. As Levinas explains our proximity which constitutes *me* through the face of the Other:

It is the signification of signs. It is the humanity of man not understood on the basis of transcendental subjectivity. It is the passivity of exposure, a passivity itself exposed. Saying does not occur in consciousness nor in a commitment understood in terms of consciousness or memory; it does not form a conjecture and a synchrony.[15]

For Levinas, proximity is not Hegel's "we" in a common present. Through the encounter with the Other who calls me, the subject first experiences the resistance to encapsulation of the Beyond. The Law of Law or the Good, is precisely the echo of the Call of the other as a prescriptive command directed toward the future that disrupts the Hegelian system and the pretense of any system to have adequately represented the totality of what "is" Good. The Law of Law "is" as rupture of the status quo. This is why Blanchot postulates the Law of Law as disaster:

> Would law be the disaster? The supreme or extreme law, that is: The excessiveness of uncodifiable law—that to which we are destined without being party to it. The disaster is not our affair and has no regard for us; it is the heedless, unlimited; it cannot be measured as terms of failure or as pure and simple loss.[16]

But in Levinas, the Good as the Law of Law is also not to be understood as simply the limit of signification, which is why he explicitly states that he disagrees with Derrida, whom he takes to have this understanding. For Derrida, the relationship between the Saying and the Said is again postulated as an unresolvable paradox which must, all the same, be respected, if one is to heed the call of responsibility to the Other. For Levinas, if we understood the Saying as the limit of ontology, the Saying would once again be reduced to a relationship synchronized with the said, and therefore, no longer disruptive of its claim to full presence. The Saying, in Levinas, is what cannot be said in the language of ontology, because the infinity of the Good, as infinity, cannot be known within finite reality.

But if Levinas postulates the Good as infinity (because we can never meet our responsibility to the Other as long as we respect her Otherness), and therefore rejects Hegel's totalized system (which tells us what the Good entails and what it demands from us as members of the community), he also disagrees with Kant. For Levinas, the call to responsibility by the Other does disrupt the Kantian notion of the free subject of morality. The Kantian subject is enthralled by duty, but duty is still self-imposed. The Kantian subject of morality is self-legislating. It is only by rising above contamination by the *heteros* that the self achieves moral freedom. For Levinas, on the other hand, the subject is bound to the Other and it is this very tie to the *heteros* that marks the ethical relation. Indeed, we can never truly be free from the Other, even when we try desperately to stifle Her call. If Kant gives us a morality of duty, Levinas gives us an ethical relationship of responsibility in which the subject recognizes autonomy as illusion, and the attempt at freedom from the heteronomous as a form of denial that is profoundly unethical. For Levinas, then, it is not just that the ethical cannot be self-grounding in the law of the transcendental subject, but that the attempt to postulate such an independent, autonomous subject would itself be unethical.

We now turn to the realm of the system of existing legal rules. How does Levinas understand the significance of the rebellion against the Hegelian system for the interpretation of legal rules? As we have seen in Hegel, legal rules are given *ethical meaning* by reference to the realized Good of relations of reciprocal symmetry. Let me emphasize that when I use the word meaning, I am not referring to institutionalized linguistic meaning in the sense of the intelligibility of sentences, but instead to ethical meaning. Hegel understood that the dilemma of legal interpretation does not turn on whether we can cement linguistic meaning. Legal rules are justified in Hegel through the appeal to the realized relations of reciprocal symmetry which give them ethical justification. The Good, in the strong sense of the ultimate universal, in Hegel, is immanent in social institutions and therefore capable of being grasped by the human mind. The Good in Hegel can tell us what measures such as progressive taxation can be justified by an appeal to the community interest, even if such measures impinge on individual rights.[17] But as we have also seen in Levinas, the Good is precisely what eludes our full knowledge. We cannot grasp the Good but only follow it as the command of the Other. It is precisely the Good, the Law of Law, as responsibility to the Other that calls us to justice. In Levinas, although there is an inevitable diremption between the Law of Law, the Good, and the actual, we can also not escape our responsibility, particularly if we are law professors, judges, and lawyers, to elaborate principles of justice which can guide us in the effort to synchronize the competing claims of individuals and to adjudicate between divergent interpretations of doctrine.

The "Postmodern" Story
of Critical Legal Studies

Within the Conference of Critical Legal Studies, there is a well-developed story that has, contrary to my reading of Levinas, represented the deconstruction of antifoundationalist philosophy as the complete loss of the Good—as if such a loss could ever be represented. Although the "irrationalists" in the conference of Critical Legal Studies rarely cite Levinas, they have been deeply influenced by Derrida, and it is to Derrida that they often attribute their own proposition that the absence of a fully cognizable Good leaves us with the irrationality of all legal and ethical choice. Ethical responsibility is reduced to a choice amongst other choices the individual can make. But as we have seen in Levinas, responsibility is not a choice at all but an irremissible necessity, since we are inevitably in proximity to the Other.

As argued in the last chapter, in a more in-depth exploration of the relationship between Derrida and Levinas, the identification of deconstruction with ethical skepticism is a serious misinterpretation. Such a misappropriation of Derrida, however, has had serious consequences for the way in which the "postmodern" story of the tangle of the three realms of the Law of Law, the law of self-legislating subjectivity, and legal rules and legal principles has been understood, at least by the "irrationalists" in the Conference of Critical Legal Studies.[18]

This misappropriation, in other words, has served as the basis of the first version of the "postmodern" story as it has been translated into law. The "irrationalist" story tells us that if there is no "real"—understood as fully cognizable—Good that can guide us in our day-to-day activities as lawyers and judges, there can be no *rational* limiting principle by which to judge competing interpretations of legal doctrine. As there is no Good, present or immanent, in social life to guide us, there is also no Kantian transcendental ego that can legislate its own law in the sphere of morality. Instead we have presented to us a self torn apart by conflicting impulses.[19] The self longs both for community and for individuality, connection and freedom. There can be no hope for a rational reconciliation or synchronization between the competing impulses. Such selves can create only a legal and social order torn apart at the center. As a result of the account of the phenomenology of the self, the Law of Law, or the Good, cannot be replaced by the second realm, the Law of the self-legislating subject, because the self cannot overcome the contradictory impulses that rend it apart. Therefore, it is an illusion that the moral self can be truly self-legislating.[20]

This means that the deconstruction of legal positivism carried forward by the Conference leaves a vacuum that cannot be filled by an ethical vision. Legal positivism argues that legal systems are self-enclosed hierarchies that generate their own elements and procedures as part of the mechanism of the self-perpetuation of the system. In Anglo-American jurisprudence, legal positivism has traditionally been based on the writing of H. L. A. Hart.[21] Hart proposed that all legal systems are based on a master rule of recognition, which establishes the initial hierarchies of the elements of the legal system.[22] From out of this master rule of recognition, Hart argued that it would be possible to directly derive two categories of secondary rules; the rules of process by which the law is applied and then the rules of prescription we think of as doctrine in a common law system. The early critique of Hart, initiated by Ronald Dworkin,[23] showed that interpretation is fundamentally an ethical enterprise, because the derivation of secondary rules cannot escape an appeal to their justification that is not based only in the mechanism for the self-generation of the hierarchy of rules. I will not repeat Dworkin's argument here, but I do want to add that the "irrationalists" in the Conference have not only shown that rules of procedure cannot escape an appeal to a substantive ethical justification, they have also shown us that the very idea of a rule as a force that pulls us down the track through each new fact situation, determining the outcome of a particular case, is false. Therefore, no line of precedent can fully determine a particular outcome in a particular case, because the rule itself is always in the process of reinterpretation as it is applied.[24] It is interpretation that gives us the rule and not the other way around.

This insight is what has come to be known as the "indeterminacy thesis," which has been mistakenly identified, at times by the proponents of the thesis themselves, with the proposition that there is no institutionalized meaning, no "real" intelligibility of the legal sentence.[25] The "proposition" should instead be understood to be that law cannot be reduced to a set of technical rules, a self-sufficient mechanism that pulls us down the track through each new fact situation. Law, in other words, cannot be reduced to a self-generated and self-validating set of *cognitive* norms. Interpretation always takes us beyond a mere appeal to the status quo. I will return to the significance of this insistence on the appeal to the beyond in relation to the system of established rules, as inherent in legal interpretation when I discuss why the philosophy of the limit is helpful in rethinking the current debates in American legal circles. It should be noted here, however, that according to the irrationalists in the Conference we cannot replace legal positivism with a rational, ethical vision. Such a vision could only be found through an appeal to the Good, the Law of Law as in Hegel, or to the Right, understood in the moral realm as the law of Kant's self-legislating subject.

As a result, ethical responsibility is reduced to an existential choice. In spite of themselves, the "irrationalists" in the Conference of Critical Legal Studies reinstate the subject-centered approach to the ethical that Levinas, and I would add Derrida, rejects. It would be a serious mistake, however, to interpret the "irrationalists" in the Conference of Critical Legal Studies as rejecting the need to make ethical commitments because they are inevitably subjective. Indeed, their insistence on the "irrationality" of personal ethical commitments can itself be understood to have an ethical dimension. Under this view, no one can proclaim his or her moral position as the truth of the real. Each one of us is free to make his or her choice. The "irrationalists," in other words, although they have not put it in this way, want to join with Levinas, to deny the ultimate hubris of ontology. The "irrationalists" want to interrupt the Logos as "the last dominating all meaning, the word of the end, the very possibility of the ultimate and the result."[26] If one interprets the "irrationalists" to expose—with Derrida and with Levinas—the ethical de-limitation of ontology, then it is possible to rethink the ethical significance of their message. Unfortunately, the "irrationalists" in the Conference have not adopted this interpretation, reverting instead to a recast existentialism. As a result, they have tended to confuse the deconstruction of the hubris of ontology with radical skepticism and with *Unsinnlosigkeit*.

The central error of the first version of the irrationalist "postmodern" story is to replace the truth of Hegelian reconciliation with the truth of castration. The Good, so the story goes, has no constituting force. The Good "is" only as absolute absence, as lack. The Good does not, in other words, leave its mark on us. On this reading, the "postmodern" conception of the Good resembles one understanding of negative theology. Levinas, on the other hand, is very careful to distinguish the Good, as otherwise than being, from negative theology. The Good does leave its mark. Indeed, as we have seen, the Good *constitutes* the subject as responsible to the Other.

> The Limits of the present in which infinity betrays itself break up. Infinity is beyond the scope of the unity of transcendental apperception, cannot be assem-

bled into a present, and refuses being recollected. This negation of the present and of representation finds its positive form in proximity, responsibility and substitution. This makes it different from the propositions of negative theology. The refusal of presence is converted into my presence as present, that is, as a hostage delivered over as a gift to the other.[27]

Derrida has also carefully distinguished himself from the ethical skepticism that proclaims the "truth" of the absent Good as lack. "The difference which interests me here is that—a formula to be understood as one will—the lack does not have its place in dissemination."[28]

The Recasting of the Story
by Feminist Critical Legal Scholars

A second version of the significance of the "postmodern" deconstruction of foundationalist philosophy has been defended by writers in feminist jurisprudence. Unlike the "irrationalists" in the Conference of Critical Legal Studies, the feminist writers do not defend ethical skepticism. The Good is not represented as absent, but as the recognition and acceptance of difference beyond any attempt to categorize others from a universal vantage point.[29] Rather than try to replace legal positivism with explicit ethical principles, we should instead simply accept the fallibility of judicial discretion as a better way to respect difference. Difference, it is argued, belies the attempt to identify universal conditions of equal personhood. It certainly belies the legitimacy of an appeal to the Good in the strong sense as an irremissible necessity for all subjects. But it also rejects the move to achieve universality even within a particular culture. The adoption of legal principles that "universalize" within a particular culture would still, so the argument goes, lead to a formal approach that is reductionist. Nor can the law of the transcendental ego replace the appeal to the Good. There are only perspectives that represent different viewpoints. The best the judge can do is to try to sensitively weigh each competing perspective, taking each seriously and refusing to condemn any of the competing perspectives as unworthy of attention.[30]

The Critique of the Feminist Critical
Version of the Story

There is an important truth in the insistence that the judge must recognize her own perspective and not pretend to speak as the law of transcendental subjectivity. But the problem, of course, is that we cannot escape the condemning power of law. Law is exclusionary. When the judge vindicates one normative interpretation over another she necessarily delegitimates one of the competing perspectives. Robert Cover has identified the silencing of competing normative perspectives through legal decision making as the "jurispathic" aspect of law. Cover does not believe we can escape this "imperial" function of the law in a complex modern state.

> It is the problem of the multiplicity of meaning—the fact that never only one but always many worlds are created by the too fertile forces of jurigenesis— that leads at once to the imperial virtues and the imperial mode of world maintenance . . . The sober imperial mode of world maintenance holds the mirror of critical objectivity to meaning, imposes the discipline of institutional justice upon norms and places the constraint of peace on the void at which strong bonds cease.[31]

As Cover points out, the "jurispathic" aspect of law is necessary for the creation of a legal system that can effectively operate as a state-organized mechanism of social control. It is, also, however, part of the development of law as a *nomos* which creates a normative legal world and which helps to re-engender a sense of belonging to a "community." The power of law to establish "universal" principles within a community both represents imperial power and its ability to regenerate the paideic pattern of law making as world of shared precepts.

> The paideic is an étude on the theme of unity. Its primary psychological motif is attachment. The unity of every paideia is being shattered—shattered, in fact, with its very creation. The imperial is an etude on the theme of diversity. Its primary psychological motif is separation. The diversity of every such world is being consumed from its onset by domination. Thus, as the meaning in a *nomos* disintegrates, we seek to rescue it—to maintain some coherence in the awesome proliferation of meaning lost as it is created—by unleashing upon the fertile but weakly organized jurisgenerative calls an organizing principle itself incapable of producing the normative meaning that is life and growth.[32]

It is precisely the "jurisgenerative" power of law to create normative meaning that makes law other than a mere mechanism of social control. Since the "jurispathic" aspect of law inheres in its "jurisgenerative" power to create unified meaning through the establishment of generalizable or universalizable standards, we cannot escape the comparison of competing normative visions of the good expressed through the appeal to legal principles. Nor do we want all differences to be recognized by the law. To do so carries within the very real danger of legally freezing well-established hierarchies. Indeed, we do need principles developed through the appeal to contextual universals by which we distinguish between differences we want to be recognized by the law from those we condemn. But of course, the question remains: Do we need an appeal to the Good which is the universal, in Levinas' sense?

Before returning to that question, we can still insist that the mistake made in this version of feminist jurisprudence is to try to *directly* translate into the practice of legal decision making the "postmodern" insight that the Good is not, as Hegel tried to show in his *Logic*,[33] fully actual in the real. But it is precisely because the Good can never be simply identified with a state of affairs that we need not fear its oppressive power to obliterate difference. The attempt at direct translation of the ethical relation into the sphere of law misunderstands the central insight of Levinas' philosophy of alternity. The ethical relation even as it is an irremissible necessity cannot be fully enacted in the actual. The ethical relation can only be conceived within time as a diachronic "power." As a result, the Good can never be fully enacted in space. That is why as a prescriptive command it points us toward the future. The Good can only be translated differently because there is not state of affairs that the Good mandates as its exact fulfillment. Still, it is only within a specific situation that we can meet our responsibility to the Good. The specific situation in the legal context is what gives us the contextual universals embodied in Law understood as the *nomos*. Of course, it is true that legal principles inevitably categorize, identify, and in that sense violate difference by creating analogies between the like and the unlike. If we cannot escape this violation of difference in a legal system, however, we can still develop principles that minimize it. Even so, law is inevitably unfaithful to the ethical relationship. But if law inevitably violates difference through the establishment of shared meaning and generalized standards, should we not then attempt to escape from legality altogether? Levinas clearly thinks not.

The Inevitability and Necessity of Law and Legal Principles

The answer for Levinas is as follows: He reminds us that we are inevitably fated to fall into law, understood now as a system of legal principles and not just as a positivist mechanism to distribute and redistribute violence and power. Why is this fall inescapable? I am never just alone with the Other. The entry of the third is inevitable, and with the entry of the third comes the need to make comparisons and to synchronize the competing demands of individuals within the space of a given legal system.

The third part interrupts the face-to-face. But the call to law and the establishment of rights should not be understood as an unfortunate empirical necessity given that we are never just alone with the Other.

> It is not that the entry of a third party would be an empirical fact, and that my responsibility for the other finds itself constrained to a calculus by the "force of things." In the proximity of the other, all the others than the other obsess me, and already this obsession cries out for justice, demands measure and knowing, is consciousness.[34]

The aspiration to a just and egalitarian state proceeds from the irreducible responsibility of the subject to the Other. Each Other has her claim, and her claim must be addressed. All claims, however, cannot be vindicated even if they must be heard. We need legal principles that guide us through the maze of competing legal interpretations, precisely because all claims cannot be vindicated. "The extraordinary commitment of the other to the third party calls for control, a search for justice, society and the State, comparison and possession, thought and science, commerce and philosophy, and outside of anarchy, the search for a principle."[35]

A principle as I use it here is not a rule, at least not as a force that literally pulls us down the tracks and fully determines the act of interpretation. A principle is instead only a guiding light. It involves the appeal to and enrichment of the "universal" within a particular *nomos*. We can think of a principle as the light that comes from the lighthouse, a light that guides us and prevents us from going in the wrong direction.[36] A principle, however, cannot determine the exact route we must take in any particular case; it does not pretend that there is only one right answer. It can, however, serve to guide us, by indicating when we are going in the wrong direction. If a principle cannot give us *one right answer,*[37] it can help us define what answers are wrong in the sense of being incompatible with its realization. For example, we might not all agree what the principle of reciprocal symmetry means, but given its historical significance as the expression of the breakdown of the vertical relations of law, we can rule out certain legal outcomes as incompatible with its realization. An example which Hegel himself often used is the legal rejection in modernity of all forms of indentured servitude. Of course, this mode of interpretation is circular, but the very structure of legal argumentation is that we argue from within the *nomos* of law. As for which principles we ultimately adopt within the *nomos,* we are left with the process of pragmatic justification based on the ability of a principle to *synchronize* the competing universals embodied in the *nomos.* A jurisprudence of principle, then, can survive the indeterminacy thesis which reminds us that a rule cannot be fully determinative of the outcome of a particular case.

This process of elaborating principles of justice involves what Levinas calls "thematization" in the said, the world of established representational systems. In Levinas, thematization is a term of art meaning the synchronization of the Good with Being in such a way as to purportedly deny the diachronic force of time. But we can also explain thematization more prosaically as the need to sound the common themes within the *nomos* so that it is possible to appeal to contextual principles. This attempt to sound the common themes still has the effect of synchronizing the Good with Being as a given state of legal affairs, because it appeals to the Good as it has manifested itself, even if only as unrealized potential of the legal system. An essential aspect of thematization is the practical use of *reason* to synchronize the competing demands and perspectives of individuals through the appeal to legal principle. Reason, in other words, is essential to thematization and thematization inheres in the narratives we develop to justify a particular state of legal affairs. As Robert Cover has explained:

> No set of legal institutions or prescriptions exists apart from the narratives that locate it and give it meaning. For every constitution there is an epic, for each

decalogue scripture. Once understood in the context of the narratives that give it meaning, law becomes not merely a system of rules to be observed, but a world in which we live.[38]

The Role of Practical Reason in Law

In this sense, law is embedded in ontology, in a shared social reality. But as the *nomos,* it is also a "critical" point within ontology. This critical point is what allows us to engage in the struggle within our *nomos* to meet the command "Be just."[39] Thematization, then, is never just descriptive. It is precisely the critical, normative dimension of law that demands reasonable assessment of competing legal principles. To quote Levinas, "Reason consists in ensuring the coexistence of these terms, the coherence of the one and the other despite their difference, in the unity of a theme; it ensures the agreement of the different terms without breaking up the present in which the theme is held."[40] Reason is not understood to ground legal principles in the traditional neo-Kantian sense. But it is a serious mistake to confuse Levinas' position with irrationalism.

In law, reason is a "practical faith" we are called upon to exercise as an essential aspect of the task of elaborating legal principles. But, of course, if reason cannot ground legal principle in the foundationalist sense through the appeal to the Law of the self-legislating subject, we must be ready to concede to the force of the better interpretation. The exercise of practical reason, in other words, demands that we continually engage in dialogue with one another. It demands that we make a Derridean double gesture. We need to recognize both that thematization in law is necessary and that no thematization into a system of justice can pretend to have the last word as the truth of a "reconstructive science."[41] We must encourage the process of interruption of any current state of legal affairs, not in the name of the "irrationality" of competing narratives, but in the name of the exercise of reason itself which demands that we participate in the acts of judgment to which the command "Be just" calls us. The Derridean double gesture invites us to new worlds as part of the very commitment to reason. The commitment to reason is essential to the exercise of ethical responsibility to the Other.[42]

Why the Concept of Postmodernity
is Rejected by Both Derrida and Levinas

Yet, both Levinas and Derrida remind us that without a foundationalist conception of reason in either the neo-Kantian or the Hegelian sense, the "secularization" of the modern world will remain incomplete. I am defining secularization as the process "where ideas and knowledge are detached from their original source, and become accessible to human reason under its own power."[43] It is the reminder of the inevitability of incomplete secularization that has led to the accusation that "postmodernity" is the "premodern" in disguise, and therefore an inherently conservative intellectual movement. It is, of course, true that both Derrida and Levinas reject the organization of time determined *teleologically* by an idea of emancipation. If one identifies modernity with a teleological organization of time guided by an idea of emancipation, then, and only then, can Derrida and Levinas be understood to reject modernity. Ironically, the very disjuncture between the modern and the "postmodern" implies the very linear, narrative organization of time that both thinkers reject. Both thinkers recognize the necessity of thematization as the projection of ideals and principles of justice. Indeed, Derrida has insisted that there is nothing less old-fashioned than the traditional emancipatory ideals.[44] It would, then, be more correct to envision the relationship between the modern call to the realization of universal principles of justice within the nomos and the "postmodern" insight that we can never escape the interplay of the three realms as a "laying beside" essential to the practice of dialogic fallibilism.[45] It reminds us of the status of the stories we tell in order to "ground" our system of justice. The stories we tell to justify one state of legal affairs over another are just that, stories. They can only be judged practically.

The Ethical Significance of the
Recognition of Incomplete Secularization

But the crucial message inherent in the recognition of incomplete secularization is even more explicitly ethical. Derrida, in particular, always wants to remind us, with Cover, of the "jurispathic" aspect of any claim to normative closure, particularly in a legal system. Derrida is only too aware of the power of law to enforce institutionalized legal meaning. Once we correctly interpret the ethical concern of the "double gesture," we can hear the message in the deconstruction of Rousseau's "delusion of presence mastered" other than as a defense of ethical skepticism, because all ethical systems are inevitably opened in violence. "There is not ethics without the presence of the other, but also, and consequently, without absence, dissimulation, detour, difference, writing. The arche—writing is the origin of morality as of immorality. The nonethical opening of ethics. A violent opening."[46]

It is, of course, possible to interpret the above passage to indicate that we can never "ethically" choose between competing normative thematizations, since they all originate in a "nonethical opening." It is this interpretation of Derrida that has led thoughtful commentators of Levinas to argue that Derrida is deaf to the ethical voice of Saying. But I want to give a different emphasis to the above passage. If all ethical thematizations are "equal" in the sense that they cannot claim to be grounded in first principles, then we must always recognize the *"equal claim"* of competing interpretations to be heard. If all interpretations are "ungrounded," then no interpretation can *theoretically* win out, shutting off from the very beginning the need for practical debate and assessment. Derrida has certainly shown us that the claim to inherent *theoretical* superiority of one ethical *system* over another is unfounded. But on the interpretation I am offering here, it would also be unethical to *theoretically* reduce to an inferior position the standing of competing normative perspectives. The real challenge we are left with as law professors, lawyers, and judges in the wake of "deconstruction" has been eloquently summarized by Cover. "The challenge presented by the absence of a single, 'objective' interpretation is, instead, the need to maintain a sense of legal meaning despite the destruction of any pretense of superiority of one *nomos* over another."[47] The truth of *"Grundlosigkeit"* is that we are to be forever left with that challenge. We are called to remain open to the invitation to create new worlds.

The Divergence Between Derrida and Levinas Rethought

I have so far emphasized the close relationship between Derrida and Levinas that is evident once the philosophy of the limit is read ethically. On an ethical reading, the philosophy of the limit does not mark the inevitable delimitation of ontology in order to drop us into the abyss of skepticism and irrationalism. Instead, the philosophy of the limit exposes ethical "transcendence" within the very iteration of the same. Derrida continuously shows us that the same is not a totality closed in upon itself. As we have seen, it is also a mistake to read Levinas as if the Good was the absolutely Other. In *Otherwise Than Being*, Levinas seeks to indicate just how the unsayable echoes in the Saying of the said. The Good "is" in the day-to-day confrontation with the Other. (In his most recent essay on Levinas, Derrida clearly echoes the cry of ethical revolt of Saying. Derrida, too, is concerned with heeding the echo of the call in the Saying of the said.)[48]

But there is a subtle difference between the two thinkers that is rarely brought to light because the ethical message of what has come to be called "deconstruction" has been obscured by the interpretation of Derrida as our latest "irrationalist." Derrida's first essay on Levinas is often interpreted to show that the very necessities of the language in which Levinas must speak of the break up of the domination of the Logos inevitably reinscribes his testament in the language of ontology.[49] Of course, Derrida does make this point. But Derrida's emphasis, as we saw in the last chapter, is not just on the inevitable fall back into ontology. He is not concerned just to show us that Levinas' project is dragged back into the "is." Instead, Derrida emphasizes the "self-transcendence" of the Same. The iteration of the same "is" as transformation. Even if Levinas is read to displace the rigid dichotomy of transcendence and immanence—and I believe this is how he should be read—he does not, like Derrida, focus our attention on the self-transcendence of the Same.

Transformative Possibility
through the Iterative

Derrida always seeks to protect the radical difference of the not yet of the Saying, but he also exposes the iteration of the Same as an infinite spiral of possibility. I am aware that Derrida is rarely read as a thinker of transformative possibility. Indeed, what I am offering is an interpretation of deconstruction as the philosophy of the limit. But I believe that the interpretation I offer is "true" to Derrida's engagement with Levinas. "Deconstruction," then, is not the witness to the paralysis of "repetition." To come around again is to re-evolve; in this specific sense it involves a re-evolution. Derrida's focus on "the deadly work of paralysis" does not mean he thinks we are helpless. Instead, he makes us think differently about the beyond. Iteration "is" as possibility because a system of representation given to us in language cannot be identical to itself and therefore truly a totality. This possibility is an "opening" to the beyond as a threshold we are invited to cross. As "a science of the threshold," deconstruction dares us to the commitment to "cross over" and perhaps, by so doing, to avoid the horror of having the door of the Law of Law finally shut in our faces.[50] Derrida, in other words, can be understood to more successfully displace the dichotomy of transcendence and immanence through the exposure of the "immanence" of ethical alternity in the iteration.

Derrida's Significance
for Legal Interpretation

This displacement is important in the legal interpretation of a system of norms. The Good, as it is interpreted as the yet unrealized potential of the *nomos,* is never simply the mere repetition of conventional norms, because there can be no mere repetition. In this sense, the Good or the Law of Law cannot be conceived as the truth of a self-enclosed system which perpetuates itself. The dissemination of convention as a self-enclosed legal system does not leave us with a fundamental lack, but with an opening. What I am suggesting is that the dissemination of convention, through *différance* as the nonfull, nonsimple, and differentiating, origin of differences, disrupts the claims of ontology to fill the universe, and more specifically the legal universe. This is the theoretical significance of Derrida's rejection of the appeal to community standards as the replacement for foundationalism.

We can now think differently about the ethical significance of the rebellion against community I discussed in the first chapter. There cannot be the effective closure upon which the communitarian insists. The Good is beyond any of its current justifications. As a result, when we appeal "back" to what has been established, we must *look* forward to what "might be." As we do so, we represent what "might be." Without a simple origin the very process of discovery of legal principles from within the *nomos* will also involve invention. It is this specific appeal to the "ought to be" that demands a vision of the Good that goes beyond the appeal to convention. The "origin" we evoke in our thematizations is ultimately a representation of the future. Legal interpretation demands that we remember the future.

Thus, the deconstructive emphasis on the opening of the ethical self-transcendence of any system that exposes the threshold of the "beyond" of the not yet is crucial to a conception of legal interpretation that argues that the "is" of Law can never be completely separated from the elaboration of the "should be" dependent on an appeal to the Good. Ethical alternity is not just the command of the Other, it is also the Other within the *nomos* that invites us to new worlds and reminds us that transformation is not only possible, it is inevitable.

There cannot be the radical immanence insisted upon by legal positivism, because the "is" of the so-called legal system is never a totality that generates its own evolution. However, even if we agreed that Law as a system of norms demanded an appeal to the Good, we would still be within legal positivism if the norms could be mandated as a self-enclosed system. Derrida then, is extremely helpful to us in the development of an understanding of Law as the nomos which is not reducible to the objective meaning of established legal conventions—because the good of the *nomos* is itself always undergoing transformation—and which, at the same time, is not just a utopian projection from the outside. Again, to quote Robert Cover:

> Law may be viewed as a system of tension or a bridge linking a concept of a reality to an imagined alternative—that is, as a connective between two states of affairs, both of which can be represented in their normative significance only through the devices of narrative. Thus, one constitutive element of a *nomos* is the phenomenon George Steiner has labeled "alternity": the other than the case; the counter-factual propositions images, shapes of will and evasion with which we charge our mental being and by means of which we build the changing, largely fictive milieu for our somatic and our social existence.[51]

This link between the Other, the more of a given state of legal affairs, is also the threshold we are constantly invited to cross through the delimitation of ontology, which in turn creates the opening for "new" interpretations. This link, the "threshold," is both the invitation to cross over, the call to interpretation, and yet a barrier to full accessibility. As both a barrier and an invitation, it is also the Derridean hymen. This call to interpretation is continually echoed in deconstruction. "As in *La Folie du jour* by Maurice Blanchot, the law does not command without demanding to be read, deciphered, translated. It demands transference. . . . The *double bind* is in the law."[52]

The Answer to Robert Cover

As we have seen, for Cover, the "double bind" in the law includes the "jurispathic" aspect of law in the very search for and assertion of "paideic" unity within the community. Law creates a normative world by imposing itself in the name of the reconciled whole. But if the "reconciled whole" is no longer thought to be the truth of the actual as in Hegel, then it is always a myth. It is made true through the very power of the state to assert its meaning and vision against that of other communities. "There is, however, danger in forgetting the limits which are intrinsic to this activity of legal interpretation; in exaggerating the extent to which any interpretation rendered as part of the act of state violence can ever constitute a common and coherent meaning."[53]

The "jurispathic" power of legal decision making concerned Cover in his "Supreme Court Foreword," but there he saw not just the necessity but the inevitability of interpretation. But, in his essay, "Violence and the Word," written shortly before his death, the mythic status of any narrative of a reconciled whole led Cover to conclude that the very act of interpretation masked the violence of the imposition of the legal sentence. Cover used the example of the criminal defendant to graphically make his point that the "community interest" with which the criminal himself was supposed to identify was clearly a myth. The criminal "goes along" with the sentence not because he recognizes the validity of what is happening to him in the name of a shared communal standard of the Good, but because of the enforcement power of the state.

> Revolutionary constitutional understandings are commonly staked in blood. In them, the violence of the law takes its most blatant form. But the relationship between legal interpretation and the infliction of pain remains operative even in the most routine of legal acts. The act of sentencing a convicted defendant is among these most routine of acts performed by judges. Yet it is immensely revealing of the way in which interpretation is shaped by violence. First, examine the event from the perspective of the defendant. The defendant's world is threatened. But he sits, usually quietly, as if engaged in civil discourse. If convicted, the defendant customarily walks—escorted—to prolonged confinement, usually without significant disturbance to the civil appearance of the event. It is, of course, grotesque to assume that the civil facade is "voluntary" except in the sense that it represents the defendant's autonomous recognition of the overwhelming array of violence ranged against him, and of the hopelessness of resistance or outcry.[54]

The "good" of the community is not the "good" of the criminal. Yet, of course, if the Law of Law had been fully actualized, there would only be the one shared Good, which is why Hegel insisted that the criminal could be "reconciled" to his sentence. According to Hegel, both the victim and the criminal experience the rift in the community caused by the criminal act. This rift unleashes "the causality of fate," in which the community seeks to overcome the rift through the punishment of the victim, who is respected as an ethical being, precisely in and through his punishment. The criminal is an ethical being since he, too, is inserted in the reign of the realized Good. Legal interpretation is fidelity to the Law of Law as the realized Good enacted even in the criminal sentence. The Hegelian system pretends to heal the rift that Cover wants to remind us cannot be healed. Thus, for Cover, the danger of legal interpretation is that because it purports to heal the rift, it blinds us to the wound of the fragmentation of our so-called community as we violate the perspective of the Other in the criminal sentence.

> Law is never just a mental or spiritual act. A legal world is built only to the extent that there are commitments that place bodies on the line. The torture of the martyr is an extreme and repulsive form of the organized violence of institutions. It reminds us that the interpretive commitments of officials are realized, indeed, in the flesh.[55]

The legal system as a mechanism of social control operates through the inscription of the sentence on the backs of its victims.[56] And yet, what Cover at least recognized in his "Foreword," was that the appeal to universality in the name of a shared good embodied in the narratives of legal opinions is not only inevitable, it is also essential to the creation of the Law as *nomos*. Therefore, we cannot escape the task of interpretation. Cover's suspicion of the power of the state led him to conclude that we can now only find shared meaning without violence in smaller communities that cannot impose their *nomos* against others through force. But this belies his own insight that the very search for "paideic" unity, even in small communities, is exclusionary and, indeed, "jurispathic."

The Derridean Gesture and the Projection of an Horizon of the Good

This is the profound sense in which Derrida, on the other hand, recognizes that we cannot escape the "double bind" of the Law of Law, of the ethical relation. The Law of Law calls us to interpretation through an appeal to justice, and this process of interpretation also projects the good of the community, which is itself only an interpretation and not the last word on what the good of the community actually could be. (As we will see in the next two chapters, justice understood as an aporia is the limit to the established good of the community or of the *nomos*.) Indeed, justice so understood could not be the "last word," once we understand that even the appeal "back" to established principle cannot avoid the projection forward of the "might be" since the origin is not simply there. We will return to a discussion of the legal significance of the recognition of the origin of the legal system as myth in chapter 5. For now, I want to emphasize that the Law of Law demands that we justify our interpretation through an appeal to the Good. What Derrida says of translation could equally well be said of legal interpretation.

> Translation, surely, as holy growth of languages, announces the messianic end,
> but the sign of that end and of that growth is "present" (*gegenwärtig*) only in
> the "knowledge of that distance," in the Entfernung, *the remoteness* that relates
> us to it . . . Yet it puts us in contact with that "language of truth" which is the
> "true language" ("*so ist diese Sprache der Wahrheit—die wahre Sprache*").
> This contact takes place in the mode of "presentiment," in the "intensive" mode
> that renders present what is absent, that allows remoteness to approach as
> remoteness, *fort:da*.[57]

But the "contact" is still there; at the same time, we cannot know its ultimate
meaning. Yet, when one legal interpretation is vindicated as to what constitutes
the good of the *nomos,* it is imposed upon the other as if the Good, in the strong
sense, had been achieved. Indeed, as Cover reminds us, this seeking to impose
or universalize one's vision of the Good is the central characteristic of redemptive
legal movements. Cover defines redemptive legal movements as follows:

> I shall use "redemptive constitutionalism" as a label for the positions of associa-
> tions whose sharply different visions of the social order require a transforma-
> tional politics that cannot be contained within the autonomous insularity of the
> association itself. . . . Redemption takes place within an eschatological schema
> that postulates: (1) the unredeemed character of reality as we know it, (2) the
> fundamentally different reality that should take its place, and (3) the replacement
> of the one with the other.[58]

I agree with Cover that the "projection" of a redeemed world and the commitment to realize it in this one should be understood as crucial to transformative
legal movements. This projection clearly entails the opposition to the current state
of legal affairs. The most obvious example of a "redemptive legal movement" is
the struggle to overthrow and outlaw apartheid in South Africa. This movement
does not, it should be noted, just plead that apartheid is wrong in South Africa.
It insists that apartheid is wrong, any time and any place. The resistance movement
does not then appeal to the cultural good of a specific context, but to the universal
Good. Apartheid violates the ethical relation as evoked by Levinas. Apartheid
does so now and will do so always. If apartheid were outlawed, the normative
view of the whites who enforced their legal sentence on the flesh of blacks would
indeed be silenced. And this silencing would be violence to their "difference."
But as Derrida, amongst others, has reminded us, it is a deserved and necessary
"violence" we are called to by any version of the Good worthy of its name. As
I have already suggested, the reminder of the violent opening of ethics is not
done to paralyze us. The double bind that inheres in the call to legal interpretation
means that we must make a double gesture as part of the very commitment to the
ethical responsibility to which we are called. We must both accept the challenge
of thematization, including the projection of a redeemed world which would
realize the emancipatory ideals, and acknowledge the status of any interpretation
we offer. The "double gesture" does, however, express the humility and indeed,

the humor, that must be kept if we are to avoid the abuses of an apocalyptic rhetoric.[59]

It would be a serious mistake, then, to read the testament of the "postmodern" story of the three realms, the Law of Law, the Law of self-legislating subjectivity, and the principles of a legal system, as the witness to the inevitability of nihilism. Of course, to tell a story is to side with diachronic allegory which "pretends to know how to tell stories," rather than the other figure of memory, the synchronic allegory, "that feigns amnesia."[60] But then we must risk the story in order to counter the mistaken account that identifies deconstruction with nihilism. The philosophy of the limit reminds us that the meaning of the "ethical" is *necessarily* displaced into the future because the Good is not fully present to the mind as it is in Hegel's system. In the next chapter I discuss just how central a conception of time is to a positivist understanding of a legal system. To summarize the central point of this chapter: Interpretation is transformation. Thus, we need to remember that we are responsible, as we interpret, for the direction of that transformation. We cannot escape our responsibility implicit in every act of interpretation. The delimitation of ontology reminds us of the positivist fallacy that the legal world is just given to us as a self-perpetuating mechanism. We are left with a reminder of the inescapability of our responsibility for the *nomos* as it is perpetuated and thus transformed.

5

The Relevance of Time to the Relationship between the Philosophy of the Limit and Systems Theory: The Call to Judicial Responsibility

Introduction

The central purpose of this chapter is to show why the deconstruction of the traditional conception of time, a conception which privileges the present, can help us understand why Justice is irreducible to the pregiven norms of any established legal system. As a result, this deconstruction can help us understand the relationship between the philosophy of the limit and Niklas Luhmann's systems theory and why an understanding of this relationship is also important for questions of justice and legal interpretation as they have been framed by the Anglo-American debates.

I want to suggest that there is an affinity between systems theory and the philosophy of the limit, in spite of the divergences I emphasize in this chapter, precisely because both rely on an antihumanist methodology. A full exploration of this affinity is beyond the scope of this chapter. At the very least, however, I will try to provoke the reader to observe this relationship differently. Yet, that being said, it also needs to be noted that the fundamental premise of this chapter, namely, that even if law in a modern, differentiated society is an autonomous system—in the unique sense of Luhmann's understanding of autonomy—the operations of that system cannot be identified as justice. This premise would seem to indicate an important disagreement between the two approaches. And indeed it does, if the observer stops with the first glance. The immediate difference would seem to be that for Derrida it is not simply that a modern legal system "requires a binary code that contains a positive value (justice) and a negative value (injustice), and that artificially excludes both contradictions. . . ,"[1] a code which for Luhmann is "of decisive significance," "as it provides the system with its own internally constituted form of contingency."[2] Instead, for Derrida, as we will see—and I am translating Derrida's insight into the language of systems theory—it is that the very idea of the "positive" value of justice carries within it a paradox or a set of aporias that cannot be resolved if justice is to meet its claim to be Justice. In turn, the system's very attempt to "de-paradoxicalize" itself, so that it can be seen as just, can in turn be defined as injustice.[3] Who is the observer, who would see the system's attempt to resolve what Derrida calls the aporias of Justice so as to validate itself as injustice? In this case, it is a woman. I will return to why this observation on the observer is relevant.

For now I want to emphasize that Derrida's understanding of the aporias of Justice cannot be separated from his understanding of the constitutive force of *différance,* and the deconstruction of the privileging of the presence that *différance* necessarily implicates.

Further, once we understand the significance of this deconstruction of the privileging of the present, we can also see why it will help give us the correct understanding of the relationship between law, justice, and the phenomenology of judging, as the last chapter has helped us to understand the relationship between the Good, in Levinas' sense of the ethical relation, and the good embodied in legal principles. As we saw in the last chapter, the Good is understood as the ethical relation that calls us to justice. At times in Levinas' writing he does not distinguish the Good, as the call to responsibility to the Other, and Justice. Levinas frequently evokes Justice as the infinite responsibility to the Other. At other times he speaks of justice more prosaically as the appeal to the embodied principles of a legal system. In the last chapter I described justice in the more prosaic sense of legal principles as involving an appeal to the good embodied in the *nomos.* As we will see in this chapter, Derrida explicitly develops a conception of Justice as a set of aporias consistent with Levinas' evocations of the Good and with his own philosophy of the limit. But as already suggested, in order to understand what is unique in Derrida's conception of Justice as aporia, we need to understand it in connection with his deconstruction of the privileging of the present.

The traditional conception of time, upon which Luhmann relies to conceptualize the reproduction of systems, defines the past and the future as modifications or horizons of the present. By time, I am not evoking chronology, but the privileging of the present as it is understood to be necessary to what Luhmann would refer to as the autopoiesis of the legal system. Without this present there would be no legal system that could serve as a system of communication for its participants, whether they be lawyers or judges. We find the deconstruction of the traditional conception of time worked through not only in Jacques Derrida's discussions of *différance* but also in Emmanuel Levinas' diachronic understanding of time. I will specifically focus on how the diachronic view of time implicit in the explanations of *différance* undermines the very possibility that Justice can ever be effectively limited to the "positive" value within the binary code that Luhmann argues is the very basis for a modern legal system if it is to be seen as a system that effectively protects expectations.[4]

As we saw in the last chapter, legal positivism, when left unchallenged, creates a system, a kingdom which reigns over possibility and excludes the dream of a truly different future. The philosophy of the limit, as we have discussed, exposes the presumption of a determinant certitude of a present Good as defined by any current philosophical or legal system. But, as I have emphasized in the last chapter, in so doing, "deconstruction" is hardly the nihilistic language exercise many critics claim it to be. As we will see in this chapter, in the definition of Justice as aporia, the philosophy of the limit protects the divide between law and Justice, and protects justice from being encompassed by whatever convention described as the good of the community. This exposure of the aporias of Justice is in and of itself ethical. The aporias, or more precisely, Justice conceived as aporia, are an uncrossable limit which continually returns us to an inherent and ultimately irresolvable paradox. Justice so conceived resists its own collapse into law or the definition by any system of the good embodied in the *nomos*. It is precisely in its rejection of any system's "deparadoxicalization" of the paradox, and in its conviction that what the system says is just cannot in truth be Justice, that the philosophy of the limit heeds the aspiration to enact the ethical relation.

As we saw in the last chapter, this ethical resistance to legal positivism is also crucial for the development of an adequate conception of legal interpretation and can help us understand judicial responsibility. To briefly summarize the argument of the last chapter: First, this ethical resistance allows us to understand why legal interpretation always involves both "discovery" and "invention." Interpretation is not an activity separable from the other two. Indeed, as we will see in this chapter, the philosophy of the limit also emphasizes precisely the necessity of "invention" in interpretation. But this process of invention and restatement of legal norms also entails a judge's "responsibility toward memory." The responsibility is not to an accurate repetition through the recollection of legal norms, but to a refutation that what has been can *ever* be conflated with Justice. Invention is inescapable if legal norms cannot be discovered purely through their mere recollection. As a result, the judge is responsible for his or her projection of the good embodied in the *nomos*.

Moreover, it is a "projection," not simply a recovery of the past or the inevitable fulfillment of the *telos* of history. It is the turn toward the future, once it is properly understood, that the philosophy of the limit demands of us. Thus, although a modern legal system cannot but make a claim of legitimacy if it is to be rendered consistent with democracy, understood broadly for our purposes here as consisting of the transition of the rule of "men" to the rule of "law," the idea of *legitimacy* as understood *within* any given legal system also cannot be identified as *justice*. The concrete good of the *nomos* is in this sense always limited by Justice. Such a broadly defined concept of legitimacy does not necessarily imply an appeal—indeed, in American law it must not imply such an appeal if it is to be a decision *consistent* with precedent—to norms external to the legal system. In the last chapter I argued instead that law should be understood to express internal norms, which in turn embody a story of the good life. The philosophy of the limit's insistence that *no* legal system can claim to have enacted Justice may surprisingly, then, be rendered consistent with Luhmann's argument against

Jürgen Habermas that the focus on legitimation through an appeal to *nonlegal* norms should be deconstructed. To quote Luhmann:

> And nowadays people look for moral rules or values to found the legal system in nonlegal norms—the famous Jellinek-Weber-Habermas line of "legitimation" or the American discussion of moral aspiration vs. original intent as a guideline for an interpretation of the constitution. My advice would be to unask such questions—or to "deconstruct" them and to replace them with the question of how the system organizes its own closure, its own social autonomy, its own immunity in fulfilling its function that nobody else takes care of.[5]

As I have already suggested, such an appeal to the *nomos* does not imply the evocation of external norms, at least not in Habermas' sense, but instead appeals to the "internal" norms of a legal system. Indeed, in the language of systems theory such an appeal can be understood as part of how a modern, democratic legal system operates, since it must be based on principles applied equally to legal subjects if such a system is to be faithful to the democratic claim that is based on the role of law and not of men. Of course, to make this suggestion is also to argue that the philosophy of the limit is not simply a restatement of the Kantian insistence that justice is an ideal of political-historical reason, and as such is irreducible to the actual conventions of any existing legal system, because Luhmann has consistently expressed his disagreement with Habermas' Kantianism.[6] We are not, in other words, just returned to the question of the legitimation of the legal system through external moral norms that Luhmann would "deconstruct."

In Kant's later writings the idea of justice or the totality of reasonable beings functions as the "as if" which is an ethical condition for the future that we must postulate if we are to preserve practical judgment from being a mere appeal to conventions. The philosophy of the limit does not, as it is often interpreted to do, reject out of hand the Kantian project, even if it refuses to connect justice directly with legitimation, through external and yet philosophically established norms, as Habermas does.[7] To do so would once again conflate description and proscription through the elaboration of established norms, even if they are external to the legal system. As we will see, Habermas' reconstructive science is obviously not a traditional Kantian project in that it tries to find prescriptive norms in the descriptive norms of speech. On one reading, Derrida is more consistent than Habermas with the quasi-transcendental analysis of Justice developed by Kantianism. Even so, the philosophy of the limit refuses to reduce the aporias of Justice to an horizon, even in the Kantian understanding of the word.

We need to analyze why Derrida rejects the definition of justice as horizon. To do so, we need to discuss more carefully how an ethical horizon has been conceived. The question of whether one can or should project an horizon of justice is itself addressed through the recognition that there is an historical specificity of types of horizons associated with the project of a horizon of rational beings as an ideal. Do we idealize a "totality" of multiple language games, as in Jean François Lyotard's paganism, or the totality of reasonable beings in Kant's own Kingdom of ends? The context of the horizon once it is specified, in other words, is not just an appeal to the Ideal of Justice, but implies some pregiven context which in turn implies some vision of the Good. I would argue that the questioning of the very concept of horizon as itself a reflection of historical specificity is, as we will see, just that—a questioning.

However, the Kantian ethical suspicion of consensus as a "reality" that dresses up convention as truth is undoubtedly evidenced in Derrida's philosophy of the limit. Like Kantianism, the philosophy of the limit rejects the identification of the ethical with "reality." This affinity does not, of course, mean that this philosophy does not challenge the metaphysical premises that underlie the Kantian split between the phenomenal and the noumenal realms. Derrida challenges this rigid dichotomy as he does all others.

But what is often missed in the interpretation of this challenge is that, as we saw in the last chapter, the Derridean deconstruction of the privileging of the present reminds us of the responsibility of judges, lawyers, and law professors for what the law "becomes." Moreover, this responsibility is connected with the very idea of judgment. Judgment is only judgment and not mere calculation or recollection if it is "fresh."[8] The judge is called upon to do just that, judge. As we will see, Derrida's remarkable insight into the limits of memory is connected to his deconstruction of the traditional conception of the modalities of time in which the present is privileged. The unique Derridean contribution to legal interpretation is to show us why the act of memory in judging involves the seemingly contradictory notion that the judge, in his or her decision, remembers the future, which is why the understanding of the traditional conception of time is relevant to a discussion of interpretation and responsibility.

The deconstruction of the privileging of the present, as we will see, is crucial if we are to correct recent misdescriptions of the process of legal interpretation which either appeal to the established conventions of the "present" or look back to the past. Even if that past is understood as a constructed "overlapping consensus,"[9] and not just the simple recollection of norms, the process of reconstruction through the overlapping consensus is still directed to the past. The deconstruction of the traditional conception of time also provides us with an account of critique that can successfully answer the argument of Stanley Fish, who asserts that critique, in any strong sense, is impossible. For Fish, we are inevitably caught in what Luhmann calls the logic of recursivity, which enforces the apparent adequation between the legal system and justice, so that the system can establish the effective normative closure and, therefore, achieve the "self-generated dynamic form of stability"[10] that makes it a system. It is this logic of recursivity that makes the following of the pregiven legal rules or norms "Doing What Comes Naturally."[11] Judges and lawyers would, as a result, be caught in a mechanism of repetition from which they could not escape. Judgment, then, cannot be separated from calculation. Memory would *just* be rote, a replication in consciousness of an objective reality. Deconstruction challenges the possibility that the lawyer or the judge can be identified with the mere instrument for replication of the system. The judge and the lawyer "act" when they remember precedent. But this deconstruction is not only relevant to the Anglo-American debates, it is also relevant to Luhmann's systems theory itself.

According to Luhmann, for a legal system to remain a system it must form a self-maintaining, even if evolving, set of operations through which what he calls normative closure can be achieved. This idea of the self-maintenance of a normatively, if not cognitively, closed system is at the very heart of his conception of law as an autopoiesis. [12] This conception of self-maintenance and its corresponding notion of recursivity implies an understanding of time. As Luhmann explains, "[s]ince autopoietic systems are *temporalized* systems depending on self-generated dynamic forms of stability they necessarily differentiate and recognize their own operations by temporal orientations." [13] In terms of its definition within the framework of law understood as an autopoietic system, recursivity means that the normativity of law can only be established by reference to the legal norms already in place as they are *authorized* and, *therefore, justified* by the system, which is why I will suggest that a very specific understanding of the appeal to the good inherent in the norms of the system itself may not be incompatible with systems theory. The legal system, in other words, grounds the validity of its own propositions by turning back on itself. Without recursivity there would be no operative, normative closure and, therefore, no system present to itself that could be considered to be self-maintaining.

Due to Luhmann's understanding of the role of time in the maintenance of any system, he explores the iterative use of temporal modalities (past presents, future presents, etc.) as they are relevant to his social theory and more specifically to his conception of law as autopoiesis. For Luhmann, following the tradition of Western metaphysics, any theory of modal forms must privilege the present. It is this privileging of the present that lies at the very heart of Luhmann's conception of social evolution as the only way to make sense of change in a legal system which nevertheless remains normatively closed. Validity, in the sense of legitimation (this is a crucial difference from Habermas), [14] is only to be found by circling within the system.

Yet, it is important to note that Luhmann is very precise in his conceptualization of his project. He studies the operations necessary for a legal system to maintain itself as a system and how these operations have historically developed and are inevitably implied, by the differentiation of a modern society. He explicitly states, however, that he does not study, and indeed does not agree with, the proposition that differences delineate the system. [15] This is how he understands his own disagreement with Derrida. And yet as Luhmann has also noted, "[w]e could take the route of Saussure and Derrida or Spencer Brown and follow the injunction always to start with difference and not with identity, with distinction and not with unity."[16]

The purpose of this chapter is to re-interpret what it means for an understanding of justice and legal interpretation to follow that injunction as it necessarily demands the deconstruction of the modalities of time. Why have I chosen to re-interpret this injunction? Again, we are correctly returned to what Luhmann considers to be the inevitable first question: "who is the observer?"[17] Here, the observer is a woman, observing a system that has systematically undermined if not outright destroyed the civil rights gains for women made in the American legal system in the late 1960s and early 1970s.

Law as Normative Autopoiesis

But let me turn now to a brief discussion of what autopoiesis means within the context of Luhmann's systems theory of law. I will not attempt to discuss autopoiesis in all its subtlety but only as it incorporates a conception of time as it is relevant to the very possibility of the establishment and maintenance of a legal system. The central thesis of autopoiesis as it has been succinctly summarized is that legal propositions or norms must be understood within a self-generating system of communication which both defines relations with the outside environment and provides itself with its own mechanism of justification. Autopoiesis conserves law as an autonomous system that achieves full normative closure through epistemological constructivism. To quote Luhmann:

> Epistemological "constructivism" concludes from this that what the system, at the level of its operations, regards as reality is a construct of the system itself. Reality assumptions are structures of the system that uses them. This can be clarified once more using the concept of recursiveness. The system controls the environment, operationally inaccessible to it, by verifying the consistency of its own operations, using for this a binary system which can record agreement or non-agreement. Without this form of consistency control, no memory could arise, and without memory there can be no reality.[18]

Practically speaking, then, recursiveness allows for the consistency control that enables the system to function as a system. The system, legal or otherwise, *is* a system only to the degree that it is operationally closed. As Luhmann himself explains:

> [S]tructures of the system can be built up only by operations of the system. This too must take place in such a way as to be compatible with the system's autopoiesis; in the case of social systems, for instance, with communication. There is accordingly no input and no output of structures or operations of the system, and at this level, there are no exchange relationships with the environment. All structures are operationally self-specified structures of the

system, which orients its operations to these structures. In this respect, too, the system is a recursively closed system.[19]

For Luhmann, then, law is a specialized system of information processing. Law maintains the consistency of legal reality through the very recursiveness of its system of communication. But, even so, the legal system is not autonomous in the sense that it is completely disengaged from the rest of society, the economy, the political arena, and so forth. Indeed, Luhmann argues that a legal system, if it is to function to resolve conflicts, necessarily engages with events that are fed to it by the outside environment. As a result, there is always a material continuum between the law and its environment, even though Luhmann would also insist that this continuum should not be understood as the causal relationship implied in the phrase "law and society." The legal system is only autonomous in the sense that it is a self-reproducing mechanism for information processing.

The postulation of operational closure explains why systems theory is a form of epistemological constructivism in which reality comes to "be" only within the recursiveness of the system. But, of course, reality is only given in language. What words mean can only be deciphered from within the relevant system of communication, not through a more general system of definition. As Luhmann explains:

> The law need not and cannot concern itself with whether particular words like "woman", "cylinder capacity," "inhabitant," "thallium" are used with sufficient consistency inside and outside the law. To that extent, it is supported by the network of social reproduction of communication by communication. Should questions such as whether women, etc., really exist arise, they can be turned aside or referred to philosophy.[20]

The operational network of law, for Luhmann, is a normative network which continually processes information through its established presuppositions. Or, to put this another way so as to explain the distinction he makes between normative closure and cognitive openness: normative closure is based in the definitional recursiveness of the law. As Luhmann has put it:

> Legal reasoning uses the distinction between norms and facts, between normative and cognitive expectations. It has to know in which respects it is supposed to learn (whether or not somebody killed another woman) and in which respects not (that she should not or be killed).[21]

Normative closure creates the seeming adequation of law and justice as part of the system's deparadoxicalization. Since the system functions through the binary code of justice and injustice, and excludes contradictory statements, the resolution of any conflict, if it is to be effective—convincing to the participants as well as to others—the society must be understood to realize the positive values of the code of justice. This formulation of law as logically recursive can, of course, be understood as a reformulation of the positivist hypothesis. The *nomos* of the law can only be found in law's *thesis*. But there is an important difference in Luhmann's conception of autopoiesis that separates him from the traditional legal positivist. In Luhmann's systems theory, the *thesis* is not an outside foundation, but the postulation of law itself as its own origin. For Luhmann, the thesis of law cannot be the will of the legislator; rather, the thesis is the already-in-place legal system, with its recursive system of normative self-reproducing definitions:

> Norms, then are purely internal creations, serving the self-generated needs of the system without any corresponding "similar" items in its environment. And nothing else is meant by "autopoiesis." Historically there is no beginning except an always renewed reconstruction of the past and also logically there are no apriorities but simply a circular, reciprocal conditioning of code and programmes.[22]

Law is a normatively closed system in the sense that the opposition between *nomos* and *thesis* is practically overcome in the functioning of the legal system. But at the same time, law is not a cognitively closed system. This distinction is connected to Luhmann's position that while the legal system's normative autopoiesis is self-referential, it is not self-transparent. Luhmann denies that any complex system can achieve perfect self-transparency. This is why Luhmann distinguishes his own systems theory from all forms of neo-Kantianism. The biological metaphor of autopoiesis is supposed to capture this distinction between self-thematization or self-referentiality, and self-transparency. A biological system can be self-referential without necessarily knowing itself to be such.[23] Because law is not self-transparent and, therefore, not able to verify all of its operations, the legal system remains cognitively open. However, it is cognitively open only in a very special sense. For example, the legal system can take account of the notion that electricity can be stolen. But even as it *recognizes* this idea, it can do so only within the normative autopoiesis that recursively defines what it means for something to be stolen. Moreover, the normative definition of theft can only be what the legal system says it is. As Luhmann has already told us, recursivity also replaces the assumption of an *a priori* which could serve as an outside ground for justice by which to justify legal principles within a legal system. Without recursivity there would be no self-reproducing system that could come full circle to claim itself as its own origin.

The Iterative Use of the Modalities of Time
Within Systems Theory

Luhmann's basic hypothesis is that time, as well as its conceptualization, is changed through the mechanisms of social evolution. Time, as Luhmann defines it, is "the social interpretation of reality with respect to the difference between past and future."[24] Modern societies can be distinguished from traditional societies because of what he calls the temporalization of being. According to Luhmann, temporalization of being discredits any theory of natural forms, which would always turn us toward the past as the fundamental pivot of a society's time frame. Temporalization of being means that the past can no longer be grounded in an initial event or origin. This loss of origin shifts the very ground of time in modern societies and is reflected in the iterative use of temporal modalities within social theory. For Luhmann, the chief features of social evolution, at least in terms of how it has changed the concept of time, are to be found in what he calls the nontemporal extension of time.

Luhmann associates his conception of the nontemporal extension of time with his basic notion of a social system as a mechanism for processing information through communication with the "outside" environment:

> This nontemporal extension of time by communication creates temporal horizons for selective behavior—a past that can never be reproduced because it is too complex and a future than cannot begin.[25]

The nontemporal extension of time in turn implies time's reflexivity. As Luhmann rightfully explains, a theory of time that is distinguishable from chronology must make use of the iteration of temporal modalities. Even though Luhmann insists that the reflexivity of time in modern society turns around our orientation to the future, the future can only be understood from within the present. The future and, indeed, the past only "are" as horizons of the present. To quote Luhmann:

> [T]he *relevance* of time (in fact, I would maintain, "relevance" as such) depends upon a capacity to interrelate the past and the future in a present. All temporal structures relate to some sort of present.[26]

The present interrelates time and reality and represents a set of constraints on the temporal integration of the future and the past. Meaning can only arise if there is this shared "present." This set of constraints establishes the recursivity of the system. Social communication demands that there be a "present" that is "there" for the temporal actors. The non-extension of time—by which Luhmann indicates the evolution of society as the continued development of the present— implies the recursivity of the systems pattern, or what Luhmann calls self-thematization. This process of self-thematization is what makes a system self-constituting in and through the present. The actors in the system can interact only because there is a shared present.

> The concept of the present contains rules for using the idea of simultaneity, which itself underlies the possibility of communication in social life.[27]

The system depends on temporal integration because without such integration it would not maintain its identity. The very distinction between the system and its environment means that there is an inevitable temporalization of the system. The system, in other words, is not there all at once in an eternal present. It is always coming to be. Recursivity is a mode of temporal integration of the past and the future as both these conceptual horizons have come to present themselves within the frame of modern society.

> As has recently been made clear, underlying this schema is the idea that the *differentiation of system and environment produces temporality* because it excludes an immediate and point-for-point correlation between events in the system and events in its environment. Everything cannot happen at once. Preserving the system requires time.[28]

In modern society the present now contains possibilities, and, in this sense, the present future has conditional possibilities. Luhmann distinguishes between societies and social systems on the basis of whether or not they are expanding or curtailing the possibilities of the present future. But even so, the nonextension of time means that the present remains the basis for the iteration of all temporal modalities even if the present view includes the future present and the present future.

According to Luhmann, once we see the future as the storehouse of possibilities of the present—both as the future present and the present future—we can no longer conceive of time as containing a turning point where it veers back to a mythical past or where the order of the present is to be apocalyptically transformed.

> It must now be recognized that the future (and this means past futures as well as our present future) may be quite different from the past. Time can no longer be depicted as approaching a turning point where it veers back into the past or where the order of this world (or time itself) is apocalyptically transformed.[29]

For Luhmann, there is also no *telos* in history which leads us to the ideal through the progressive realization of the potential that inheres in the origin and which ultimately has the power to make itself real. Luhmann believes himself to be enriching the iterative use of temporal modalities so as to develop a unique modern conception of time.

> For modern society, it is especially important that we be able to distinguish between our future presents and our present future. We can even speak, if necessary, about the future of future presents, the future of past presents (*modo futuri exacti*), and so on. This iterative use of modal forms has always been a problem for the theory of modalities. For example: why not speak of the "future of futures" like the "heaven of heavens" (*coelum coeli*)? Only phenomenological analysis can justify the selection of meaningful combinations of modal forms. What it shows, in fact, is that all iteration of temporal forms must have its basis in a present.[30]

For Luhmann, rooting the iteration of all temporal modalities in the present has implications for the way we think about the historical time of systems history.

> Historical time is constituted as the continuity and irreversibility of this move-
> ment of past/present/future as a whole. This unity of historical time lies in the
> fact that the past and future horizons of each present intersect with other (past
> or future) presents and their temporal horizons. This guarantees each present a
> sufficient continuity with other presents—not only temporally, but materially
> and socially as well.[31]

It is because the future and past move around the present that Luhmann can
speak of his theory of time as reflexive. The horizons of the past and the future
are reflexively integrated and thematized into a system through the present. Once
we accept Luhmann's proposition that the past and the future are reflexively
integrated into the present, we can understand exactly what he means when he
insists that the future cannot begin.[32] For Luhmann the future is both the *present
future*, as the conditional possibilities inherent in any complex modern social
system, and the *future present*, expressed as the utopian projections of social
critics. These projections of the utopian future, however, are only expressible as
the negations of the present and, therefore, are contained in the very systems
history they purport to reject. They serve as images to give body to the aspirations
of the future present.

A future that cannot begin inheres in the reflexive view of time Luhmann
associates with complex modern societies based on advanced technology. An
open-ended future present which is necessary for the cognitive opening of the
system ironically involves the loss of the future as the promise of a truly "new
beginning." However, it should be remembered that the present of the systems
theory, which is not a simple present because it is relativized through the horizons
of the past and the future, still constitutes reality.

This view of the time of social systems and of world history has specific
implications for legal interpretation, the conception of justice, and the possibility
of social criticism. For Luhmann, if there is no *telos* of history, the pull of the
regulative ideal cannot be introduced *into* social theory or systems history, which
is why he is a critic of the reconstructive science of Jürgen Habermas.[33] This is
what Luhmann means when he says that history has been neutralized. History no
longer has normative implications. Luhmann uses legal positivism as one of the
examples of what the neutralization of history entails.[34] The past can no longer
provide us with an origin that can serve as the basis for normative justification
for the present or for the projection of a truly different future as the truth of the
past. In Luhmann's conception of the legal system's autopoiesis, justice can only
be what the legal system defines it to be. The idea of justice as an external moral
norm which justifies the system is rejected as inconsistent with an explanation of
how the system reproduces itself. The horizon—Habermas' ideal speech situation
or Kant's Kingdom of ends, for example—is only an ethical horizon to the degree
that the projected ideal is beyond the logic of recursivity. The "ought to be," in
other words, cannot be captured by the present. Kantianism, in all its forms,
maintains a transcendental divide between the is and the ought. But in Luhmann,

any norm, legal or otherwise, only means something to the degree that such a norm expresses the present understanding developed through the network of legal operations. The legal system can develop, but only as the legal system. For Luhmann, the victory of legal positivism inheres in the very mode of the temporalization of modern society.

The Deconstructive Challenge to Luhmann's Conception of the Modalities of Time Inherent in Systems Theory

Derrida's philosophy of the limit challenges the idea that a theory of modal forms must have its basis in the present. (But it should be remembered here that Luhmann's theory of time studies the time framework necessary for systems maintenance.) As we will see, this challenge is crucial for the development of an antipositivist conception of legal interpretation in which the divide between justice and law is always maintained, but not in the Habermassian manner of the projection of an external norm or set of norms that serve as a criterion for the definitive establishment of justice.

But first I will turn to the deconstruction of the traditional conception of time which privileges the present. In order to do so, we must turn with Derrida around *différance*. Heidegger forcefully pointed to the privileging of the present in traditional conceptions of time in Western metaphysics. Derrida clearly recognizes the explosive power of Heidegger's attempt to follow through on the implications of *Dasein's*[35] finitude and its potential to undermine the traditional conception of time. But it is not this aspect of Heidegger's analysis that is crucial for the deconstruction of the traditional conception of temporal orientation. Therefore, I will focus instead on the significance for legal theory of Derridean *différance*. Because *différance* is not a traditional philosophical concept it is difficult to define it directly. Indeed, Derrida himself circles around the play of *différance* as it operates within several different theoretical parameters.

Différance can be understood as the "truth" that being is only represented in time; therefore, there can be no all encompassing ontology which claims to tell us the truth of all that is. There is a similarity here between Derrida and Luhmann insofar as both stress, even in different ways, the temporalization of Being. Luhmann's analysis is sociological, focusing on how the temporalization of Being results from the shift in the conception of time associated with modernity. Derrida's analysis, on the other hand, is quasi-transcendental. For Derrida, the temporalization of Being inheres in the conditions of the presentation of Being and not in the specific historical conditions of modernity. *Différance,* to use Derrida's word, *temporizes.* It breaks up the so-called claim to fullness of any given reality, social or otherwise, because reality only "presents" itself in intervals so that, to return to Luhmann, there can no longer be sufficient continuity between each present with other presents.

An interval must separate the present from what is not in order for the present to be itself, but this interval that constitutes it as present must, by the same token, divide the present in and of itself, thereby also dividing, along with the present, everything that is thought on the basis of the present, that is, in our metaphysical language, every being, and singularly substance or the subject.[36]

The intervals through which reality is "presented" also make possible the presentation of reality out of what would otherwise be sheer density, "or the night in which all cows are black."[37] In order for reality to "present" itself, it must already be spaced, which implies temporization and time. "The present," in other words, is what is already past and, therefore, "presented." But this condition is only reachable as the "effects" of temporization, one of which is time, itself a diachronic force. Time, understood in this way, cannot function as both an integration and a unit of the past and future through the present, as in Luhmann. Any reality is always already divided against itself. Thus, the disruption of temporizing turns us toward the past, even if only in a very specific sense, because this past can just as well be conceived as the trace of the future.

It is because of *différance* that the movement of signification is possible only if each so-called "present" element, each element appearing on the scene of presence, is related to something other than itself, thereby keeping within itself the mark of the past element, and already letting itself be vitiated by the mark of its relation to the future element, this trace being related no less to what is called the future than to what is called the past, and constituting what is called the present by means of this very relation to what it is not: what it absolutely is not, not even as past or a future as a modified present.[38]

The statement that the trace is related "no less to what is called the future than to what is called the past" may seem strange indeed. Yet it is precisely this insistence on the constitutive power of the "not yet" of the never has been that separates the Derridean understanding of temporalization from Luhmann's sociological analysis of the unique conception of time in modernity and, more specifically, the time inherent in any self-perpetuating system, and sets Derrida against Luhmann's assertion that the future cannot begin.

For Derrida, the future has already begun—although it is, of course, inappropriate to use the word beginning here since temporization belies an absolute beginning—as the trace of the unreachable origin. Derrida would agree with Luhmann, then, that there is no way back to the origin. As we approach the origin it recedes and the receding of the origin is inevitable because we have always already begun once there is a reality that has been presented. The origin only "is" as this recession of the never has been of an absolute beginning; this is why it can also be related to the future of the not yet. The past is not the past of chronology, which can be traced back through a linear succession of moments. Nor is it one of the horizons that extends back from the present, what Luhmann would call the present past. Rather, the past is the primordial constitution of temporality, which in turn is the condition of presentation. The present, as a result, itself becomes a sign, pointing beyond itself.

Derrida would, however, also agree with Luhmann that the recognition that we can never grasp the origin has implications for the way we think about the future. The central difference is that for Derrida it is the present that is forever postponed, because the present "moment" must refer to the trace of the not yet of never has been that cannot be conceived as simply a modification of the now. In order to be what it is, the now, or the present, must refer back to an anterior/posterior that is the basis for presentation. As we have seen, this "movement" of temporalization is already "there" in presentation. As a result, the "present" is always belated. It cannot arrive except as constitutive power of the not yet of the never has been, which can be evoked as either the "not yet" past or future. The future in this specific sense of the "not yet" cannot be reduced to the present future or future present. It remains the "not yet," but as that power it has always already begun. This is why *différance* implies a diachronic view of time. Time disrupts the very pretense of full presence at the very moment that it makes presentation possible. Time, in this primordial sense, is the *delimitation* of the ontology of presence.

We can now turn to what the diachronic view of time means for the engagement between Luhmann's systems theory and Derrida's philosophy of the limit. Luhmann claims that his epistemological construct view is "postontology." And, of course, it is in the sense that Luhmann gives to postontology. For Luhmann, ontology claims privileged access to an "external reality" outside of the autopoietic system. He replaces ontology with epistemological constructivism. (As Luhmann well understands, his own conception of postontology demands philosophical as well as sociological exploration.)

But in another, more profound sense, the very idea of recursiveness implies exactly what Derrida means by the ontology of the full presence. Recursiveness implies a view of time that necessarily privileges the present. The whole point of Luhmann's theory of autopoiesis is to show us how a legal system makes itself "real" through operative closure in the present. Through autopoietic closure, the system becomes the only "reality." As such it fills the universe; it becomes a kingdom which reigns over possibility and excludes the dream of a truly different future. Derrida challenges this idea that the system can reign in the beyond of the not yet through the demonstration of the significance of the play of *différance*.

> It is the domination of beings that *différance* everywhere comes to solicit, in the sense that *sollicitare*, in old Latin, means to shake as a whole, to make tremble in entirety. Therefore, it is the determination of Being as presence or as beingness that is interrogated by the thought of *différance*. Such a question could not emerge and be understood unless the difference between Being and beings were somewhere to be broached. First consequence: *différance* is not. It is not a present being, however excellent, unique, principal or transcendent. It governs nothing, reigns over nothing and nowhere exercises any authority.

It is not announced by any capital letter. Not only is there no kingdom of *différance*, but *différance* instigates the subversion of every kingdom. Which makes it obviously threatening and infallibly dreaded by everything within us that desires a kingdom, the past or future presence of a kingdom.[39]

Recursiveness establishes the kingdom or the system as, at the very least, *de facto* ontology (which, of course, Luhmann would recognize, since epistemological constructivism both recognizes "reality" as a construct and yet preserves the notion of "reality"); *différance*, on the other hand, explodes from within its very claim to rule over the future by reducing the future to a horizon of the present. There is a sense, of course, in which Derrida would agree with Luhmann that the future cannot begin, because the very idea of the not yet is both anterior and *posterior* and, therefore, not merely "future" in the traditional meaning of the word. But, as we have seen, the very posterity of the future as the not yet of the never has been means that it has already begun as a constitutive force that disrupts the presence of the present. The future "is" as *redemption* from enclosure in the present.

The Significance of Time for a Conception of Law

Within a legal system, the future as the promise of Justice "is" as the possible deconstruction of law or right. The destabilization of "the Kingdom" is also the destabilization of the functional or practical identity of *nomos* and *thesis* within a given legal system. As we have seen, in Luhmann, the logic of recursivity functions so as to postulate itself as its own origin, therefore urging *nomos* and *thesis* into accord. It is this endless process of turning in on itself that replaces the myth of origin.

Derrida agrees with Luhmann—and we will return to the significance of this agreement in his discussion of Rousseau—that there is no "real" normative origin from which all the values and norms of the legal system can be returned so they can be adequately assessed. But, unlike Luhmann, Derrida does argue that this origin cannot ever fully be displaced by the logic of recursivity:

Since the origin of authority, the foundation or ground, the position of the law can't by definition rest on anything but themselves, they are themselves a violence without ground. Which is not to say that they are themselves unjust, in the sense of "illegal." They are neither legal nor illegal in their founding moment. They exceed the opposition between founded and unfounded, or between any foundationalism or anti-foundationalism. Even if the success of performatives that found law or right (for example, and this is more than an example, of a state as guarantor of a right) presupposes earlier conditions and conventions (for example in the national or international arena), the same "mystical" limit will reappear at the supposed origin of said conditions, rules or conventions, and at the origin of their dominant interpretation.[40]

Law, as a construct, is always deconstructible. The endless deconstruction of law destabilizes the machine and exposes the cracks in the system. As a result of this destabilization, the displacement of the origin can never be completed through the functioning of the legal system or through the postulation of a Master Rule of Recognition which supposedly replaces the founding moment of violence with a norm of foundation.[41] This destabilization is itself done in the name of legal *transformation* and reform and, ultimately, in the name of Justice. To quote Derrida:

> The structure I am describing here is a structure in which law (*droit*) is essentially deconstructible, whether because it is founded, constructed on inter-pretable or transformable textual strata (and that is the history of law (*droit*), its possible and necessary transformation, sometimes its amelioration), or because its ultimate foundation is by definition unfounded. The fact that law is deconstructible is not bad news. We may even see in this a stroke of luck for politics, for all historical progress. But the paradox that I'd like to submit for discussion is the following: it is the deconstructible structure of law (*droit*), or if you prefer of justice as *droit,* that also insures the possibility of deconstruction. Justice in itself, if such a thing exists, outside or beyond law, is not deconstruct-ible. No more than deconstruction itself, if such a thing exists. *Deconstruction is justice.*[42]

Why *is* deconstruction justice? There are several levels on which this question must be answered. Deconstruction, as we have seen, undermines the legal ma-chine that claims to find authority in its own functioning. The tyranny of the "real," and with it the appeal to a present "reality" as the basis of the Justice, denies possibilities of legal reform that have yet to be articulated. The attempt to positively establish the nature of justice is rejected as incomplete because descrip-tive justification, the appeal to what is, still stands in for prescriptive justice. If we say this is what justice is through descriptive justification, no matter how sophisticated the argument, if a victim's claim can still not be adequately trans-lated, her claim goes unnoticed. To identify any existent state of affairs as justice is to impose silence on the Other who cannot or dares not speak in that system.

Justice, if it is defined immanently, reinstates a circular mode of justification that turns on what already is. Therefore, such an appeal still collapses prescription and description. This refusal of the collapse of a prescription into description is one dimension of deconstruction's insistence on the maintenance of the divide between the is and the ought, law and justice. This resistance is in and of itself ethical. It is important to note again that Luhmann's project is to conceptualize what a legal system "is," not to philosophically show how it is necessarily delimited by its very structure, which separates the internal from the external as a matter of self-definition. We will return to the divergence between Derrida and Luhmann, in particular with regard to how each understands the relationship between difference and any system's own self-delimitation, shortly. For now, I want to emphasize their shared differences with Kantianism.

But if justice is not immanent to any legal system, how can we conceive of justice as transcendent without simply reverting to Kantian metaphysics in which the is and the ought are clearly divided into two realms, the phenomenal and the noumenal. In other words, how can the philosophy of the limit destabilize the traditional dichotomy between nature and freedom, so crucial to Kantian morality while at the same time insisting on Justice as transcendent to any set of immanent norms in any legal system? As we have seen, this destabilization can itself only be conceived within the deconstruction of the traditional modalities of time. The legal system is never simply present to itself so as to generate its own purely immanent norms. This destabilization of the relation between the immanent and the transcendent is itself done in the name of justice but is not Justice. Justice "is" the limit of the immanent norms of the legal system to the extent that these norms are identified as Justice. But for Derrida, this limit is not projected as a transcendental ideal. Rather, it is an unsurpassable aporia. Justice, in other words, operates, but it operates as aporia. From the standpoint of the observer, justice is the refusal to accept as valid the system's own attempts at "deparadoxicalization."

Derrida's Definition of Justice as Aporia

Derrida gives us three examples of the operational force of Justice as aporia.[43] The first aporia is between "épokhe and rule." If law is just calculation, then it would not be self-legitimating, because the process of legitimation implies an appeal to a norm. The judge is called to judge, which means that she not only states what the law is, she confirms its value as what ought to be.

> In short, for a decision to be just and responsible, it must, in its proper moment if there is one, be both regulated and without regulation: it must conserve the law and also destroy it or suspend it enough to have to reinvent it in each case, rejustify it, at least reinvent it in the reaffirmation and the new and free confirmation of its principle. Each case is other, each decision is different and requires an absolutely unique interpretation, which no existing, coded rule can or ought to guarantee absolutely. At least, if the rule guarantees it in no uncertain terms, so that the judge is a calculating machine—which happens— we will not say that he is just, free and responsible. But we also won't say it if he doesn't refer to any law, to any rule or if, because he doesn't take any rule for granted beyond his own interpretation, he suspends his decision, stops short before the undecidable or if he improvises and leaves aside all rules, all principles.[44]

But at the same time, the judge is called to judge according to law. That is part of the responsibility of a judge: he must judge what is right, which means he appeals to law, to rules and not only to his opinion. So the judge is caught in a paradox. He must appeal to law and yet judge it through confirmation or rejection.

But this act of judgment would not be a "true" judgment, fresh, if it were simply calculation of law. As a result:

> It follows from this paradox that there is never a moment that we can say *in the present* that a decision *is* just (that is, free and responsible), or that someone *is* a just man—even less, *"I am* just."[45]

To be just, is to be in the throes of this paradox.

The second aporia is the "undecidable," an aporia which is close to the first, and to some degree reflects a transcendental deduction of the conditions of a decision.[46] A legal decision is an interpretation which "exists" in the first aporia. If a decision is merely calculation, it is not a decision.

> There is apparently no moment in which a decision can be called presently and fully just: either it has not yet been made according to a rule, and nothing allows us to call it just, or it has already followed a rule—whether received, confirmed, conserved or reinvented—which in its turn is not absolutely guaranteed by anything; and, moreover, if it were guaranteed, the decision would be reduced to calculation and we wouldn't call it just. That is why the ordeal of the undecidable that I just said must be gone through by any decision worthy of the name is never past or passed, it is not a surmounted or sublated (*aufgehoben*) moment in the decision.[47]

The third aporia[48] is, perhaps, most significant for the purposes of our discussion here, because it most clearly distinguishes the Kantian divide between the noumenal and the phenomenal from the Derridean conception of Justice as the limit of the immanent as aporia. The third aporia is created by the very urgency of justice. As we have seen, every case calls for a decision and a "fresh" judgment. The judge is called to decide now. In Habermas or Lyotard, two modern interpreters of Kant, justice ultimately "is" only as the projection of the horizon of the ideal. The content of the ideal differs in Habermas and Lyotard, but not the Kantian mode of argumentation.[49] But we are not in Habermas' ideal speech situation now, nor are we in Lyotard's paganism. And yet, we must judge. As a result, Derrida states:

> One of the reasons I'm keeping such a distance from all these horizons—from the Kantian regulative idea or from the messianic advent, for example, or at least from their conventional interpretation—is that they are, precisely, *horizons*. As its Greek name suggests, a horizon is both the opening and the limit that defines an infinite progress or a period of waiting.[50]

Justice does not wait. We judge in our present. But the ideal cannot guide us precisely because it is the ideal and thus not present. For Habermas, truth and rightness in the ideal speech situation demand the projection of a regulative ideal to guide us. As a regulative ideal, it is not realizable. Yet, we do not have the ideal speech situation and, indeed, as an ideal we cannot have it.

There is another concern. In spite of ourselves, the ideal will not be other to the real, therefore ideal; it will only be a rationalized projection of our current norms.[51] Justice demands the recognition of the possible contamination of the ideal itself. One classic example is that very ideal of the rational "man" crucial to traditional liberal conceptions of justice, which may rest on just that, a conception of the norm as masculine to the exclusion of feminine forms of reasoning. In order to prevent the justification of one norm as justice, Derrida appeals to the overflowing of the performative, inherent in the very act of interpretation.

> Paradoxically, it is because of this overflowing of the performative, because of this always excessive haste of interpretation getting ahead of itself, because of this structural urgency and precipitation of justice that the latter has no horizon of expectation (regulative or messianic). But for this very reason, it *may* have *avenir, a "to-come," which I rigorously distinguish from the future that can always reproduce the present.* Justice remains, is yet, to come, *à venir*, it has an, it is *à-venir*, the very dimension of events irreducibly to come. It will always have it, this *à-venir*, and always has. Perhaps it is for this reason that justice, insofar as it is not only a juridical or political concept, opens up for *l'avenir* the transformation, the recasting or refounding of law and politics. "Perhaps," one must always say perhaps for justice.[52]

The legal system as the present norm silences the perhaps. The machine may or may not operate. But, as a machine, in Derrida's sense, it demands only calculation of those who operate it. For Derrida, judgment begins where calculation ends.

Here we see the affinity of Derrida's conceptualization of the aporias of Justice with Levinas' "Jewish humanism," in which Justice provides the sanctity for the Other. Justice does not, then, begin with the "I" that strives to establish *his* rights and protect *his* due share of the pie. The right of the Other is infinite, meaning that it can never be reduced to a proportional share of an already established system of ideality, legal or otherwise. Justice understood as distributive justice always implies an already-established system of ideality in which the distribution takes place. For Levinas, distributive justice is never a question of Justice, but only of right. It is the Other as other to the present that echoes in the call to Justice. The echo breaks up the "present," because the Other is there before the conception of a system of ideality and remains after.

The Relationship between Derrida and Levinas'
Deconstruction of the Modalities of Time

Levinas also deconstructs the modalities of time, even as they are incorporated into Luhmann's unique conception of social theory. Even if his deconstruction proceeds differently from Derrida's, Levinas offers us a concept of the future as irreducible to the evolution of the present that also has implications for the way in which the relationship between justice and law is understood.

Levinas elaborates a unique sense of the future which he connects to what he calls the infinity of time. Like *différance,* the infinity of time can also be understood as an inevitable temporalization of Being so that presentation is possible. For Levinas, the infinity if time implies that temporalization is a diachronic force that cannot be suppressed. Time is *always* disrupting the presence of the present as it also makes presentation possible. The infinity of time is not, then, the eternal *now,* all that is in its full presence, a conception that is associated with the traditional reading of Hegel. The infinity of time disrupts the fullness of presence. As it does so it promises us hope of a new beginning because there can "be" no mere reproduction of what is or what has been, because there is no past or present simply "there" to be repeated.

> Resurrection constitutes the principal event of time. There is therefore no continuity in being. Time is discontinuous; one instant does not come out of another without interruption by an ecstasy.[53]

For Levinas, it is the very infinity of time as the overreaching of the in-finite of the present that opens us to the beyond as other than an horizon of the eternal present. This beyond can also be understood as the future which can never be closed off.

> The future does not come to one from a swarming of indistinguishable possibilities which would flow toward any present and which I would grasp; it comes to one across an absolute interval whose other shore is absolute Other.[54]

The future as the "not yet" remains other than the present. Again we see the contrast with Luhmann's understanding of the time frame of systems maintenance such that future time is understood within the system's operations, which is necessary for the sake of reducing the future to the "present future" or the "future present." It is Levinas' denial of the reflexivity of the present that leads him to insist that the future does not come "from a swarming of indistinguishable possibilities." The "Other" of the "not yet" is "present" as the recommencement that inheres in the diachronic "force" of time. "Time is the non-definitiveness of the definitive, an ever-recommencing altering of the accomplished—the 'ever' of the recommencement."[55]

"To be" infinitely and eternally has usually been taken to mean "to be" without limits and, therefore, necessarily outside of time. Time, as traditionally conceived, is only a limit—the integrative force of the present that operates as a set of constraints. But Levinas shifts our understanding of infinity by making it "the infinity of time" which resists the illusion of totalization that lies at the root of the Hegelian conception of the infinite. Infinition in Levinas is the rupture of continuity that is expressed in time. In this sense, Levinas and Luhmann offer us very different meanings of what is entailed by the non-extension of the temporal. It is important to note again, however, that Luhmann's conception of time involves his explanation of why a system is possible. In Luhmann, time turns back on itself because it is inevitably rooted in the present. The time of the system evolves, but it does not recommence, if one means by a recommencement a "new beginning." According to Luhmann, the iterative use of time can only be understood through the evolution of the present. As we have seen, for Luhmann, the very notion of recommencement, let alone of resurrection, would involve an appeal to a lost origin that he believes is necessarily gone. This is why Luhmann argues that apocalyptic visions inevitably veer back to the past. But in Levinas, recommencement and resurrection do not appeal to the lost origin. Indeed, the opposite is the case. Time recommences precisely because it is discontinuous. It is the discontinuity of time that disrupts the very idea of an appeal to an origin as an absolute beginning. The past that has never been and yet must be for presentation to be possible disrupts the very idea of the beginning, at least as traditionally conceived. And yet, in another very specific sense, the future is always beginning as the recommencement that inheres in the infinity of time. But this recommencement is not just continuity in the sense of a present future or future present. There is no simple "return" through the present that defines change only as evolution. This is why Levinas can say that the time in which being and infinition are produced goes beyond the possible, if the possible is understood as the future present or the present future.

As with Derrida, Levinas' conception of time has implications for his under-standing of justice. For Levinas, Justice is messianic. The *"avenir"* is not just the limit created by the aporias Derrida indicates, but instead inheres in the otherness of the Other that cannot be encompassed by any present system of ideality. The Other is other to the system. Incorporation into the system is the denial of the Other. Justice is sanctity for her "otherness." Nonencompassable by the system, the Other is also noncalculable. The right of the Other, then, is infinite, meaning that it can never be reduced to a proportional share of an already-established system of ideality, legal or otherwise. It is the Other as other to the present that echoes in the call to justice. The echo breaks up the "present," because the Other is there before the conception of a system of ideality and remains after.

For Derrida and Levinas, if for different reasons, the future is distinguished from the present that merely reproduces itself. Justice, in other words, whether as a limit, as echoed in the necessary demand of the Good, or as the call of the Other that cannot be silenced, is the opening of the beyond that makes "true" transformation to the "new" possible. Without this appeal to the beyond, transformation would not be transformation, but only evolution and, in that sense, a continuation. The very concept of continuation as evolution of the system implies the privileging of the present.

The Relationship between Systems Theory
and the Philosophy of the Limit Rethought

But what is the "bottom line" in terms of the relationship between systems theory and the deconstruction of the privileging of the present carried out by both Derrida and Levinas? On one reading, particularly of Derrida, such a deconstruction demands that sociology, conceived for our purposes here as Luhmann's systems theory, must be rejected because such a theory, which studies how systems come to be identified as systems replicates the identity logic that Derrida deconstructs. Many writers who have been identified as "postmodern" have reached that conclusion.[56] Some feminists, for example, have suggested that there is no "system" of gender reproduction. Gender is only a masquerade and, because gender can always be restyled, it is both a philosophical and political mistake to try to explain how "men" and "women" are reproduced as "men" and "women."[57] The very concept of social "reality," let alone systems "reality," is rejected. In terms of the relationship between sociology and a quasi-transcendental analysis such as Derrida's philosophy of the limit, this understanding of deconstruction has led to the inescapable conclusion that sociology, even in its most sophisticated forms, such as Luhmann's systems theory, is misguided. (Of course, other "postmodern" feminists have reached the opposite conclusion: the contrary "postmodern" position insists that sociology replaces philosophy.)[58]

The politics of this rejection can be stated simply and, again, I will use the example of gender identity. The politics inherent in the deconstruction of gender identity involves an implicit appeal to freedom. We are always free. We are always free to restyle ourselves, to make up our own "gender" or lack thereof. Nietzsche's influence, interpreted through one reading of Foucault, is obviously evident here in the emphasis on the aesthetic recreation rather than, as in Levinas, on the enactment of the ethical relationship.[59] As I argued in the third chapter, Derrida does not deny the importance of the Nietzschean moment, particularly if one thinks that moment in the context of gender identity as the possibility of the restylization of one's own sexual identity. As we have seen, Derrida's deconstructive intervention into Lacan shows us both why the recognition of phenomenological symmetry for women is possible, in spite of the system of gender meaning which denies women that recognition, and why the "new choreography of sexual identity" can never be foreclosed by the system of gender reproduction so eloquently described by Lacan. I have also argued elsewhere[60] that it is a serious misreading of Derrida to argue that he denies that *systems* do indeed perpetuate themselves so as to provide the meaning within which "facts" are defined. He does not, as I argued, deny *on the level of sociological analysis,* that there is no such "thing" as a woman. Lacan tells us that within the current system of gender identity women are defined as just that, "things," mirrors, and fantasy objects for men.

But there is a horrifying "reality" that is at least seemingly connected to that definition of women as "things."[61] In the United States, women are murdered five times as often as men,[62] and every eighteen seconds a woman is raped, while the number of rapes perpetuated against men is statistically non-significant.[63] Similarly, a woman is battered every fifteen seconds while the number of husband batterers is statistically insignificant.[64] In their individual lifetimes, nearly forty percent of all women will be victims of a violent assault.[65] Of course, these statistics are also influenced by race and class; women are not equally subjected to abuse and crime.

Yet, even with the crucial addition of the recognition of race and class within the category of "Woman" itself, there is an obvious difference that makes a difference between the lives of women and men. The role of systems theory is to give us an explanation, not just an empirical account of how a given system not only defines the difference between the genders, but also why this system seems to perpetuate violence against women in a way that it does not against men. Of course, no one would deny that the horrifying murder rate in the United States affects all human beings although, again, not equally. Even so, there is still a difference even in the types of crime women and men endure. In other words, if we are to adequately understand the conditions in which women have to live within this system of gender reproduction, we need an explanation of how the system operates. Although Luhmann has not spoken to the question of whether or not gender can be understood as a system, given his definition of systems, I would argue that we could reach the conclusion that the reproduction of gender identity in the Lacanian sense can and should be understood as a system, because in Lacan there is no outside referent such as biology. Gender is embedded in linguistic structures which are self-replicating and which give meaning to sexual difference.

More importantly, I am suggesting that we need sociological analysis, at the same level of abstraction as that of systems theory, to account for the "facts" of violation of women. Without that, we are left with the horrifying reality, but with no explanation.

Luhmann argues that there are no conservative implications in his systems theory. I agree with him; I would also argue, however, that his conception of a system is crucial to an adequate feminist understanding of our social reality. In addition, I want to emphasize again that *nothing* in Luhmann's analysis necessarily denies that there are concrete conceptions of the Good embodied in "*internal*" legal norms which can provide for the evolution of the system. The classic example in constitutional law of such an evolutionary shift of the system itself is the decision in *Brown v. Board of Education,* which challenged the social reality of segregation.[66] Justice Warren argued that, at the very least, the doctrine of "separate but equal" could never meet the standards of equality as they had been defined in legal doctrine, at least not in a racist society. "Separate but equal," under this system, meant in our social "reality," separate but *un*equal. Justice Warren relied on the embodied good of the *nomos* to justify his decision.

The preliminary suggestion I am making here, in accordance with other thinkers deeply sympathetic with Luhmann's project, is that "normative closure" in Luhmann's very specific sense does not mean that the appeal to internal norms, including the idea of law as *nomos,* with its implicit appeal to the good embodied in internal norms, is foreclosed. Such an appeal would allow for legal reform and, as I have already suggested, *Brown v. Board of Education* is a classic example of the kind of reform that can easily be included in Luhmann's systems analysis.[67] Normative closure as Luhmann defines it then can allow legal reform, including reform as seemingly drastic as that enunciated in *Brown v. Board of Education,* if such reform rests on internal rather than external norms.

We have not yet reached the question of Levinas' sense of the Good as an irremissible necessity for all subjects, as this conception addresses Luhmann's systems theory. Levinas does not hesitate to call his understanding of the Good "religious." Luhmann's sympathy for the Good, in this sense, is evidenced in his own work on religion.[68] Perhaps his own view of Levinas' evocation of the Good would be close to Wittgenstein's "Whereof one cannot speak, thereof one must be silent."[69] I am just speculating here, because Luhmann has never directly addressed Levinas. Even so, given my speculation, his main challenge would not come from Levinas—although Levinas is clearly not satisfied with silence before the Saying—but from what I have called the philosophy of the limit.

Why do I argue that it is the philosophy of the limit that is Luhmann's most serious challenge? We have already seen, in the example of gender, that we need both a sociology and a quasi-transcendental analysis of the conditions which not only make a system possible but also delimit it, precisely at the moment that a system is a system. Luhmann has succinctly summarized his own disagreement with Derrida on just this point.

> Information is, according to Gregory Bateson's oft-cited dictum, "a difference that makes a difference." Regardless of what one thinks of their ontological and metaphysical states or their incarnation as a script (Derrida) or similar approaches, differences direct the sensibilities which make one receptive to information. Information processing can only take place if, beyond its pure facticity, something has been experienced as "this way and only this way" which means that it has been localized in a framework of differences. The difference functions as a unity to the extent that it generates information, but it does not determine which pieces of information are called for and which patterns of selection they trigger off. Differences, in other words, do not delimit a system; they specify and extend its capacity for self-delimitation.[70]

For Luhmann, in other words, differences are always relational to the semantic code which ultimately encompasses them, redefines them, or rejects them in the process of its own operation. Undoubtedly we hear the echo of Hegel in Luhmann's own dialectical account of how difference, even if it is constitutive of the system, is, in the end, constituted by it. In this sense, Luhmann is incorrect to suggest that the metaphorical or ontological status given to difference does not matter. For Derrida, as we have seen throughout this book, the relational concept of difference is precisely what must be deconstructed. I have argued that the impulse for such a deconstruction is ethical, in that a relational concept of difference cannot pay respect to the otherness of the Other. Again, to return to the example of sexual difference, feminine sexual difference, as we have seen, is erased, not recognized in the definition of Woman's otherness as only given meaning in relation to Man. Yet, as I have also suggested, the example of gender "difference" is an excellent example of how difference is encompassed in the system's own operations so as to redefine its self-delimitation. I am clearly making a distinction here between the transcendental and the system, even if in a peculiar sense. As a result, we need to ask, with Luhmann, whether or not the quasi-transcendental analysis of Derrida's logic of parergonality cannot also be seen as empirical. What Luhmann said of Kant could be said of Derrida:

> But it can occur in many other cases as well where distinctions are used as justifications. Thus, for example, every justification of the law in terms of transcendental theory must answer the question whether the distinction between transcendental and empirical is itself transcendental or empirical. If the distinction is a transcendental one, then the empirical is also something transcendental. But the distinction itself may be an empirical one since Kant, an empirical individual, introduced the distinction at a specific time in history, nearly at the end of the 18th century (in his *Critique of Pure Reason*).[71]

I have already suggested that there may be a systems analysis of the understanding of justice as aporia, which would turn us back to the observer who "sees" the very definition of justice as involving an unresolvable paradox. But ultimately, I would suggest that the decision as to whether or not the distinction between the empirical and the transcendental is itself empirical or transcendental, is undecidable in Derrida's specific sense of the word. If it is undecidable, then, one could only have an ethical positioning *vis-à-vis* the *decision* as to whether or not the system is self-delimited or delimited by the Other. But then, if this book has had a central point, it is that this ethical positioning *vis-à-vis* the Other is a difference that makes a difference. Interestingly enough, Luhmann may himself recognize a difference that remains different—even if paradoxically—beyond any attempt to root it in a system. That difference is love.

> What will have to be conceded more radically than ever before is that love itself cancels out all the characteristics which could have served as the basis and a motive for it. Every attempt to see through the other person ends up in empty space, in the unity of true and false, of sincere and insincere, a vacuum in which there is no criterion of judgement. Therefore it is not possible to say everything. Transparency only exists in the relationship of system and system, and by virtue, so to speak, of the difference of system and environment which constitutes the system in the first place. Love and love alone can be such transparency.[72]

Indeed, Luhmann ends "Love as Passion" with a poem that beautifully evokes Levinas' own understanding of the face to face.

> A face in front of
> one
> neither now any more subject
> only
> reference
> intangible
> and fixed.[73]

Does the in between of love which demands the recognition of the otherness of the Other take place in the present? Or does it demand another time frame? Obviously these questions cannot be answered here. But they can lead us to my next intervention.

Of course, the simple point, and yet it is a point that must be restated in the context of this discussion, is that Derrida continually deconstructs the rigid dichotomies upon which Western metaphysics has been thought to rest. A classic example is the dichotomy between the internal and the external, the immanent and the transcendent. In the last chapter I argued that the deconstruction of these dichotomies has significance for the evocation of the *nomos* of law and a conception of legal interpretation. The significance of this deconstruction within the legal system is that Derrida can be reinterpreted as a thinker of *transformative* possibility. Luhmann's systems theory allows for evolution, but it must be *within* the system. In a specific sense, systems theory does not allow radical transformation precisely because the system must rely on the distinction between internal and external, if it is to remain a system. Derrida, unlike Habermas, does not appeal to "external" norms to legitimate the system. Nor, on the other hand, does he argue that the system can only appeal to *internal* norms, as if there could be a rigid distinction between the internal and the external, as the boundaries yield the conception of what is internal and external can be redefined.

We can now summarize the differences between Luhmann and Derrida that make a difference. Derrida's philosophy of the limit makes three interventions into systems theory that are important for our discussion here. The first is the deconstruction of the rigid dichotomy between the external and the internal, which we have already discussed and which is central to the argument of chapter 4. The second—and the second is why I have renamed deconstruction the philosophy of the limit—is that conditions of delimiting a system as a system necessarily imply a beyond to the system. No matter how the boundaries of the system are redrawn, the beyond to the system will necessarily be implied. This second intervention is what Derrida has called the "logic of parergonality."[74]

The third intervention, the one we have focused on in this chapter, engaged in by both Derrida and Levinas, is the deconstruction of the privileging of the present. But we now need to add a further distinction between what it is that

Derrida focuses on and what it is that Luhmann focuses on in systems theory. The two can be understood to focus on different interactions with otherness, and these different interactions may involve different conceptions of time.

Yet, this being said, the "time" of the ethical relation and the "time" of the self-maintenance of the system, although different, also need not be mutually exclusive. Although I am aware that Luhmann would disagree with this reformulation of his own conception of time, I want to reformulate it as follows: If he is understood to be giving us a partial and, yet, necessary "truth," which is that systems operate through a conception of the present in order to be self-perpetuating systems, then the *difference* between his sociological project, Levinas' ethical philosophy of alterity, and Derrida's philosophy may not be as great as would first appear. Both conceptions of time might be necessary for an adequate understanding of how human beings engage with the Other and with Otherness. Luhmann himself recognizes that the system is other to the individual, the individual is never reduced to a cog in the mechanism. But his focus, when he has law, and not love, in view, is not on the *individual* in the ethical relation to the Other. His focus is instead on the system. I am suggesting in my discussion of Derrida and Levinas that the shift in focus to the individual and her responsibility to the Other also demands a shift in the conception of time.[75] This shift in focus can not be separated from Justice as conceived by Derrida, because it is Justice that is our singular responsibility to the Other. As in the example of the judge, the judge's responsibility is to give justice to the parties who are before him or her. The judge's responsibility is to the actual individuals, not to the system. On a sociological plane, the system is "real." But any system can be subjected to a "quasi-transcendental" analysis which shows us the limit of that reality, and which further shows us that the system thereby maintains the possibility of its transformation. Again, this quasi-transcendental analysis does not show that change will happen, but only that transformative change cannot be foreclosed. In this sense, sociological explanation can never simply displace the quasi-transcendental analysis of the philosophy of the limit. But it is also important to note that the study of the operations of the system should not be identified with the engagement with Justice to which the Good calls us.

Systems theory has a crucial place in explaining the self-maintenance of a legal system, but such a theory cannot explain *justice,* because Justice, at least as defined by Derrida, is precisely the limit of the legal system. Derrida's conception of Justice as aporia cannot be separated from his understanding of the temporalization of Being through *différance. Différance* disrupts the present that would allow for the self-identity of the system. No system, in other words, can philosophically be defined as ever perpetuating self-identity with itself, which does not mean that Derrida in any way denies the social reality that systems have great staying power. Why would I choose to focus on the limit of the legal system as justice and its relation to the deconstruction of the present that disrupts the system, rather than the perpetuation of or the explanation for the system through the present?

I am returned now to Luhmann's ironic challenge to those who deny the "truth" of the system.

> There is no conservative bias in such a theory. . . . Autopoietic systems are systems organizing dynamic stability. If the observer does not heed to this advice,—and his own autopoiesis does not force him to do so—it would be advisable to change the topic of interest and to observe the observer.[76]

He turns us toward the observer. Perhaps it is my own autopoiesis as a woman that demands that I begin with difference, the future, and Justice, because the "present" of this social system and legal system is profoundly threatening to women. You might say that the legal system and, certainly, the "system" of gender reproduction is so bad for my system that I have no choice but to observe these systems in this way. I am, of course, offering a sociological explanation for why I choose this entry into "reality" and, more specifically, into our legal system. There is, I am sure, a "systems" explanation for why a woman would become interested in "deconstructing" the system rather than in participating in it. In spite of this explanation, however, the deconstruction of the privileging of the present can also help us understand why a system cannot be self-enclosed so as to foreclose transformation rather than just evolution. Derrida's concept of iterability helps us to understand why re-evolution, not just evolution, is possible. Using the example of gender hierarchy again, if systems theory can explain our subordination, the deconstruction of the full presence of the system can give us the hope for transformation. Perhaps, as women, we need that hope to survive the system.

But it is important to note the significance of Luhmann's first question, "who is the observer?"[77] for the very question implies that there can be different observations of the system and, therefore, at least in a limited sense, the possibility of critique, if not rejection. This insistence on the stance of the observer as an *individual* distinguishes Luhmann from the recent version of legal positivism of Stanley Fish,[78] who would deny that "critical" observation in any profound sense is possible. But the distinction between transformation and evolution remains at the heart of the debate of what deconstruction and, more generally, "postmodern" philosophy amounts to in law. I will now turn to how Fish's understanding of deconstruction differs from my own, particularly as this difference relates to the distinction between evolution and transformation.

The Significance of the Distinction between Evolution and Transformation

For Stanley Fish, "postmodern" insight, and more specifically, legal positivism leaves us only with a sociological analysis of how the legal system becomes a self-enclosed system. For Fish, the identification of law with justice is inevitable. What deconstruction or "postmodern" philosophy has shown us is that all reality, including the self, is socially constructed. This, in turn, means for Fish that "we" are what our reality makes us. We could not be otherwise. As we have just seen, this is not Luhmann's position, which begins with the question of who is the observer. Indeed, Luhmann's theory involves a very expansive conception of individuality. For Luhmann, the differentiation of society leads to ever-greater attention paid to the concrete individual. Further, according to Luhmann, "the alienation effect" of the outside observer allows for the examination of what remains latent or manifest in any system. On the level of systems theory, such an examination may not directly serve as a critical exposure—Luhmann indeed would insist it does not—but on the level of politics, there is no reason why it cannot. Luhmann's reconstruction of individuality is important as a response to Fish because he shows us how society itself, and the understanding of the social construction as individuality, may reinforce rather than erase the possibility of the critical observer. The result of Fish's position is that social criticism and radical transformation are impossible. For Fish, to have social criticism in legal interpretation or a critical observer, let alone a standpoint by which to know when "real" transformation had happened, we would have to appeal to a transcendental viewpoint. Since we have no *transcendental* or *outside* viewpoint, it follows that there can be no social criticism and no critical consciousness. Change can take place only as slow evolution, but not through transformation, and the players may well never note the change. The system is run differently, but there is no true *difference* from the system. There is only evolution, not transformation.

For Fish, in other words, law is always evolving, but at the same time, and in spite of his remarks to the contrary, law is not *deconstructible*. As Derrida reminds us, the deconstructibility of law is possible only through the paradox that it is only the *undeconstructibility* of Justice that makes deconstruction possible.

> 1. The deconstructibility of law (*droit*), of legality, legitimacy or legitimation (for example) makes deconstruction possible. 2. The undeconstructibility of justice also makes deconstruction possible, indeed is inseparable from it. 3. The result: deconstruction takes place in the interval that separates the undeconstructibility of justice from the deconstructibility of *droit* (authority, legitimacy, and so on).[79]

Because for Fish there is no divide between justice and law, the deconstruction of law is not possible. In this sense, Fish in not a deconstructionist, but a legal positivist.

The significance of Fish's positivism for legal interpretation is as follows. We have seen in the discussion of the aporias of Justice that judgment as judgment demands the suspension of rule following, otherwise application of the law would not be judgment, but only calculation. Fish, unlike Derrida, does not indicate the aporias of Justice. Instead he argues that what "is" is a system of rules from which no one can extract himself or herself. The suspension of rule following that Derrida rightfully argues is necessary for judgment is exactly what Fish insists cannot exist. As a result, "Doing What Comes Naturally" does not include judging. The problem, of course, is that a judge who does not judge cannot claim to do justice. And yet, the claim of legitimacy of law cannot be separated in its articulation from at least some concept of the good as embodied in the "internal" norms of law. This claim is part of running the very machine Fish calls law. Fish cannot avoid the confrontation with the *nomos* of law as easily as he thinks.

Fortunately, as we have seen, there is also an effective challenge to legal positivism through the deconstruction of the traditional conception of time, which helps us solve the dilemma inherent in Fish's own work. There is no system present to itself which can fill the universe, and ourselves as containers for that universe, and by so doing "foreclose" the future or reduce it to the continuation of the present.

> This *same time* never is, will never have been and will never be *present*. . . .
> There is only the promise and memory, memory as promise, without any
> gathering possible in the form of the present. This disjunction is the law, the
> text of law and the law of the text.[80]

Deconstruction calls us to that promise and leaves us with that hope. The utopianism, if it can be called that, is in Levinas' reminder "that what took place humanly has never been able to remain closed up in its site."[81] As suggested in the last section, this reminder is crucial for distinguishing between evolution and transformation. The impossible, Justice, is what makes us confront the possible as the limit to what has been established, even as the *nomos* of the law.

Given this confrontation, we can now see how to rethink the significance of Derrida's deconstruction of Rousseau's political theory and its implications for legal interpretation. As discussed in the last chapter, many of Derrida's critics claim that the deconstruction of Rousseau theoretically undermines the very possibility of political and ethical thought by showing that it must rely on an origin that does not exist. However, once we put Derrida's thought within the understanding of time and temporalization I have presented here, we can see why this is not the case. For Derrida, as we discussed in the last chapter, the Rousseauian community postulates an originary instant of coming together without a trace of what has gone before. This originary instant is the festival based on an unmediated unity in the face-to-face relations of the participants. As Derrida points out, Rousseau's vision privileges the living voice, speech is the vehicle of co-equals who are literally present to one another as they codetermine their fate as if they could start again from the absolute beginning, the origin.

There is also a more profound point that has been completely missed and one which shows the significance of Derrida's temporalization for legal interpretation. Derrida shows us how the inevitable failure to find the origin as the full presence that Rousseau so desperately seeks opens up the space for the conditional mood. Derrida wants us to see that what masks itself as simple discovery is in fact discovery through projection of the ought to be. Rousseau argues from the logic of discovery, as if we could just discover the origin in which the oppositions of nature and spirit, man and woman, and so forth, did not exist so as to rend the soul apart. Rousseau seeks reconciliation in the past as if it were "there." But the power of his message actually lies in its eschatological anticipation, in Derrida's sense of the "not yet." If there is no simple origin that we can find our way back to in the future, then we cannot escape the conditional mood of political and ethical vision. We project forward the truth of the past of the never has been as the "ought to be." As Derrida reminds us again and again, when we remember the past to find the ethical truth of the origin, we are, in truth, remembering the future. But we do so within the rhetoric of memory, because the future only is as the anterior/posterior.

> Memory is the name of what is no longer only a mental "capacity" oriented toward one of the three modes of the present, the past present, which could be dissociated from the present present and the future present. Memory projects itself toward the future, and it constitutes the presence of the present. The "rhetoric of temporality" *is* the rhetoric of memory.[82]

But this rhetoric is also a tension toward the future as the ought to be since memory can never exactly reconstitute what was.

> The memory we are considering here is not essentially oriented toward the past, toward a past present deemed to have really and previously existed. Memory stays with traces, in order to "preserve" them, but traces of a past that has never been present, traces which themselves never occupy the form of presence and always remain, as it were, to come—come from the future, from the *to come*. Resurrection, which is always the formal element of "truth," a recurrent difference between a present and its presence, does not resuscitate a past which had been present; it engages the future.[83]

In this sense legal interpretation must be both *discovery* and *invention* because there can be no simple origin of legal meaning, whether we call it intent of the founders of the Constitution or some other name. We cannot escape the conditional mood of legal interpretation. In this sense, interpretation is always an act; moreover, an act for which we cannot escape responsibility. It is this insistence on the inevitable responsibility for our acts of judging that separates Derrida from Fish. The remembrance of precedent cannot just be reduced to calculation.

The Example of *Roe v. Wade*[84] and its Progeny: The Act of Remembrance of Judging

We can now turn to how this understanding of responsibility inherent in the reconceptualization of the relation between discovery and invention can help us shift our conception of the judge's role in "perpetuating" precedent. I will use *Roe v. Wade* to demonstrate my own understanding. (This example, of course, returns us to the woman as the observer of the system.) In *Roe,* the Supreme Court was presented with whether or not the constitutional right to privacy recognized in previous decisions such as *Griswold v. Connecticut*[85] should apply to abortion. *Roe,* as Catharine MacKinnon has *described* the decision, "guaranteed the right to choose abortion, subject to some countervailing considerations, by conceiving it as a private choice, included in the constitutional right to privacy."[86] MacKinnon, among others has challenged the normative bases of the decision in the right to privacy. My focus, however, is not on the normative basis for the decision, but on the mistaken "phenomenology" of judging that has now been used to justify the undermining of the principles on which *Roe* was based. The argument, supposedly legal, not moral, goes something like this: there is no origin in the Constitution itself for the right of privacy, let alone for the right of privacy to be "applied" to abortion.

We will now turn to the question of whether or not the judges, when they enunciated the decision in *Roe,* were unfaithful to their designated role as judges. The charge is that they did not simply recollect precedent and then enunciate its reading as if this could be done without involving an *evaluation.* Instead, they made up the law to fit the "new" situation, the demand of women for reproductive rights.[87] It is not just that the judges had competing constitutional views which could be understood to "fit" the example of abortion and they chose the wrong one—although I think it is evident that they had such norms available for their imaginative "recollection."[88] There is no *firmly rooted* constitutional precedent for the judge to recollect that could justify *Roe.* If the only correct act for the judge when enunciating a legal decision is the recollection of past decisions that are understood to be based on the intent of the fathers, or some other notion of the foundational origin of constitutional meaning, then there can be *no* justification for *Roe* that is consistent with this view of judging.[89] I have argued, elsewhere[90] and in the course of this chapter, that this understanding of the relationship of law and judging completely misunderstands the role of interpretation in legal decisions because such interpretations always involve the justification, not merely the perpetuation, of the norms "embodied" in past decisions. Even if judging was understood to primarily involve memory in the sense of recollection of precedent, memory itself can never just capture the past. Derrida's analysis of the limit to memory, as well as the responsibility to it, is thus crucially important to an adequate understanding of what judicial memory involves. This more adequate understanding of the phenomenology of memory in judging can be used in turn to critique any justification for the reversal of *Roe* as the correction of an irresponsible act of judging.

We can use the progeny of *Roe* to show that the deconstruction of the traditional conception of the modalities of time has implications for the way we think about the role of the judge. The judge can never be reduced to the instrument of the system who simply recollects precedent. Her subjective role is not merely the passive one of recollecting what is there in the origin. She also cannot just do what comes naturally, that is, follow the rules as if such a following were a form of automatic writing. She is responsible for her memory and the future which she promotes in the act of remembrance itself.

I am using responsibility in the sense that we are accountable for our own actions and our judgments. We are responsible precisely because we cannot be reduced to automatons who cannot choose to do other than what comes naturally. Responsibility has often been thought to turn on a positive account of a transcendental or autonomous subject. Only a subject that can rise above circumstances, so the argument goes, can be held accountable, because only an autonomous subject can achieve meaningful freedom to choose. If we cannot do otherwise, then responsibility becomes a misnomer. But such a view, which completely identifies the subject with the "machine" or system, depends on the myth of full presence and the privileging of the present that has been deconstructed. Similarly, the machine or system is not just a self-replicating presence. The machine is *only presented* through its enforcers. The very functioning of the machine demands its enforcers. It is our irreducibility and the irreducibility of the machine to a self-contained context that make our responsibility inescapable. This is not, admittedly, a *positive* account of the subject. But deconstruction reinforces an account of the irreducibility of the subject to a context which is necessary for the strong sense of responsibility that Derrida emphasizes. We have to think again about the responsibility to memory that is demanded by deconstruction and the very deconstructibility of law.

> The sense of a responsibility without limits, and so necessarily excessive, incalculable, before memory; and so the task of recalling the history, the origin and subsequent direction, thus the limits, of concepts of justice, the law and law (*droit*), of values, norms, prescriptions that have been imposed and sedimented there, from then on remaining more or less readable or presupposed. As to the legacy we have received under the name of justice, and in more than one language, the task of a historical and interpretive memory is at the heart of deconstruction, not only as philologico-etymological task or the historian's task but as responsibility in face of a heritage that is at the same time the heritage of an imperative or of a sheaf of injunctions.[91]

In this unique sense, genealogy becomes a part of judicial integrity itself.[92] The tradition, or even the system, through the critical observer, is called to remember its own exclusions and prejudices. We are called upon to remember the history in which women did not have the right to an abortion. We have to remember what the general conditions of women were during those times in history in which abortion was disallowed. Genealogy is not invoked for the sake of debunking. Genealogy, in the sense that I use it, is crucial to the integrity to justice that demands that we also examine the existing limits of actualized concepts of justice, particularly as these exist in, and perpetuate, the patriarchal order of society. Integrity to Justice, the attempt to be just with Justice, demands no less than this responsibility, to expose the limits of what has been established as law through the perpetuation of the legal system, as well as in other circumstances, its confirmation or reinstatement.

> This responsibility toward memory is a responsibility before the very concept of responsibility that regulates the justice and appropriateness (*justesse*) of our behavior, of our theoretical, practical, ethico-political decisions. This concept of responsibility is inseparable from a whole network of connected concepts (property, intentionality, will, conscience, consciousness, self-consciousness, subject, self, person, community, decision, and so forth) and any deconstruction of this network of concepts in their given or dominant state may seem like a move toward irresponsibility at the very moment that, on the contrary, deconstruction calls for an increase in responsibility.[93]

In *Roe*, Justice Blackmun confessed that the question of when life begins was not one the Justices could answer.[94] Blackmun, however, was able to *decide* whether and when a fetus becomes a *legal* person. In a profound sense, Blackmun responsibly operated within the first aporia of justice. He imaginatively recollected a legal norm from within our heritage that would allow us to make crucial distinctions about the status of the fetus for the purposes of law. He had to make a fresh judgment in the new conditions created by women's demand for the right to abortion. In this sense, he applied the norm of privacy developed in *Griswold* to a new situation. This "application" clearly was also a judgment about what right women should have to privacy and why abortion was part of that right. In terms of the second aporia, he was called to make a decision in response to the woman's movement's call to justice, and he did. Once we read Blackmun's judgment within the aporias of justice, we can see his decision as the kind of activism that is *inevitable* in judgment and decision, but an activism exercised in accordance with responsibility and the call to justice. As we will see, Rehnquist is no less an activist, just less responsible, and deaf to the call of justice for women. Blackmun constructed the trimester framework[95] based upon the State's shifting interests in the respective lives of the woman and fetus. In dissent, Justice Rehnquist found himself "in fundamental disagreement" with almost every segment of the *Roe* framework.[96]

Sixteen years later, in *Webster v. Reproductive Health Services*,[97] Chief Justice Rehnquist failed to recollect precedential history. First, he maintained that *stare decisis* is a constitutional principle applicable only where used to recollect "good" law. Then, by identifying *Roe* as "unsound in principle and unworkable in practice,"[98] he substituted his own standards in lieu of those which already existed, while maintaining that differences in fact justified not revisiting *Roe*.[99] We can now see just how deconstruction, with its emphasis on responsibility to history, differs from the position that would argue that all judges do is make things up as they go along. Rehnquist was responsible for considering the history in which women were not allowed to have abortions and what that meant for the exercise of their bodily integrity. But, equally important, he was called by the demand of Justice for women to consider the reasons for the compromise in *Roe*. The *Webster* decision certainly shows why the deconstructibility of law promotes anxiety. As women, our rights can always be undermined. But we cannot protect against the deconstructibility of law by denying its possibility. Our only protection is in the call to responsibility, which is precisely why the recognition that law is always deconstructible increases rather than decreases responsibility.

For Rehnquist, the fact that the *Roe* framework was difficult to apply statutorily led him to question whether it had any constitutional basis. To quote Rehnquist:

> In the first place, the rigid *Roe* framework is hardly consistent with the notion of a Constitution cast in general terms, as ours is, and usually speaking in general principles, as ours does. The key elements of the *Roe* framework—trimesters and viability—are not found in the text of the Constitution or in any place else one would expect to find a constitutional principle. Since the bounds of the inquiry are essentially indeterminate, the result has been a web of legal rules that have become increasingly intricate, resembling a code of regulations rather than a body of constitutional doctrine.[100]

Therefore, although Rehnquist acknowledged that "[s]tare decisis is a cornerstone of our legal system,"[101] he nevertheless felt that the *indeterminacy* of the *Roe* framework was sufficient justification to ignore it as precedent.

Perhaps the most striking aspect of Rehnquist's decision was its undermining of the principle which justified the erection, and I use that word deliberately, of the *Roe* framework.[102] This is most clearly shown in Rehnquist's interpretation of the preamble of the contested law restricting abortion.[103] The preamble stated:

> "findings" by the [Missouri] state legislature that "[t]he *life* of each human being *begins at conception*," and that "unborn children have protectable interests in life, health, and wellbeing." The Act further requires that all Missouri laws be interpreted to provide unborn children with the same rights enjoyed by *other persons*, subject to the Federal Constitution and [Supreme Court] precedents.[104]

As Rehnquist explained, "[t]he preamble can be read simply to express . . . a value judgment favoring childbirth over abortion."[105] Of course, that value judgment, cast as a finding of fact, undermines the fundamental basis upon which the *Roe* Court limited the states' interference with a woman's right to choose whether to have an abortion. The preamble establishes that life begins at conception and that a "fetus is a 'person' "[106] with "protectable interests in life, health, and wellbeing."[107] Therefore, the case for a woman's right to choose whether to terminate her pregnancy "collapses, for the fetus's right to life would then be guaranteed specifically by the [Fourteenth] Amendment."[108] By allowing the Missouri statute to stand, the *Webster* plurality authorized the supersession of the woman's privacy right. Rehnquist interpreted the preamble of the statute in deliberate disregard of the genealogical considerations demanded by integrity. These considerations are demanded by the call of the Other for Justice.

Likewise, in *Akron v. Akron Center for Reproductive Health*,[109] in dissent, Justice O'Connor (joined by Justices White and Rehnquist) characterized:

> [t]he *Roe* framework . . . [as] clearly on a collision course with itself. As the medical risks of various abortion procedures decrease, the point at which the State may regulate for reasons of maternal health is moved further forward to actual childbirth. As medical science becomes better able to provide for the separate existence of the fetus, the point of viability is moved further back toward conception.[110]

This, she felt, would render the principle of the trimester approach worthless. The compelling state interest at the point of viability in the potential life of the fetus would clash with the woman's right to decide whether to terminate the pregnancy. This looming confrontation would create in fact what Justice O'Connor already believed true. O'Connor appealed to what was already understood as the state's interest in protecting the fetus, to undermine the woman's call for Justice.

> The choice of viability as the point at which the state interest in potential life becomes compelling is no less arbitrary than choosing any point before viability or any point afterward. Accordingly, I believe that the State's interest in protecting potential human life exists throughout the pregnancy.[111]

O'Connor, then, engaged in an irresponsible act of judging not by imaginatively recollecting her projection of the future, but by failing her responsibility to remember the actual conditions women would again face if the *Roe* framework was dismantled. Those conditions had been graphically described. They needed to be addressed. Instead, O'Connor appealed to the state's interest in the law, rather than to justice for women. Viability, as essential to the *Roe* framework, was clearly a compromise. As we have seen, in my interpretation, the compromise should be understood within Blackmun's attempt to operate within the aporias of justice. The call of women was for Justice. What they got, indeed the only "thing" they could get from the legal system, was law. But the law, the new application of the norm of privacy, was an act of responsibility to memory in that it recognized the actual conditions in which women had been denied the right to abortion. Of course, the fetus can itself be recognized as Other, with infinite right. But whether or not this recognition is to be embodied in law, the Justices must directly confront the woman as Other, they cannot simply follow along with the system which, as constituted, allows the rights of women to go unnoticed.

We can now return to why the deconstruction of the traditional conception of the modalities of time has implications for the way we think about the role of the judge. What we have seen is that when the judge remembers the past she does so through the "ought to be" implicit in the not yet of the never has been. But we can also see the difference between this conception of the future of justice and the traditional Kantian projection of an horizon. In the first place, it should be obvious that such horizons, as traditionally defined within our heritage, have projected rational persons as interchangeable, yet it is unclear whether an ideal premised on interchangeability can really help us justify abortion. Here we see a specific example in which the projected ideal, premised on interchangeability, may itself be contaminated by history, in this case patriarchal ignorance of the specificity of femininity. Secondly, as the slogan from the 1970s asserted, "women want abortion now." Thus, in this demand, we are returned to the third aporia of justice: Justice does not wait.

We do not remember through the logic of recursivity, although Justice O'Connor implicitly relied on such a logic when she appealed to an established state interest. If we undermine the "right of abortion," we can only do so through a direct appeal to competing conceptions of the concrete Good embodied in the nomos. Changing technology, which is what O'Connor pointed to, is not the issue. According to the philosophy of the limit, an "is" cannot simply undermine an "ought." Judicial interpretation is not the calculation that "fits" pieces into a puzzle. Judicial interpretation demands judgment. Judgment demands more than a *description* of how two cases "fit" together. When the judge 'judges' she *justifies* precedent. As a result, the question of fit can never be legitimately used to enunciate an articulated norm, because the judge must justify her decision and, indeed, is even called upon to justify her decision by the system of modern law. If the norm is wrong, then it must be condemned through evaluation, understood within our legal system as an appeal to the *nomos* of the law. I have suggested that a part of this evaluation must be a recognition of the conditions of women and the conditions in which the right of abortion had been denied. Both aspects of this evaluative process are demanded by the exercise of responsibility to memory. The question is not whether *Roe* fits into our constitutional scheme, because every new decision raises the question of whether our constitutional system is acceptable or, in the terms of systems theory, whether the established *nomos* of the law is reconcilable with its own projection of a communal good. Again, we are returned to the first aporia of justice. *Roe* was an attempt at fresh judgment based on this responsibility to memory. Privacy may not have been the "best norm." I believe that it is not.[112] But the attempt was still made to heed the call to Justice, not as an external norm, but as the embodied good of the *nomos*. In Blackmun's dissent there is also an implicit appeal irreducible to the *Good* implicit in the *nomos*. The appeal, I think, can best be understood as an appeal to Justice in Derrida's sense of Justice as aporia and yet, as a call that demands that the judge respond. In the recent decisions, we find the failure to heed the call, hidden by the rhetoric of fit. And yet, even Rehnquist recognized that it is only *good* law that is to be followed. Unless one can show that there is a past present or a present past that merely evolves, reliance on the logic of recursivity, including the rhetoric of fit, is an impossibility. It is precisely the contribution of deconstruction to show us that such a present past does not exist. By doing so it shows us why we cannot avoid appealing to the "ought to be" when we interpret precedent. Integrity demands that we face the call to Justice and the endless transformative demands on the legal system which justice demands of us. We are left with a simple command and an infinite responsibility. Be just with Justice.

6

The Violence of the Masquerade:
Law Dressed Up as Justice

From our childhood, most of us are familiar with the fairy tale "The Emperor's New Clothes." Throughout this book I have challenged a reading of "deconstruction" that has been proposed by its friends and its foes in legal circles. My decision to re-name deconstruction the philosophy of the limit has to do with the attempt to make the ethical message of deconstruction "appear." The more accepted readings understand deconstruction to expose the nakedness of power struggles and, indeed, of violence masquerading as the rule of law. With this exposure, the intervention of deconstruction supposedly comes to an end.[1] The enemies of "deconstruction" challenge this exposure as itself an act of violence which leaves in its stead only the "right" of force and, as a result, levels the moral differences between legal systems and blurs the all-too-real distinctions between different kinds of violent acts. We have seen this critique specifically evidenced in the response to Derrida's writing on Rousseau. I have countered this interpretation as a fundamental misreading, especially insofar as it misunderstands the Derridean double gesture.

At first glance, however, the title of Jacques Derrida's essay, "Force of Law: The 'Mystical Foundations of Authority,' "[2] seems to confirm this interpretation. It also, in turn, informs Dominick LaCapra's subtle and thoughtful commentary,[3] which evidences his concern that Derrida's essay may—in our obviously violent world—succumb to the allure of violence, rather than help us to demystify its seductive power. I refer to LaCapra's text because it so succinctly summarizes the political and ethical concern that deconstruction is necessarily "on strike" against established legal norms as part of its refusal to positively describe justice as a set of established moral principles.

To answer that concern we need to examine more closely the implicit position of the critics on the significance of right as established, legal norms that "deconstruction" is accused of "going on strike" against. This becomes extremely important because it is precisely the "on strike" posture not only before established legal norms, but also in the face of the very idea of legal norms that troubles LaCapra. Undoubtedly, Derrida's engagement with Walter Benjamin's text, "The

Critique of Violence,"[4] has been interpreted as further evidence of the inherent danger in upholding the position that *law* is always deconstructible. It is this position that makes *possible* the "on strike" posture toward any legal system.[5] But it is a strike that supposedly never ends. Worse yet, it is a strike that supposedly cannot give us principles to legitimately curtail violence. This worry is a specific form of the criticism addressed in chapter 2 that deconstruction, or the philosophy of the limit as I have renamed deconstruction, can only give us the politics of suspicion. I, on the other hand, have argued throughout that deconstruction, understood as the philosophy of the limit, gives us the politics of utopian possibility. As we saw in the last chapter, the philosophy of the limit, and more specifically the deconstruction of the privileging of the present, protects the possibility of radical legal transformation, which is distinguished from mere evolution of the existing system. But we still need to re-examine the stance on violence which inheres in Derrida's exposure of the mystical foundations of authority if we are to satisfactorily answer his critics. To do so we will once again return to the ethical, political, and juridical significance of his critique of positivism. The case we will examine in this chapter is *Bowers v. Hardwick.*[6] But let me turn first to Derrida's unique engagement with Benjamin's text.

Walter Benjamin's text has often—and to my mind mistakenly—been interpreted to erase human responsibility for violence, because the distinction between mythic violence—the violence that founds or constitutes law (right)—and the divine violence that is its "antithesis" because it destroys rather than founds, expiates rather than upholds, is ultimately undecidable for Benjamin. The difference between acceptable and unacceptable violence as well as between divine and mythic violence is ultimately not cognitively accessible in advance. We will return to why this is the case later in this essay. Law-making or founding violence is then distinguished, at least in a preliminary manner, from law-preserving or conserving *force*. We will see the significance of this further distinction shortly. If this undecidability were the end of the matter, if we simply turned to God's judgment, there would be no *critique* of violence. Of course, there is one interpretation already suggested and presented by LaCapra that Benjamin—and then Derrida—does erase the very basis on which the critique of violence proceeds.[7] But this interpretation fails to take notice of the opening reminder of Benjamin's text, to which Derrida returns us again and again, and which structures the unfolding of Benjamin's own text. To quote Benjamin:

> The task of a critique of violence can be summarized as that of expounding its relation to law and justice. For a cause, however effective, becomes violent, in the precise sense of the word, only when it bears on moral issues. The sphere of these issues is defined by the concepts of law and justice.[8]

Critique, in this sense, is hardly the simple glorification of violence per se, since Benjamin carefully distinguishes between different kinds of violence.[9] Indeed, both Benjamin and Derrida question the traditional positivist and naturalist justifications for violence as legitimate enforcement for the maintenance of an established legal system or as a necessary means to achieve a just end. In other words, both thinkers are concerned with *rationalizations of bloodless* bureaucratic violence that LaCapra rightfully associates with some of the horrors of the twentieth century.[10] Benjamin's own text speaks more to the analysis of different kinds of violence and more specifically to law as law conserving violence, than it does to justice. But Derrida explicitly begins his text, "The Force of Law," with the "Possibility of Justice."[11] His text proceeds precisely through the configuration of the concepts of justice and law in which the critique of violence, understood as "judgement, evaluation, examination that provides itself with the means to judge violence,"[12] must take place.

As we have seen, it is only once we accept the uncrossable divide between law and justice that deconstruction both exposes and protects *in the very deconstruction of the identification of law as justice* that we can apprehend the full *practical* significance of Derrida's statement that "deconstruction is justice."[13] What is missed in the interpretation I have described and attributed to LaCapra is that the undecidability which can be used to expose any legal system's process of the self-legitimation of authority as myth, leaves us—the us here being specifically those who enact and enforce the law—with an *inescapable responsibility* for violence, precisely because violence cannot be fully rationalized and therefore justified in advance. The "feigning [of] presence"[14] inherent in the founding violence of the state, using Derrida's phrase, disguises the retrospective act of justification and thus *seemingly,* but only seemingly, erases responsibility by *justification.* To quote Derrida:

> Here we "touch" without touching this extraordinary paradox: the inaccessible transcendence of the law before which and prior to which "man" stands fast only appears infinitely transcendent and thus theological to the extent that, so near him, it depends only on him, on the performative act by which he institutes it: the law is transcendent, violent and non-violent, because it depends only on who is before it—and so prior to it—on who produces it, founds it, authorizes it in an absolute performative whose presence always escapes him. The law is transcendent and theological, and so always to come, always promised, because it is immanent, finite and so already past.
>
> Only the yet-to-come (*avenir*) will produce intelligibility or interpretability of this law.[15]

Law, in other words, never can catch up with its projected justification. Therefore, there can be no insurance of a metalanguage in relation to the "performativity of institutional language or its dominant interpretation."[16] As we saw in the last chapter, this insistence that there can be no metalanguage in which to establish the "external" norms by which to legitimate the legal system separates Derrida from Habermas. The question then becomes, what does it mean practically for the field of law that we cannot have such insurance, other than that it separates Derrida from Habermas' neo-Kantianism? For LaCapra this lack means that we cannot in any way whatsoever *justify* legal principles of insurance. If we cannot justify legal principles, then, for LaCapra, we will necessarily be left with an appeal to force as the only basis for justification. To quote LaCapra:

> A second movement at least seems to identify the undecidable with force or even violence and to give to violence the power to generate or create justice and law. Justice and law, which of course cannot be conflated, nonetheless seem to originate in force or violence. The extreme misreading of this movement would be the conclusion that might makes right—a conclusion explicitly rejected at one point in Derrida's essay but perhaps insufficiently guarded against at others.[17]

For LaCapra, in spite of his clear recognition that Derrida explicitly rejects the idea that might makes right, there is still the danger that undecidability will lead to this conception of law and the role of legal argument and justification within legal interpretation. But, indeed, the opposite position is implied. Might can never justify right, *precisely* because the establishment of right can never be fully rationalized. It also does not lead to the replacement of legal argument through an appeal to principle with violence, as LaCapra seems to fear it might, if taken to its logical conclusion.

To emphasize once again why deconstruction does not reduce itself to the most recent and sophisticated brand of legal positivism developed in America which, of course, asserts that might does indeed make right, it is useful to again contrast "deconstruction" *as* the force of justice against law with Stanley Fish's insistent identification of law with justice.[18] Fish understands that as a philosophical matter law can never catch up with its justifications, but that as a practical reality its functional machinery renders its philosophical inadequacy before its own claims irrelevant. Indeed, the system sets the limit of relevance. The machine, in other words, functions to erase the mystical foundations of its own authority. My critical disagreement with Fish, a disagreement to the support of which I am bringing the force of "deconstruction," is that the legal machine he celebrates as a marvel, I abhor as a monster. Once again, as in the last chapter, we are returned to the divergent viewpoints of different observers.

In the case of law, there is a reason to be afraid of ghosts. But to see why I think the practical erasure of the mystical foundation of authority by the legal system must be told as a horror story, let me turn to an actual case that embodies the two myths of legality and legal culture to which Fish consistently returns us. For Fish, contemporary American legal interpretation, both in constitutional law and in other areas, functions primarily through two myths of justification for decision.[19] The first is "the intent of the founding fathers," or some other conception of an original foundation. The second is "the plain meaning of the words," whether of the relevant statutes or precedent, or of the Constitution itself. In terms of "deconstruction," even understood as a practice of reading, the second can be interpreted as the myth of full readability. These myths, as Fish well recognizes, conserve law as a self-legitimating machine by returning legal interpretation to a supposed origin that repeats itself as a self-enclosed hermeneutic circle. This, in turn, allows the identification of justice with law and with the perpetuation of the "current" legal system.[20]

To "see" the violence inherent in being *before the law* in the many senses of that phrase which Derrida plays on in his text, let us imagine the scene in Georgia that sets the stage for *Bowers v. Hardwick*.[21] Two men are peacefully making love, little knowing that they were *before the law* and soon to be proclaimed guilty of sodomy as a criminal offense. Fish's glee is in showing the impotence—and I am using that word deliberately—of the philosophical challenge or political critique of the legal system. The law just keeps coming. Remember the childhood ghost story "Bloody Bones" to help you envision the scene. The law is on the first step. The philosopher desperately tries to check the law—but to no avail—by appealing to "outside" norms of justice. The law is on the second step. Now the feminist critic tries to dismantle the law machine which is operating against her. Again, the law simply wipes off the criticism of its masquerade and here, heterosexual bias, as irrelevant. The law defines what is relevant. The law is on the third step. It draws closer to its victims. Fish admires precisely this *force of law*, the so-called *potency*, to keep coming in spite of its critics and its philosophical bankruptcy, a bankruptcy not only acknowledged but continually exposed by Fish himself. Once it is wound up, there is no stopping the law, and what winds it up is its own functions as elaborated in the myths of legal culture. Thus, although law may be a human construct insofar as we are all captured by its mandates, its constructibility, and therefore its potential deconstructibility, has no "consequences."[22]

In *Bowers* we do indeed see the force of law as it makes itself felt, in spite of the criticisms of "the philosophers" of the opinion. Justice White concludes and upholds as a matter of law that the state of Georgia has the right to make homosexual sodomy a criminal offense.[23] Some commentators, defending the opinion, have relied precisely on the myth of the intent of the founding fathers. The argument is that there is no evidence that the intent of the founding fathers was to provide a right of privacy or any other kind of right for homosexuals.

The arguments against the philosophical justification of this position repeated by Fish are obvious. The concept of intent is problematic when speaking of living writers, for all the reasons discussed in writing on legal interpretation. But in the case of interpreting dead writers who have been *silent* on the issue, the subtle complexities of interpreting through intent, are no longer subtle, but are manifestly ludicrous. The process of interpreting intent *always* involves construction once there is a written text that supposedly introduces the intent. But *here,* there is only silence, an absence of voice, simply because the *founding* fathers never addressed homosexuality. That this silence means that there is no right of homosexuality and they thought it so self-evident as never to speak of it, is clearly only one interpretation and one that can never be clarified except in the infinite regress of construction. Since the process involved in interpreting from silence clearly entails construction, the judge's own values are involved. In this case we do not even need to go further into the complexities of readability and unreadability of a text, because we are literally left with silence, no word on homosexuality.

But in Justice White's opinion we are, indeed, returned to the problem of the readability or the unreadability of the text of the Constitution and of the precedent that supposedly just "states" its meaning. Justice White rejects the Eleventh Circuit's[24] holding that the Georgia statute violated the respondent's fundamental right "because his homosexual right is a private and intimate association that is beyond the reach of state regulation by reason of the Ninth Amendment and the Due Process Clause of the Fourteenth Amendment."[25] The Eleventh Circuit relied on the line of precedent from *Griswold*[26] through *Roe*[27] and *Carey*[28] to read the right of privacy to include "homosexual activity." Justice White rejects this reading. He does so, as we will see, by narrowly construing the right supposedly implicated in this case and then by reading the language of the holding of each case in a "literalist" manner implicitly relying on "the plain meaning of the words." Do we find any language in these cases about homosexuality? Justice White cannot find any such language. Since he cannot find any such language, Justice White concludes that "the plain meaning of the words" did not mandate this extension of the right of privacy to "homosexual activity." To quote Justice White:

> Accepting the decisions in these cases and the above description of them, we think it evident that none of the rights announced in those cases bears any resemblance to the claimed constitutional right of homosexuals to engage in acts of sodomy that is asserted in this case. No connection between family, marriage, or procreation on the one hand and homosexual activity on the other has been demonstrated, either by the Court of Appeals or by respondent.[29]

We do not need to develop a sophisticated philosophical critique to point to the flaw in Justice White's "literalist" interpretation of the cases. We can simply rely on one of the oldest and most established "principles" of constitutional interpretation: the principle that cases should be narrowly decided. If one accepts that this principle was operative in the cases associated with the establishment of the "right of privacy,"[30] then the reason none of these cases "spoke" to homosexuality was that the question of homosexuality wasn't before them. Judges under this principle, or in Luhmann's terms, under this system, are to decide cases, not advance norms or speculate about all possible extensions of the right. When and how the right is to be extended is dependent on the concrete facts of each case. In spite of what he says he is doing, Justice White, like the commentators already mentioned, is interpreting from a silence, and a silence that inheres in the principle that constitutional cases in particular should be construed narrowly. Need I add here that if one is a homosexual, the right to engage in homosexual activity might have everything to do with "family, marriage, or procreation,"[31] even though Justice White argues the contrary position? As a result, his very interpretation of the "privacy" cases—as being about "family, marriage, or procreation"—could be used against him. Can White's blindness to this obvious reality be separated from his own acceptance of an implied heterosexuality as legitimate and, indeed, the only right way to live?

Justice White's opinion does not simply rest on his reading of the cases, but also rests on an implicit conception of the readability of the Constitution. For White, the Constitution is fully *readable*. Once again, he does not find anything in the Constitution itself that mentions the right to homosexuality. Therefore, he interprets the Eleventh Circuit as creating such a right out of thin air, rather than on a reading of the Constitution and of precedent that understands what is *fundamental* and necessary to privacy as a right "established" by the Constitution. For Justice White, to simply create a "new" fundamental right would be the most dangerous kind of activism, particularly in the case of homosexuality. And why is this the case for Justice White? As he explains:

> Proscriptions against that conduct have ancient roots. Sodomy was a criminal offense at common law and was forbidden by the laws of the original 13 states when they ratified the Bill of Rights. In 1868, when the Fourteenth Amendment was ratified, all but 5 of the 37 States in the Union had criminal sodomy laws. In fact, until 1961, all 50 States outlawed sodomy, and today, 24 States and the District of Columbia continue to provide criminal penalties for sodomy performed in private and between consenting adults. Against this background, to claim that a right to engage in such conduct is "deeply rooted in this Nation's history and tradition" or "implicit in the concept of ordered liberty" is, at best, facetious.[32]

For White, not only is the danger of activism always to be guarded against, but it must be specifically forsaken in a case such as this one. Again, the *justification* for his position turns on his implicit conception of the readability of the Constitution. To quote Justice White, "[t]he Court is most vulnerable and comes nearest to illegitimacy when it deals with judge-made constitutional law having little or no cognizable roots in the language or design of the Constitution."[33]

I have critiqued the charge of judicial activism elsewhere as a fundamental misunderstanding of the inevitable role of normative construction in legal interpretation[34] once we understand that interpretation is also evaluation.[35] Fish has his own version of this critique. The point I want to make here is that for Fish, the power of law to enforce its own premises as the truth of the system erases the significance of its philosophical interlocutors, rendering their protest *impotent*. The concrete result in this case is that the criminal sanctions against gay men are given constitutional legitimation in that it is now proclaimed to be legally acceptable for states to outlaw homosexual love and sexual engagement.

Is this a classic example of the conserving violence of law? The answer, I believe, is unquestionably yes. But more importantly, given the analysis of Justice

White, it demonstrates a profound point about the relationship, emphasized by Derrida, between conserving violence and the violence of foundation. To quote Derrida, and I quote in full, because I believe this quotation is crucial to my own response to LaCapra's concern that Derrida yields to the temptation of violence:

> For beyond Benjamin's explicit purpose, I shall propose the interpretation according to which the very violence of the foundation or position of law (*Rechtsetzende Gewalt*) must envelop the violence of conservation (*Rechtser-haltende Gewalt*) and cannot break with it. It belongs to the structure of fundamental violence that it calls for the repetition of itself and founds what ought to be conserved, conservable, promised to heritage and tradition, to be shared. A foundation is a promise. Every position (*Setzung*) permits and promises (*permet et pro-met*), it positions *en mettant et en promettant.* And even if a promise is not kept in fact, iterability inscribes the promise as the guard in the most irruptive instant of foundation. Thus it inscribes the possibility of repetition at the heart of the originary. . . . Position is already iterability, a call for self-conserving repetition. Conservation in its turn refounds, so that it can conserve what it claims to found. Thus there can be no rigorous opposition between positioning and conservation, only what I will call (and Benjamin does not name it) a *différantielle* contamination between the two, with all the paradoxes that this may lead to.[36]

The call for self-conserving repetition is the basis for Justice White's opinion, and more specifically, for his rejection of "reading into" the constitution, *in spite of an interpretation of precedent,* a fundamental liberty to engage in "homosexual sodomy." As White further explains:

> Striving to assure itself and the public that announcing rights not readily identifiable in the Constitution's text involves much more than the imposition of the Justices' own choice of values on the States and the Federal Government, the Court has sought to identify the nature of the rights qualifying for heightened judicial protection.[37]

To summarize again, the result for White is that "fundamental liberties" should be limited to those that are "deeply rooted in the Nation's history and tradition."[38] For Justice White, as we have also seen, the evidence that the right to engage "in homosexual sodomy" is not a fundamental liberty is the "fact" that at the time the Fourteenth Amendment was passed, all but five of the thirty-seven states in the union had criminal sodomy laws and that most states continue to have such laws. In his dissent, Blackmun vehemently rejects the appeal to the *fact* of the existence of antisodomy criminal statutes as a basis for the continuing prohibition of the denial of a right, characterized by Blackmun not as the right to engage in homosexual sodomy but as "the right to be let alone."[39]

Quoting Justice Holmes, Blackmun reminds us that:

> It is revolting to have no better reason for a rule of law than that so it was laid down in the time of Henry IV. It is still more revolting if the grounds upon

which it was laid down have vanished long since, and the rule simply persists from blind imitation of the past.[40]

Derrida gives us insight into how the traditional positivist conception of law, in spite of Justice Holmes' remark and Justice Blackmun's concern, consists precisely in this self-conserving repetition. For Fish, as we have seen, it is the practical power of the legal system to preserve itself through the conflation of repetition with justification that makes it a legal system. Of course, Fish recognizes that repetition as iterability also allows for evolution. But evolution is the only possibility when *justification* is identified as the functioning of the system itself. Law, for Fish—in spite of his remarks to the contrary—is not deconstructible and, therefore, is also not radically transformable. As a system it becomes its own "positive" social reality in which the status of its own myths cannot be challenged.

It is, however, precisely the status as myth of its originary foundation and the "plain meaning of the words"—or in more technical language, the readability of the text—that Derrida challenges in the name of justice. We are now returned to LaCapra's concern about the potentially dangerous equalizing force in Derrida's own argument. LaCapra reinterprets what he reads as one of Derrida's riskier statements. Let me first quote Derrida's statement: "Since the origin of authority, the foundation or ground, the position of law can't by definition rest on anything but themselves, they are themselves a violence without ground."[41] LaCapra reformulates Derrida's statement in the hope of making it less subject to abuse. To quote LaCapra: "Since the origin of authority, the foundation or ground, the position of the law can't by definition rest on anything but themselves, the question of their ultimate foundation or ground is literally pointless."[42]

My disagreement with LaCapra's restatement is as follows: it is not that the question of the ultimate ground or foundation of law is pointless for Derrida; instead, it is the question of the ultimate ground, or correctly stated, lack of such, that *must* be asked, if we are to heed the call of Justice. That no justificatory discourse *can* or *should* insure the role of a metalanguage in relation to its dominant interpretation, *means* that the conserving promise of law can be never be fully actualized in a hermeneutical circle that successfully turns back in on itself and therefore grounds itself.

Of course, there are, at least at first glance, two kinds of violence at issue here; the violence of the foundation or the establishment of a legal system and then the law-conserving or jurispathetic violence of an actual legal system. But Derrida demonstrates in his engagement with Benjamin's text just how these two kinds of violence are contaminated. To concretize the significance of this contamination, we are again returned to *Bowers*. The erasure of the status of the intent of the founding fathers and the plain meaning of the words as legal myths is the basis for the *justification* of the jurispathic or law-conserving violence of the decision. The exposure of the mystical foundation of authority, which is another way of writing that the performativity of institutive language cannot be fully incorporated by the system once it is established, and thus, become fully self-justifying, does show that the establishment of law is violence in the sense of an *imposition* without a *present* justification. But this exposure should not be understood as succumbing to the lure of violence. Instead, the tautology upon which Justice White's opinion rests—that the law is and therefore it is justified to be, because it is—is exposed as tautology rather than justification. The point, then, of questioning the origin of authority is precisely to undermine the conflation of justification with an appeal to the origin, a conflation made possible because of the erasure of the mystical foundation of authority. LaCapra's reformulation may be "riskier" than Derrida's own because it can potentially turn us away from the operational force of the legal myths that seemingly create a self-justifying system. The result, as we have seen, is the violence of Justice White's opinion in which description is identified as prescription, criminal persecution of homosexuals defended as the necessity of the rule of law.

But does the deconstructionist intervention lead us to the conclusion that LaCapra fears it might? That conclusion being that all legal systems, because they are based on a mystical foundation of authority, have "something rotten"[43] at the core and are therefore "equal."[44] In one sense, LaCapra is right to worry about the equalizing force of Derrida's essay. The equality between legal systems is indeed that all such systems are deconstructible. But, as we have seen throughout this book, it is precisely this equality that allows for legal transformation, including legal transformation in the name of the traditional emancipatory ideals. Derrida reminds us that there is "nothing . . . less outdated"[45] than those ideals. As we have seen in *Bowers,* achieving them remains an aspiration, but an aspiration that is not just impotent idealism against the ever functioning, non-deconstructible machine.

As we have seen, Derrida is in disagreement with Fish about deconstructibility of law. For Fish, since law, or any other social context, defines the parameters of discourse, the transformative challenges to the system are rendered impotent because they can only challenge the *system* from within the constraints that will effectively undermine the challenge. "There is" no other "place" for them to be but within the system that denies them validity or redefines them so as to manage the full range of the complaint. But for Derrida "there is" no system that can catch up with itself and therefore establish itself as the only reality. To think that any social system, legal or otherwise can "fill" social reality is just another myth, the myth of full presence. In Fish, it is practically insignificant that law is a social construct, because, social construct or not, we can not *de*construct the machine. Derridean deconstruction reaches the opposite conclusion. As Derrida explains, returning us to the excess of the performative language that *establishes* a legal system:

> Even if the success of the performatives that found law or right (for example, and this is more than an example, of a state as guarantor of a right) presupposes

earlier conditions and conventions (for example in the national or international arena), the same "mystical" limit will reappear at the supposed origin of their dominant interpretation.

The structure I am describing here is a structure in which law (*droit*) is essentially deconstructible, whether because it is founded, constructed on interpretable and transformable textual strata, (and that is the history of law (*droit*), its possible and necessary transformation, sometimes its amelioration), or because its ultimate foundation is by definition unfounded. The fact that law is deconstructible is not bad news. We may even see in this a stroke of luck for politics, for all historical progress.[46]

The deconstructibility of law, then, as Derrida understands it, is a theoretical conception that *does* have practical consequences; the practical consequences are precisely that law cannot *inevitably* shut out its challengers and prevent transformation, at least not on the basis that the law itself demands that it do so. It should not come as a surprise, then, that the Eleventh Circuit, the court that held that the Georgia statute violated the respondent's fundamental rights, rested on the Ninth Amendment as well as on the Fourteenth Amendment of the Constitution. The Ninth Amendment can and, to my mind, *should* be interpreted to attempt fidelity to the deconstructibility of even the "best" constitution, so as to allow for historical change in the name of Justice. The Ninth Amendment can also be understood from within the problematic of what *constitutes* the intent of "the founding fathers." The intent of the constitution can only be *to be just,* if it is to meet its aspiration to democratic justification. This intent need not appeal to "external" legal norms but to "internal" legal norms embodied in the interpretation of the Bill of Rights itself. The Bill of Rights clearly attempts to spell out the conditions of *justice* as they were understood at the time of the passage of the Constitution. But the Ninth Amendment also recognizes the limit of any *description* of the conditions of justice, including those embodied in the Bill of Rights. An obvious example is the call of homosexuals for Justice, for their "fundamental liberty." The Ninth Amendment should be, and indeed was, used by the Eleventh Circuit to guard against the tautology upon which Justice White's opinion rests.[47] Silence, in other words, is to be constructed as the "not yet thought," not the "self-evident that need not be spoken."

But does this interpretation of the Ninth Amendment mean that there is no legitimacy to the conservation of law? Can a legal system completely escape the promise of conservation that inheres in its myth of origin? Certainly Derrida does not think so. Indeed, for Derrida, a legal system could not aspire to justice if it did not make this promise of conservation of principle and the rule of Law. But it would also not aspire to justice unless it understood this promise as a promise to Justice. Again we are returned to the recognition, at least in my interpretation of the Ninth Amendment, of this paradox.

It is precisely this paradox, which, for Derrida, is inescapable, that makes Justice an aporia, rather than a projected ideal.[48] To try exactly to define what Justice *is* would once again collapse prescription into description and fail to heed the humility before Justice inherent in my interpretation of the Ninth Amendment. Such an attempt shuts off the call of Justice, rather than heeding it, and leads to the travesty of justice, so eloquently described by Justice Holmes.[49] But, of course, a legal system if it is *to be* just must also promise universality, the fair application of the rules. As a result, as we saw in the last chapter, we have what for Derrida is the first aporia of Justice, *epokhe,* and rule. This aporia stems from the responsibility of the judge not only to state the law but to *judge* it.

> In short, for a decision to be just and responsible, it must, in its proper moment
> if there is one, be both regulated and without regulation: it must conserve the
> law and also destroy it or suspend it enough to have to reinvent it in each case,
> rejustify it, at least reinvent it in the reaffirmation and the new and free
> confirmation of its principle.[50]

Justice White failed to meet his responsibility precisely because he replaced description with judgment, and indeed, a description of state laws a hundred years past, and in very different social and political circumstances.[51]

But if Justice *is* (note the constative language) only as aporia, if no descriptive set of current conditions for justice can be identified *as* Justice, does that mean that all legal systems are equal in their embodiment of the emancipatory ideals? Is that what the "equality" that all legal systems are deconstructible boils down to? And worse yet, if that is the conclusion, does that not mean that we have an excuse to skirt our responsibility as political and ethical participants in our legal culture? As I have argued throughout this book, Derrida explicitly disagrees with that conclusion: "That justice exceeds law and calculation, that the unpresentable exceeds the determinable cannot and should not serve as an alibi for staying out of juridico-political battles, within an institution or a state or between one institution or state or others."[52]

But let me state this positioning *vis-à-vis* the deconstructibility of law even more strongly. The deconstructibility of law is, as I have argued for the last two chapters, exactly what allows for the possibility of transformation, not just the evolution of the legal system. This very openness to transformation, which, in my interpretation of the Ninth Amendment, should be understood as institutional humility before the call to Justice, as the beyond to any system, can itself be *translated* as a standard by which to judge "competing" legal systems. It can also be *translated* into a standard by which we can judge the justices themselves as to how they have exercised their responsibility. Compare, for example, Justice White's majority opinion with Justice Blackmun's dissent.[53] Thus, we can respond to LaCapra's concern that all legal systems not be conceived as equally "rotten." All judges are not equal in the exercise of their responsibility to Justice, even if justice can not be determined once and for all as a set of established norms.

The idea of right and the concrete, practical importance of rights, it must be noted, however, is not denied. Instead, the basis of rights is reinterpreted so as to be consistent with the ethical insistence on the divide between law and justice.

This ethical insistence protects the possibility of radical transformation within an existing legal system, including the new definition of right. But the refusal of the idea that only current concepts of right can be identified with justice is precisely what leads to the practical value of rights. Emmanuel Levinas once indicated that we need rights because we cannot have Justice. Rights, in other words, protect us against the *hubris* that any current conception of justice or right is the last word.

Unfortunately, in another sense of the word, Justice White is "right" about our legal tradition. Homosexuals have been systematically persecuted, legally and otherwise, in the United States. Interestingly enough, the reading of deconstruction I have offered allows us to defend rights as an expression of the suspicion of the consolidation of the boundaries, legal and otherwise, of community. These boundaries foreclose the possibility of transformation, including the transformation of our current conceptions of "normal" sexuality as these norms have been reflected in the law and used as the basis for the denial of rights to homosexuals. What is "rotten" in a legal system is precisely the erasure of its own mystical foundation of authority so that the system can dress itself up as justice. Thus, Derrida can rightly argue that deconstruction

> hyperbolically raises the stakes of exacting justice; it is sensitivity to a sort of essential disproportion that must inscribe excess and inadequation in itself and that strives to denounce not only theoretical limits but also concrete injustices, with the most palpable effects, in the good conscience that dogmatically stops before any inherited determination of justice.[54]

It is this "rottenness" in our own legal system as it is evidenced in Justice White's opinion that causes me to refer to the legal system, as Fish describes it, as a monster. The difference in Luhmann's terms turns on what is observed and why.

But for LaCapra, there is also another issue, separate if connected to the potential equalization of legal systems due to their inherent "rottenness." That danger is a danger of an irresponsible turn to violence, because there can be no projected standards by which to judge *in advance* the acceptability of violent acts. For LaCapra, this danger inheres in the complete disassociation of cognition and action that he reads as inherent in Benjamin's text, and perhaps in Derrida's engagement with Benjamin. As LaCapra reminds us in a potential disagreement with Derrida's formulation of this disassociation:

> As Derrida himself elsewhere emphasizes, the performative is never pure or autonomous; it always comes to some degree bound up with other functions of language. And justificatory discourse—however uncertain of its grounds and deprived of the superordinate and masterful status of metalanguage—is never entirely absent from a revolutionary situation or a *coup de force*.[55]

But Derrida certainly is not arguing that justificatory language has nothing to do with revolutionary situations. His argument is instead that the justificatory language of *revolutionary* violence depends on what has yet to be established, and of course, as a result, might yet come into being. If it did not depend on what was yet to come, it would not be *revolutionary* violence. To quote Derrida:

> A "successful" revolution, the "successful foundation of a State" (in somewhat the same sense that one speaks of a "felicitous" performative speech act) will produce *après* coup what it was destined in advance to produce, namely, proper interpretative models to read in return, to give sense, necessity and above all legitimacy to the violence that has produced, among others, the interpretative model in question, that is, the discourse of its self-legitimation. . . . There are cases in which it is not known for generations if the performative of the violent founding of the state is "felicitous" or not.[56]

That separation of cognition and action by *time* means that no acts of violence can truly be justified at the time they take place, if by truly justified one means cognitive assurance of the rightness of action. I believe that this interpretation of Derrida's engagement with Benjamin is the reading that does full justice to the seriousness with which both authors take the command "thou shalt not kill."[57] Thus, we can only be just to Benjamin's text and to Derrida's reading if we understand the responsibility imposed upon us by Benjamin's infamous statement about divine violence. "For it is never reason that decides on the justification of means and the justness of ends, but fate-imposed violence on the former and God on the latter."[58] Since there can be no cognitive assurance in advance of action we are left with our responsibility for what we do. We cannot escape responsibility by appealing to established conventions. Revolutionary violence cannot be rationalized by an appeal to what "is," for what "is" is exactly what is to be overturned. In this sense, each one of us is put on the line in a revolutionary situation. Of course, the inability to know whether or not the situation actually demands violence also means there can be no justification for not acting. This kind of undecidability is truly frightening. But it may not be more frightening than the justifications for violence—whether they be justifications for the death penalty or the war machine—put forward by the state. LaCapra worries precisely about the day-to-dayness of extreme violence in the modern/postmodern state.[59] But so does Benjamin in his discussion of the police.[60] The need to have some standards to curtail violence, particularly this kind of highly rationalized violence, should not be confused with a justification for revolutionary violence. The problem is not that there are not reasons given for violence. It is not even that these reasons should better be understood as rationalizations. It is rather that revolutionary violence cannot be rationalized, because all forms of rationalization would necessarily take the form of an appeal to what has already been established. Of course, revolutionary movements project ideals from within their present discourse. But if they are *revolutionary* movements they also reject the limits of that discourse. Can they do so? Have they done so? Judgment awaits these movements in the future. Perhaps we can better understand Benjamin's refusal of human rationalizations for violence by appealing to Monique Wittig's myth, *Les Guérillères.*[61] In *Les Guérillères,* we are truly confronted with a revolutionary situation, the overthrow of patriarchy with its corresponding enforcement of heterosexuality. In the myth, the Amazons take up arms. Is this mythic violence governed by fate? Is the goal the establishment of a new state? Would this new state not be the reversal of patriarchy and therefore its reinstatement? Or does this "war" signify divine violence—the violence that truly expiates. The text presents those questions as myth, but also as possibility "presented" in literary form.

How could the women in the myth know in advance, particularly if one shares the feminist premise that all culture has been shaped by the inequality of the gender divide as defined by patriarchy? If one projects an ideal even supposed by feminine norms, are these norms not contaminated by the patriarchical order with which the women are at "war"? Rather than a decision about the resolution of this dilemma, Wittig's myth symbolizes the process of questioning that must inform a revolutionary situation, which calls into question all the traditional justifications for what is. I am relying on this myth, which challenges one of the deepest cultural structures, because I believe it allows us to experience the impossibility of deciding in advance whether the symbolized war against patriarchy can be determined *in advance,* either as mythic or divine, or as justified or unjustified.

Yet, I agree with LaCapra that we need "limited forms of control."[62] But these limited forms of control are just that, limited forms. Should we ever risk the challenge to these limited forms? Would LaCapra say never? If so, my response to him can only be "Never say never." And why? Because it would not be just to do so.

Derrida's text leaves us with the infinite responsibility undecidability imposes on us. Undecidability in no way alleviates responsibility. The opposite is the case. We cannot be excused from our own role in history because we could not know so as to be reassured that we were "right" in advance.

Conclusion:
"The Ethical, Political, Juridical Significance of the End of Man"

If this book has a central purpose it has been first to show the *ethical* and then the *juridical* significance of the so-called "postmodern" rebellion against "metaphysics" and, more specifically, against Hegel. This shared ethical rebellion is, of course, the reason for grouping together philosophers as different as Theodor Adorno, Jacques Derrida, Jacques Lacan, and Emmanuel Levinas. But I had a more specific reason for insisting on this grouping. My argument can be summarized as follows: It is the intersection of the specific deconstructive intervention of Derrida into Levinas' ethical philosophy of alterity, combined with his deconstruction of Lacan's political pessimism of the possibility of dismantling the gender hierarchy, that can be figured as a "new," "different" ethical configuration.

I want to emphasize the specificity of Derrida's deconstructive intervention in the work of Hegel, Levinas, and Lacan. I use the phrase deconstructive intervention deliberately. It is a mistake to think of "deconstruction" as a systematic social theory which encompasses a positive political analysis. But, as I have also argued, the relation between systems theory and more specifically Luhmann's systems theory is much more complicated than it has been understood to be.[1] The two as I have suggested do not simply foreclose one another, although, as I have also argued, the deconstruction of the privileging of the present does show us that the very definition of a system as a system implies a beyond to it and that the time of the system and the time of the ethical relation to the Other are not the same. But this philosophical position, as we have seen, does not mean and should not be confused with the rejection of the centrality of the ethical. On the contrary, the philosophy of the limit can also be interpreted as a unique kind of ideological critique.

I will return to why I can risk the expression "ideological critique," an expression associated with the critical social theory of the Frankfurt school and certainly not with deconstruction. First, however, we need to explore in more depth the question: Why "new"? Why "different"? Simply put, this intersection, now figured as an ethical configuration, makes the question of *sexual difference* crucial to how we even dare to dream of the enactment of the ethical relation, even if we realize that its full enactment is impossible if we are to remain faithful to the ethical asymmetry that inheres in the respect for the Other as Other. But, as we have seen, Derrida also shows that this respect for difference demands the recognition of a "strange" phenomenological symmetry. This "strange" phenomenological symmetry is that we are the same precisely in our difference as egos. It is in this insistence on phenomenological symmetry in which the Other is recognized as ego that, for Derrida, there is an unsurpassable "Hegelian" moment in the philosophy of alterity. But we also need to remember that in *Glas,*[2] among other texts, Derrida further shows the limit of Hegel in his own recognition of this "strange" symmetry, precisely because he denies its strangeness and attempts to encompass this symmetry in a relational *concept* of difference. This relational concept of difference falters precisely when it projects the Other as conceptualized only in relation to me. In other words, it tames the otherness of the Other by making her mine. To summarize: for Derrida, Hegel remains a classic example of how the so-called recognition of identity through difference not only privileges identity over difference, but does so through the projection of the Other as only the Other to me and, therefore, not truly other at all. For Derrida, the classic example in Hegel—emphasized in the first instance by Simone de Beauvoir—is the ironic denial of Woman's otherness, her feminine specificity, in her very projection of her as the Other to Man. But for de Beauvoir, the recognition of phenomenological symmetry also meant the rejection of ethical asymmetry. As a result, she completely rejected Levinas' ethical philosophy of alterity as another excuse for the continuing oppression of women or, in the terms I have used here, the perpetuation of the illusion that women were not beings recognizable as phenomenologically symmetrical to men.

In her thoughtful essay relied on earlier in this book,[3] I argued that Luce Irigaray also criticizes Levinas' own elaboration of his project precisely because it cannot recognize the "strange" symmetry of the Other as Other. To summarize once more, the reason for this failure is his own sentimentalization of Woman. The very symbol of the subject burdened by her responsibility is the pregnant mother who then joyously gives birth to a baby *boy*. Much can be said about the masculine privilege inherent in this symbolization and Irigaray says it. But, when Irigaray later addresses the need for the recognition of feminine difference in the law as "sexuate" rights[4] she seems once again to fail to fully understand the practical, legal significance of the recognition of phenomenological symmetry. (I have retranslated Irigaray's program of sexuate rights into a program of equivalent rights, which I believe is consistent with a "vision" of equality that does indeed respect the strange symmetry of the Other as singular being.)[5] In other words, Irigaray's own engagement with Levinas leaves some concern that she makes the opposite mistake of de Beauvoir in that she recognizes ethical asymmetry and the specificity of sexual difference at the expense of the "strange" phenomenological symmetry that keeps the asymmetry of the ethical relationship from degenerating into a bad excuse for violation. Derrida's contribution in this debate has been precisely to insist on the need to recognize the "strange" phenomenological symmetry as crucial to the respect for the otherness of the Other as Other and particularly of the otherness of Woman, as irreducible to the "relational" other, to Man. In this sense, Derrida attempts to salvage what is valid in Levinas' philosophy of alterity, while recognizing his masculine bias. This attempt, as we will see in a moment, is crucial to legal discourse.

But for now, I want to recall the other figure in the intersection which makes up the ethical configuration I have traced throughout this book. That figure, as we have seen, is Jacques Lacan. Why is Lacan relevant in the specific context of Derrida's engagement with Levinas? This engagement, as I have argued, emphasizes the thinking of sexual difference as crucial to the aspiration of the enactment of the ethical relationship, an aspiration that dreams the possibility of the recognition of phenomenological symmetry at the same time that it respects ethical asymmetry. It would be impossible to summarize the rich analysis of Lacan's understanding of the psychosexual dynamics of the gender hierarchy. But to build to the understanding of ideological critique I want to advocate, it is necessary to be reminded of two of Lacan's central insights. For Lacan, "ego" identity, as it has come to be defined within ego psychology, is reflected as ideology in the "old-fashioned" sense that it is false to the "social" reality of how "identity" is formed under the gender hierarchy. Lacan never denied his Hegelian roots in the sense that the development of an "individual" identity was dependent on a pregiven social reality and, more specifically, the realization of the relations of mutual recognition. But in Lacan's analysis these relations are impossible and, therefore, the illusion of a self-sufficient subject is not only a myth, it is based in the masculine imaginary that, as we have seen, is protected by a woman reduced to his mirror. The feminine is erased in the assumption of identity, achievable only by entering into what Lacan calls the realm of the symbolic, the realm of conventional meaning. The pregiven "social reality" that gives meaning to the very idea of an ego identity is the reality of the gender hierarchy. In Lacan, sexual difference and gender identity are based on the cultural significance attributed to the importance of having the penis. Having the penis is identified with being potent, able to satisfy the mother's desire, which is why Lacan associates the "reality" of having the penis with the fantasy that having the penis is having the phallus. The fantasy is that because Mommy wants Daddy, those with the penis can bring the Mother back. This illusion is, of course, fantasy, given the reality that the other, including Mommy, can always leave. But the male child is able to solve his primary narcissistic wound that Mommy does not want me alone by projecting this fantasy that he has what Daddy has. Thus, he can bring her back by identifying himself through the phallus. The result is the fort/da game that Freud observed.[6] Woman, on the other hand, is now identified as the castrated Other. If the penis is identified with the phallus, not only on the level of fantasy, but also as reinforced by a cultural system of patriarchal pregiven conventions, then, Woman, who lacks the penis, is also "seen" as lacking the affirmative qualities associated with the phallus. But from within her own feminine "identification" she is also the one who cannot bring the desired Other back. As a result, women suffer a severe sense of inadequacy—not, now, because they do not have a penis, but because they cannot make up for their primary narcissistic wound.[7]

The meaning given to the "fact" of lack of the phallus does not inhere for Lacan in anatomical difference per se. The meaning has to do with how one "recovers" from the primary narcissistic wound and why the fantasy that the penis is the phallus becomes a compensation in our patriarchal society. The feminine, defined as lack, is a cultural construct that is necessary for the self-perpetuation of the gender hierarchy because the very illusion of masculine self-sufficiency demands that the devalorized Other be there to serve as a mirror. The Man needs to believe that he can bring Mommy back. There is no reciprocity here. Instead, there is the subjection of Woman. But the condition of the Man is not a happy story either. For the greatest fear is to lose "it." If the imagined phallus is taken away, Man is reduced to a "girl" or, more crassly put, a "cunt." The boy can take the place of "daddy" only because he has "it." But the symbolic "Daddy"—not the real father, but the imagined figure who represents the symbolic of patriarchal conventions—can always take "it" away. Taking "it" no longer implies literal castration, but the loss of the affirmative qualities associated with potency. (If one needs, here, a concrete example of how language reinforces phallic qualities as affirmative, think for example of the familiar phrase in academic circles of the "seminal idea").

Lacan's world of the gender hierarchy is played out as the horror story of "wimps" and "ghosts"—boys endlessly in fear of Daddy, girls defined as lack. This horror story is beautifully allegorized in Samuel Beckett's *Happy Days*.[8] The one aspect of engagement that never happens in this play is that the two meet face to face and talk. That, they cannot do. And yet, Winnie keeps hoping, keeps calling to Willie, with only the occasional response that never becomes the back and forth we associate with conversation.[9] The story in Lacan is not simply a denial of the subject. It is a story of how the subject is *constituted* through the gender hierarchy. Gender identity, on this account, blocks any ascension to individuality, *particularly* if individuality is defined as the power of "innovative capability"[10] the ability to play one's own role rather than assume as "real," the masquerade we call gender identity.[11]

My second point has been to show that Lacan's analysis always turns on the establishment of the Law of the Father as an unshakable "social reality" because it has become frozen into the unconscious if, indeed, it is not the unconscious. Yet, of course, any analysis of the Law of the Father also turns on an analysis of the cultural constructs which mark this Law as the law. Lacan's story is the story of repetition compulsion which makes political transformation, particularly in terms of the aspiration to a society of reasonable beings, an illusion. Masculine subjectivity is, on this analysis, not something men just get over—and, I may add here, unfortunately, because then the "cure" would just be the gift of a few books—when they read a little philosophy or even become *established* as academic philosophers. The appeal of Lacan's analysis to feminists is that it is helpful in explaining the profound hold that the gender hierarchy has over Western culture, including its philosophical theories of political transformation. Under a Lacanian analysis the law of gender identity will be replicated in the laws of an existing legal system. Therefore, there can be no rigid divide between the "formal" justice of the public realm and the "informal" realm of sexual and family relations. What, specifically, does it mean that "formal" justice cannot be separated from informal justice? It means that one could not hope for the sustaining of legal reforms unless the gender hierarchy, as it plays a constitutive role in identity, is challenged. As this century comes to an end and we watch the long-fought-for civil rights of women systematically overturned, we have reason to think about this connection as it helps us to shed light on an underlying truth of our social, political, and legal reality. I have, as a result, focused on the question of legal transformation throughout the second half of this book.[12]

I now want to summarize Derrida's deconstructive intervention into Lacan's analysis as it specifically relates to the intersection I have recast into an ethical configuration. I will then turn to how that ethical configuration can serve as the basis for ideological critique. Derrida's intervention has been to show how Lacan's insight that any concept of sexuality cannot be separated from what shifts in language turns against Lacan's own political pessimism. As Derrida reminds us, the subject and first of all the speaking subject, depends upon the system of differences and the movement of différance. It is within the gender context that Derrida has very specifically shown the ethical significance of this understanding of the subject. Simply put, the subject, including the masculine subject, cannot be frozen into its gender role precisely because of the performative aspect of language inherent in an understanding of language as a system of differences. It is always possible to play out our gender roles differently. Derrida's endless playing with the insight that masculine privilege is based on a fantasy, the fantasy that having the penis is having the phallus, is an explicitly ethical and political "act."

This exposure itself can serve as a form of ideology critique.[13] Now we see why I can justify this deconstructive intervention as "ideology critique" in a very traditional manner. First, as we have seen, Derrida's deconstructive intervention into Levinas' work uncovers the moment of phenomenological symmetry in the ethical relationship of alterity, so that ethical asymmetry is protected from the degeneration into violation of the Other. But, he also shows with Lacan how the recognition of women as others, not the Man's Other, is blocked by the psychical fantasy of Woman. Thus, the psychical fantasy of Woman stands in the way of the aspiration to the ethical relationship which demands the recognition of phenomenological symmetry. In the very traditional sense of ideology critique, which demands that there be some notion of falsity and thus of truth, Derrida shows that the gender hierarchy, and with it, imposed heterosexuality, is "ideology" in that it is not and cannot be made "true" to lived, individual sexuality. In turn he shows that the gender hierarchy violates the moment of universality that inheres in the recognition of the phenomenological symmetry of the Other.

For Lacan, on the other hand, it is ethically and politically irrelevant that gender hierarchy is not "true," at least in the sense that there is no outside referent in which the process of interpretation of sexuality and sexual difference comes to an end such as biology or a theory of constituted essences. The Law of the Father has been established as law and replicates itself through the linguistic code of the symbolic. As a result, meaningful transformation is foreclosed, at least within patriarchal culture. Women can appropriate the phallus—and who better to know how this is done than a woman law professor—but the phallus remains the very symbol of potency and of power. Put simply, to enter into the masculine world, women must take up the masculine position. How does one challenge the erection of the phallus as the "transcendental signifier"? Here again, Derrida's intervention is politically important. Derrida shows us that the phallus takes on the significance it does only as the metaphor for what the mother desires. Because the erection of the phallus as the transcendental signifier is based on a reading, the symbolic significance of the phallus can be reinterpreted. Thus, the discovery of anatomical sexual difference can also be reinterpreted (if the phallus is not read through the fantasy projection of what it means to have a penis). As a result, the divide into two genders, which is also the basis of the divide into heterosexuality and homosexuality, may also yield to other interpretations. Lacan himself undermines the very concept of homosexuality as perversion, because under his own analysis there can be no "correct" progression to a mature, normal sexuality through the proper development of the libidinal drives, as he also strips away the pretense that masculine "superiority" is in any way mandated by nature. But even if gender identity is just a role into which we are cast by the rigid structures of culture, we still play it, like automatons, as we take up our positions in the gender hierarchy.

Derrida's "ideological critique" has two prongs. We do not just end with the exposure of gender identity and heterosexuality as "ideology" because the divide into males and females can never be justified as true in the sense of an accurate description. In Derrida, gender hierarchy is also ideology in the sense that it denies the phenomenological symmetry of each one of us. Gender hierarchy is thus not only false, it is unethical.

His experimental "writing style," particularly as it develops as a dialogic engagement with a feminine interlocutor, should be read as an expression of the dream that we can express and live our lives and sexuality differently and, yes, maybe even talk to one another without being hopelessly blocked by the masculine imaginary. In Derrida's writing of the "dialectic" as a dramatic exercise, the "part" of the feminine is allowed to play out its disruptive force against the psychical fantasy of Woman.[14] The feminine is played out through the recognition of the "strange" phenomenological symmetry which denies that the individual woman can be adequately defined by her definition within the masculine-identified symbolic. Of course, this ideological critique, combined with the experimental writing of the "dialectic" cannot replace direct political action. But then no philosophical or social theory can replace such action. What it can do is show us that any conception of "dialogue" will itself be an illusion if it does not address itself to the way in which dialogue is blocked by the perpetuation of the gender hierarchy and with it the psychical fantasy of Woman.

Who can be the subject of dialogue? Who can truly develop a "fallibilistic consciousness"[15] so as to open himself (or herself) to the Other? These questions are of concern to social theory as well as to any conception of participatory democracy that does not ignore the reality of social life and the possibility of transformation that does not end in restoration. The question of what kind of human being one would have to become to live in a "new" society was and remains central to the tradition of romantic idealism. Friedrich Schiller eloquently addressed it in *On the Aesthetic Education of Man*,[16] because of his anguish over the disintegration of the French Revolution into the worst kind of violence. Indeed, it would not be an exaggeration to write that the question haunts debates over how extensive change can or, indeed, even should actually be.[17] In the social theory of Jürgen Habermas, for example, the question of motivation to participate in relations of dialogic reciprocity is at least partially answered through Kohlberg's theory of individual moral development. In Habermas' revision of Kohlberg's theory the possibility of a "seventh" stage, the stage of "dialogic" or, more precisely, a "post-conventional" personality has been historically realized. Habermas' social theory of the moral subject is thus evolutionary. The "postconventional" personality is precisely the person of a "fallibilistic consciousness" who can achieve reflexive role distancing from his own existential and moral convictions. The person is post-conventional because his moral judgments rest on reflection, not the mere acceptance of the conventions of the society in which he lives. One learns, in Kohlberg's sense, to apply universal standards of right, even when they go against one's "gut" instinct. In Habermas, this capacity is associated with the recognition of the Other as an equal subject in dialogue. It also implies, at least on the interpretation of reflexive role distancing that Habermas has given us, the ability to identify with the Other precisely as a subject of dialogue. In everyday language, reflexive role distancing demands that one can imagine being in the other's shoes. One can, in other words, play out, at least in the imagination, the roles into which the other has been placed. Of course, the first *ethical* criticism of Habermas' conception of the "postconventional" personality is that it never *directly* addresses just how the recognition of the Other's phenomenological symmetry as a subject of dialogues is blocked by the gender hierarchy. Following Kohlberg, he simply assumes the postconventional personality has developed beyond that point. Would that it were "true," and that we lived in a society in which that "truth" had been realized. But there is another criticism related to whether or not one can truly imagine being in the other's shoes.

Luce Irigaray, on the other hand, has emphasized that the two sexes cannot be in the same position, even in the sense of being formally conceptualized as subjects of dialogue. The irreducibility of one sex to the other also means that one sex cannot fully experience or imagine what the Other "is" or the extent of her suffering. This irreducibility of the "two" sexes leads Irigaray to evoke the hope for a new alliance between the two "sexes" to rest on wonderment,[18] which recognizes the irreducible difference between them, and not on the imagination in which one imagines oneself as the Other. Very simply, no man can know or fully imagine what it is like to have an abortion, although he can clearly wonder about it and respect the suffering entailed if that right to abortion is denied to women. Continually in both Derrida and Levinas, humility before the otherness of the Other is emphasized as crucial to the aspiration to enact the ethical relationship.

But this respect for the otherness of the Other also has implications for the way in which one thinks about "the subject of dialogue," a conception different from Habermas' Kohlbergian analysis. What is often missed in discussions of Jacques Lacan is the historical dimension of the way in which "the era of the ego" comes to be established precisely in connection with the psychical fantasy of Woman upon which it is based.[19] The historical reading of Lacan not only goes against the "poststructuralist" interpretation, but also against those analysts associated with Lacanianism who argue that feminism, or any other form of rebellion against the gender hierarchy, necessarily puts individual sanity at risk.[20] For Lacan, the closed thinking of the ego is precisely what blocks "fallibilistic" or "dialogic" consciousness. Lacan specifically notes that it is not a coincidence that philosophy is no longer written in the form of the dialectic. The Other is assimilated, not listened to. But, in the case of women and the gender hierarchy, Woman is assimilated as the necessary basis for the illusion of the ego's self-sufficiency. For Lacan, "the era" of ego identity is inherently connected to the role of the masculine imaginary in fantasizing the ideal of self-sufficiency.

To even begin to dream of the "subject of dialogue" we then have to challenge the law which establishes the gender hierarchy. The Law of the Father not only has to be undermined, it has to be delegitimated. I have already suggested that Derrida's deconstructive intervention engages in that process of delegitimation, particularly once it is understood as a form of ideological critique. It does so first—and this step we need to recall is taken with Lacan—by demonstrating that masculine superiority is a "sham" in the Lacanian sense that it is imaginary and connected to the macho illusion of self-sufficiency. Secondly, it does so by turning Lacan's own insight into the relationship between *significance* and sexual identity against Lacan himself. As we have seen, Derrida shows that the Law cannot protect itself against reinterpretations that could potentially destabilize the gender hierarchy itself. This delegitimation and this destabilization have political consequences in that they indicate that the conditions for a "subject of dialogue" and of "participatory" democracy demand the undermining of the gender hierarchy. Without this challenge to gender hierarchy, in other words, the "era of the ego" cannot be transformed and, thus, in any meaningful way surpassed. Both Lacan and Derrida specifically connect what has now come to be called the philosophy of consciousness with gender hierarchy and with the subjection of women. To summarize, within the ethical configuration I have offered, the psychical fantasy of Woman blocks both the recognition of the strange phenomenological symmetry of the Woman as an Other, a singular being, like the man's self and the ethical alterity of the Other whose otherness can never be reduced to any conception of Her or to any man's relationship to Her.

We can now return to the differences between Theodor Adorno's and Max Horkheimer's *Dialectic of Enlightenment*[21] and the analysis I have offered here. I do not want to deny the affinity of the ethical configuration I have offered with critical theory, particularly as developed by Adorno. But an affinity implies not only similarity, but also difference. First, however, we will focus on the affinity between Adorno and Derrida. As we saw in the first chapter, Adorno shares with Derrida a critique of Hegelian totalization in the name of the remain(s), the otherness of "things" that can never be adequately captured by any imposed definitions.

Such an exposure refuses the *idea* that what "reality" is can ever be reduced to our conception of it. In that sense, Adorno and, even more militantly, Derrida deny the move we now associate with the recent versions of "pragmatism."[22] The "conversation of mankind," for Derrida, does not do away with the Other to us as "material" reality. In this sense, Derrida is closer to Charles Peirce in his understanding that there "is" a reality labeled by Peirce as secondness. In his beautiful essay on the death of his friend Paul de Man, he spoke of the secondness of death itself.[23] "It" is not interpretation all the way down for Derrida. Paul de Man is dead, and that death and one's powerlessness before it has all the force of hitting against a barrier that Peirce called secondness. Derrida's philosophy of the limit exposes *the limit* of the move to objective "spirit,"[24] particularly in the form of "the conversation of mankind," as the answer to all our questions.

Adorno's display of the nonidentity is also against the imposed identity of the Hegelian system in which difference is ultimately recaptured by the Concept. This exposure was shown to be ethical in its impulse. In the place of the Concept was put the constellation, a metaphor for how one could uncover the object as it speaks to us, not as we define it. Both Derrida and Adorno remain "materialists" in the specific sense just described.

In *The Dialectic of Enlightenment*, Adorno and Horkheimer also show how the very historical consolidation of the subject of reason turns against itself. The critique is not only that reason in modern capitalism is reduced to instrumental rationality in which objects and, indeed, human beings are valued and understood through their usefulness in the system of exchange. It is also, as we saw, that the subject of reason has to violate himself by controlling his own empirical self. Thus Adorno, in his *Negative Dialectics,* is not critical only of Hegel, but also of the Kantian division between the noumenal and the phenomenal self. The subject that pulls itself together so as to radically separate itself from its empirical being as a creature of the flesh does so only at the cost of violence to himself. The very symbol of the violence to the self imposed by the attempt to become a subject of reason in control of himself is Odysseus, who ties himself to the mast to "protect" himself from the seduction of the sirens. The sirens, in turn, promise the happiness so tempting to creatures of the flesh. But the rumors abound about the horrible reality that results if the subject gives into the temptation of seduction. The negative connotation associated with the popular designation of the "siren" as the temptress continues to express this fear of the seductress as a threat to the subject's control. The very idea, then, of the subject of reason, at least if defined in the traditional Kantian manner, splits the subject from part of himself. This splitting, and the endless battle for control over the Other in oneself, is the basis for resentment toward those who seem to be having "too much fun." Adorno and Horkheimer, in other words, connect the Nietzschean insight that resentment is the motor of the modern, particularly the Christian, subject in his relations with those who he views as his Other, with the Kantian conception of the autonomous subject.

The emphasis in Adorno and Horkheimer is on the violation to the individual of the denial of one's self as a creature of the flesh. In Levinas, on the other hand, we saw that the Kantian aspiration to autonomy from the *heteros* is itself condemned as a violation of the call to responsibility. In Levinas, the violation inherent in the Kantian conception of the self is to the Other. As we saw, both Derrida and Irigaray were concerned, if in different ways, with his perpetuation of the myth of the Mother. Within the psychical fantasy of Woman the Mother becomes the illusionary Other to the seductress, the evil siren.

But we also saw in Derrida a suspicion of the Levinasian prescription that the dissatisfaction of the subject enslaved by the infinite call to responsibility was sublime. Here again, there are echoes of Adorno in Derrida in that both thinkers are concerned with the violation to the creature of the flesh inherent in a strong Kantian conception of autonomy. Returning to the symbol of Odysseus, the very image is of a subject tied up in knots in the effort at control. To confuse being tied up in knots with freedom is precisely the confusion that Adorno and Horkheimer expose. But in spite of this similarity, in Adorno there is a clearer obsession with the repressed promise of happiness that can never be completely obliterated by the era of the subject or, in Lacan's phraseology, of the historical era of the ego than there is in Derrida. Derrida's concern is, in this sense, closer to the Levinasian obsession with the Other and his responsibility to Her. Although it is not absent, and I have discussed the implicit appeal to something like happiness in his criticism of Levinas, there is less emphasis on self-violation. In this sense, Derrida should be understood as positioned between Levinas and Adorno and Horkheimer.

But, of course, Adorno and Horkheimer were also concerned with the implications in the relation to otherness implied by the resentment of the subject ever subjected to his own effort at control. In the *Dialectic of Enlightenment,* they specifically draw attention to the connection between resentment and anti-Semitism. Derrida, in like manner, has been vigilant in the exposure of the ethnocentrism of the Western philosophical tradition.

But, we now need to turn to the evident differences between Adorno and Horkheimer and Derrida. One I have just suggested: that Derrida remains closer to Levinas with his concern with the call of responsibility of the Other. This concern is not just with Being, but as we saw in Derrida's engagement with Levinas' critique of Heidegger, with the awe implied in the recognition of the "being" of the Other.

But there are two further differences on which I now focus because they have been emphasized in this book. The first is that, like Lacan, Derrida does not emphasize the self-referentiality of logocentrism but, instead, the self-referentiality of *phallo*gocentrism. As already discussed in this Conclusion, this explicit emphasis on the connection between the era of the ego and the gender hierarchy is shared by both Derrida and Lacan. Thus, Derrida's specific intervention is not simply to engage in the exposure of the limit of logocentrism, but of the gender hierarchy as constituted in the era of the ego. I do not want to deny that, particularly in his aphorisms, Adorno had glimmers of insight into the relationship between the era of the ego and the devalorization and subordination of the feminine. Strong feminist readings of Adorno have focused on these moments of insight. But these moments of insight were never systematically developed into the position that the question of sexual difference was central to philosophical discourse and to the aspiration to enact the ethical relationship.

I have suggested this position on the significance of gender hierarchy in philosophy is neither ahistorical nor lacking in ethical and political importance, if one thinks that ideological critique, as I have defined it in this conclusion, has ethical and political significance. Thus, it is not the case, as some political critics of Derrida have suggested, that there is no "social" basis to deconstruction if one means by social basis an appeal to how important relationships are constituted within a particular culture or historical period. For me at least, the political and ethical meaning of living under a gender hierarchy in which the feminine is pushed under is not "ineffable."[25]

But in spite of the interpretation I have just given of how both Lacan and Derrida can be read historically and socially, it is undoubtedly the case that Derrida remains committed to traditional philosophical discourse to a degree that Adorno would have rejected. Yes, Derrida endlessly exposes the *limit* of philosophy, but he does so *philosophically,* through a quasi-transcendental inquiry, even if it is one that undermines the traditional assumptions of phenomenol-

ogy. This insistence on the limit should not be confused with the denial of the
possibility of reconstruction. It simply demands that we think about the status of
projects of reconstruction differently. More specifically, it demands that we think
through the realization that justice can never be reduced to the conventions of
what "is." This effort is philosophical precisely insofar as it refuses to replace
philosophy with sociology. (But, as we also saw in the discussion of the relation
between Derrida and Luhmann, deconstruction does not seek to simply displace
sociology.) It is not a coincidence, then, that one of Derrida's recent texts,
published in the winter of 1990, is entitled "Du Droit à Philosophie."[26] At the
heart of this text is an essay in which Derrida plays off the many meanings of the
title, "Of the Right of Philosophy To Right."

We come now to the ethical, legal, and political significance of this difference
from Adorno and, even more evidently, from Horkheimer. For Adorno, the "end
of philosophy," which must come with the full acknowledgment of the horror of
the Holocaust,[27] left him only with "negative dialectics." For Adorno, the violence
of the idealist attempt to find "truth" in theory can only be exposed by demonstrating its "nontruth." To pretend that in this fallen world we could give an affirmative
account of the conditions of truth or of justice would only further perpetuate the
violence of idealism. Even in art, the possibility of redemption can only be shown
negatively. To try to abstractly portray the conditions of redemption, to give form
to the hope of reconciliation as if it existed now, only promotes accommodation
to a fallen world. As a result, Adorno does not reflect on the conditions of justice
and the relation of these conditions to positive law, either through a quasi-
transcendental inquiry or through empirical analysis. Such a reflection is foreclosed by his negative dialectics. Thus, as I have argued in the first chapter, even
if his negative dialectics carries within it an ethical message that can be decoded,
this message cannot be translated into an account of justice and its relation to
law.

Yet, Derrida does give us such an account, which can neither be identified
simplistically as "negative" or as "positive," if by a positive account we mean
the elaboration of justice as a given set of descriptive conditions. If the second
half of this book has had a central purpose, it has to have been to reinterpret the
Derridean double gesture so as to answer Thomas McCarthy's question: "[H]ow
is tolerance of difference to be combined with the requirements of living *together*
under *common* norms?"[28]

It should be noted, however, that it is a mistake to reduce Derrida's account
of justice as three aporias[29] to the "tolerance of difference." Respect for difference,
as we saw in the discussion of *Bowers v. Hardwick*[30] and *Roe v. Wade*[31] is
undoubtedly crucial to a society whose laws aspire to justice. But to reduce justice
to "tolerance of difference" would be to again identify justice with a positive
description or with established legal values or norms. This reduction follows from
the mistake of trying to *directly* translate deconstruction or, as I have relabeled
it, the philosophy of the limit, into a "positive" political or legal program. It is

perhaps no coincidence that the political significance of deconstruction has been emphasized in law. In law, the question of the relationship between rights, law, and justice is unavoidable once judging is understood as inevitable in the process of interpretation, a process which can never be reduced to merely following the rules. The realization that if justice is *identified* with positive "law" or with any given conception of rights, it undermines the very concept of justice is, of course, not specific to deconstruction. To return to the example in the Introduction, John Rawls is always careful, even in his later work which displays a break with Kantianism, to distinguish his conception of "overlapping consensus" from any *actual* consensus established by the "conversation of mankind."[32] For Rawls, the very idea of a constitution rejects the reduction of justice to politics. In this sense, his, too, remains a quasi-transcendental inquiry, if by quasi-transcendental we mean nothing more than the attempt to establish the conditions of justice *prior* to the actual legal contests that constitute the day-to-day reality of adjudication and legislation. The idea that justice is prior to politics is, for Rawls, a crucial aspect of the constitutional tradition and to his own theory of constitutional essentials.

But if there is one important difference between Rawls' conception of an "overlapping consensus" and his theory of "constitutional essentials" and Derrida's account of the three *inescapable* aporias of justice, it lies in the degree of accommodation to the established norms, even if those norms are validly established through an "overlapping" rather than an actual consensus. Derrida's account gives greater attention to the necessary "utopian" moment in the vigilant insistence on the maintenance of the divide between law, established norms, and Justice. The difference, in other words, lies in Derrida's suspicion of even a quasi-transcendental inquiry if it is understood as a procedure to establish *identifiable norms* as "constitutional essentials." The danger of an "overlapping consensus," as we saw in the chapter on time,[33] is that it still turns us to the past in a way that can potentially limit legal transformation. Rawls himself always emphasizes tolerance of difference as at the center of his suspicion of communitarianism. But even so, he is more concerned than is Derrida to reconcile his theory of "constitutional essentials" with established norms. In the end, even if both inquiries are quasi-transcendental, Rawls' analysis is ultimately more conservative than Derrida's account of Justice as the three aporias. Simply put, Derrida's account is no more "ineffable" than Rawls'; it is more utopian. Yet, if this utopian moment demands that we always recognize the *status* of any positive principles, it does not deny the necessity for their elaboration within law, understood as a shared *nomos*. It only demands that we recognize that these principles cannot be identified as Justice, even if this identification is done through an "overlapping consensus." Deconstruction keeps open the "beyond" of currently unimaginable transformative possibilities precisely in the name of Justice. And so, we are left, as I have argued, with a command, "be just with Justice," and an infinite responsibility to which we can never close our eyes or ears through an appeal to what "is," even the "is" of "constitutional essentials."

But perhaps the only way to end this book is with the voice of a woman who knows there is no ending, at least not when it comes to the dream of Justice. In response to a question as to why she did not become a lawyer, the narrator of Ingeborg Bachmann's novel *Malina* gives the following answer:

> Fine, as you wish. I'll express myself more clearly and get right to the point. I'd only like to add that there are warning signs. You know which ones I mean. Since justice is so oppressively near and what I am saying does not exclude the possibility of its being no more than a longing for the unattainable, pure greatness. That's why it is simultaneously both oppressive and near, but in the nearness, we call it injustice.[34]

Notes

Introduction

1. See Jacques Derrida, *The Truth in Painting,* trans. Geoffrey Bennington and Ian McLeod (Chicago and London: University of Chicago Press, 1987).

2. Heidegger in his later work crosses out ~~Being~~; see Martin Heidegger, *Early Greek Thinking,* trans. David Farrell Krell and Frank A. Capuzzi (Harper & Row, 1985).

3. Jürgen Habermas, for example, has described what he believes to be the crux of the Enlightenment in his lectures on modernity. For Habermas, modernity is not only inseparable from, but is indeed defined by Enlightenment ideals. See Jürgen Habermas, *The Philosophical Discourses of Modernity,* trans. Frederick Lawrence (Cambridge: Massachusetts Institute of Technology Press, 1987). Cf., further, John Rawls, "The Domain of the Political and Overlapping Consensus," in *New York University Law Review,* vol. 64, no. 2 (1989).

4. For a conception of the rule of law, see John Rawls, *A Theory of Justice* (Cambridge: The Belknap Press, 1971), pp. 235–43.

5. Thomas Nagel, *Partiality and Equality* (Princeton: Princeton University Press, 1991).

6. Michael Sandel, *Liberalism and the Limits of Justice* (Cambridge: Harvard University Press, 1982).

7. Alasdair MacIntyre, *Whose Justice? Which Rationality?* (Notre Dame: University of Notre Dame Press, 1988).

8. Jürgen Habermas, *Theory of Communicative Action,* vols. 1 and 2, trans. Thomas McCarthy (Boston: Beacon Press, 1984).

9. See generally Habermas, *Philosophical Discourses of Modernity.*

10. Andrew Arato and Jean Cohen, *Civil Society and Political Theory,* ed. Thomas McCarthy (Boston: Massachusetts Institute of Technology Press, forthcoming, 1991).

11. An example of someone who has questioned the political relevance of deconstruction

is Seyla Benhabib, in "Deconstruction, Justice, and the Ethical Relation," in the forthcoming *Cardozo Law Review*, vol. 13 (1991).

12. Jacques Derrida, "Force of Law: The 'Mystical Foundation of Authority,'" in *Cardozo Law Review*, vol. 11, nos. 5–6, (1990), p. 971.

13. See, e.g. Thomas McCarthy, "The Politics of the Ineffable: Derrida's Deconstructionism," in *Philosophical Forum*, vol. 21, nos. 1–2 (Fall-Winter 1989–90). Cf. Richard Bernstein, "Serious Play: The Ethical-Political Horizon of Jacques Derrida," in the *Journal of Speculative Philosophy* (Pennsylvania State University Press), 1987. Although Bernstein clearly does not understand Derrida's ethical and political theory, he recognizes from the outset, in a simplistic sense, that Derrida's ethics is based on a tolerance of difference which is the very basis of liberalism. Understanding Derrida's unique contribution, we must grapple with Derrida's sympathy for a kind of liberal insistence on difference; however, even as we see this sympathy on his part, we must recognize Derrida's severance from the liberal tradition by virtue of the fact that his insistence is a Utopian moment that cannot be erased.

14. McCarthy, ibid., and cf. Nancy Fraser, "The French Derrideans: Politicizing Deconstruction or Deconstructing the Political?" in *Unruly Practices: Power, Discourse, and Gender in Contemporary Social Theory*, (University of Minnesota, 1990).

15. Fraser, ibid.

16. Peter Dews, *Logic of Disintegration* (London: Verso, 1987).

17. See Ingeborg Bachmann, *Malina* (New York: Holmes and Meier Publishers, Inc., 1990). In *Malina*, the smothering of women by the definition of objects demands a new experimental style which does not just redefine who women are. In order to let the object speak, this time, woman as object, the system of definition must be broken upon. The seemingly jarring style of the novel is what allows for the woman's experience to be decoded beyond the definition imposed upon her by her lover Ivan.

18. See *Beyond Accommodation: Ethical Feminism, Deconstruction and the Law* (New York: Routledge, 1991).

Chapter 1

1. Theodor W. Adorno, *Negative Dialectics*, trans. E. B. Ashton (New York: The Continuum Publishing Co., 1973), p. 139.

2. Immanuel Kant, *Foundations of the Metaphysics of Morals*, trans. Louis White Beck (Indianapolis: Bobbs-Merrill Company, Inc., 1959), pp. 30–31.

3. Adorno, *Negative Dialectics*, p. 145.

4. Michael Theneuissen, *Sein und Schein, der Kritische Funktion Heggschen Logik* (Frankfurt am Main: Suhrkamp, 1978), pp. 148–49.

5. Ibid.

6. Adorno, *Negative Dialectics*, p. 191.

7. Theodor W. Adorno, *Minima Moralia: Reflections from Damaged Life*, trans. E. F. N. Jephcott (London: New Left Books, 1974), p. 50.

8. I am using realism in the popular sense rather than in the strict philosophical sense,

but there is a relationship between the two that cannot be entirely ignored, particularly as certain forms of moral realism deny the possibility of radical transformation, and also particularly as this realism has been used in moral theory. As the counterexample of a unique understanding of this realism, which could be reinterpreted in moral theory so as not to foreclose radical transformation, see Sabina Lovibond, *Realism and Imagination in Ethics* (Minneapolis: University of Minnesota Press, 1983).

9. Adorno, *Minima Moralia*, p. 16.

10. Ibid., p. 200.

11. Ibid., p. 167.

12. Adorno, *Negative Dialectics*, p. 144.

13. Ibid., p. 161.

14. Ibid., p. 38.

15. Ibid., p. 143.

16. Ibid., p. 27.

17. Ibid., p. 172.

18. Ibid., p. 160.

19. Ibid., p. 167.

20. Ibid., p. 145.

21. Ibid., p. 11.

22. Robert Neville, *Hegel and Whitehead: Contemporary Perspectives on Systematic Philosophy,* ed. George R. Lucas, Jr. (Albany: State University of New York Press, 1986), p. 91.

23. Ibid., p. 92.

24. Richard Rorty continues to make this mistake. See "Philosophy in America Today," in *Consequences of Pragmatism* (Minneapolis: University of Minnesota Press, 1982), pp. 211–30.

25. Adorno, *Negative Dialectics*, p. 161.

26. Ibid., p. 158.

27. Ibid., p. 159.

28. Adorno, *Minima Moralia*, p. 247.

29. Adorno, *Negative Dialectics*, p. 163.

30. On one reading this understanding differs from Benjamin's. Cf. "The Language of Man," in *Reflections: Essays, Aphorisms, Autobiographical Writings,* ed. Peter Demetz, trans. Edmund Jephcott (New York: Harcourt Brace Jovanovich, 1978).

31. Adorno, *Negative Dialectics*, p. 163.

32. Ibid.

33. Ibid.

34. Ibid., p. 161.

35. Ibid., p. 174.

36. Theodor W. Adorno, *Against Epistemology; A Metacritique: Studies in Husserl and the Phenomenological Antinomies,* trans. Willis Domingo (Oxford: Basil Blackwell, 1982), p. 162.

37. Fred R. Dallmayr, *Twilight of Subjectivity: Contributions to a Post-Individualist Theory of Politics* (Amherst: University of Massachusetts Press, 1981), p. 137.

38. Adorno, *Negative Dialectics,* p. 357.

39. Theodor W. Adorno, "The Idea of Natural History," trans. Bob Hullot, *Telos,* no. 60 (Summer 1984), pp. 111–24.

40. Adorno, *Negative Dialectics,* p. 203.

41. Ibid., p. 204.

42. Ibid., pp. 203–4.

43. Ibid., p. 203.

44. Arthur Schopenhauer, *The World as Will and Representation,* vol. 1, trans. E. F. J. Payne (New York: Dover Publications, 1969), p. 104.

45. Adorno, *Negative Dialectics,* p. 299.

46. Schopenhauer, *The World as Will and Representation,* p. 104.

47. Theodor W. Adorno and Max Horkheimer, *Dialectic of Enlightenment,* trans. John Cumming (New York: Herder and Herder, 1972), p. 103.

48. Adorno, *Negative Dialectics,* p. 404.

49. Ibid., p. 400.

50. Ibid., p. 38.

51. Ibid., p. 281.

52. Ibid., p. 283.

53. Ibid., p. 232.

54. Ibid., p. 289.

55. Ibid., p. 241.

56. Ibid., p. 238.

57. Ibid.

58. Ibid., p. 264.

59. Ibid., p. 262.

60. Ibid.

61. Ibid., p. 220.

62. Ibid., pp. 283–84.

63. Hans-Georg Gadamer, *Truth and Method* (New York: Crossroad, 1975).

64. Rorty, "Philosophy in America Today."

65. Sabina Lovibond, *Realism and Imagination in Ethics.*

66. Ibid., p. 195.

67. Adorno, *Minima Moralia,* p. 274.

68. Adorno, *Negative Dialectics*, p. 172.

69. Charles S. Peirce, *The Collected Papers of Charles Sanders Peirce, 1931–1934*, ed. Charles Hartshorne and Paul Weiss (Cambridge, Mass.: The Belknap Press of the Harvard University Press, 1960), p. 130. Cf. his "Evolutionary Love," in *Philosophical Writings*, ed. Justus Buchler (New York: Dover, 1955), pp. 361–74.

Chapter 2

1. Iris Young, "The Ideal of Community and the Politics of Difference," in *Soc. Theory & Prac.*, vol. 12, no. 12 (1986).

2. Ibid., pp. 1–2.

3. See generally Martin Heidegger, *Identity and Difference*, trans. Joan Stambaugh (New York: Harper and Row, 1st ed., 1969). For Heidegger, the mediated synthesis of relation determines what is to be related and how it is to be related. The relation precedes what is related, and what is related is unknown to the relation. Heidegger's "belonging together" is part of Identity. Such a question can be understood as Heidegger's challenge to those who think within the Hegelian framework.

4. See Georg W. F. Hegel, *Natural Law*, trans. T. M. Knox (Philadelphia: University of Pennsylvania Press, 1975), pp. 93–94.

5. See ibid.

6. Law and economics scholars such as Judge Richard Posner continue to make this mistake. Cf. Richard Posner, *The Economics of Justice* (Cambridge, Mass.: Harvard University Press, 1981).

7. Gillian Rose, *Hegel Contra Sociology* (Atlantic Highlands, N.J.: Humanities Press, 1981), pp. 54–55 (footnote omitted).

8. Hegel, *Natural Law*, p. 72 (footnote omitted).

9. See Rose, *Hegel Contra Sociology*, p. 56.

10. See ibid., p. 55 (quoting Georg W. F. Hegel, *Jener Schriften*, neu. hrsg. von Hans Brockard und Hartmut Buchner (Hamburg: Felix Meiner, 1979), pp. 458–59).

11. This is Robert Nozick's critique of John Rawls. See Robert Nozick, *Anarchy, State, and Utopia* (New York: Basic Books, 1974).

12. See Rose, *Hegel Contra Sociology*, p. 69 (quoting Georg W. F. Hegel, *System der Sittlichkeit*, Hrsg. von Georg Larson, ed. Philosophische Bibilothek, Bd. 144a (Hamburg: Felix Meiner, 1967), p. 53).

13. I have argued that the Hegelian view of the subject divested of sovereignty meets Michael J. Sandel's requirements for a reformulated conception of the subject and the community. Drucilla Cornell, "Toward a Modern/Postmodern Reconstruction of Ethics," *University of Pennsylvania Law Review*, vol. 133, no. 2 (1985), p. 360. The community would no longer be understood as an external, coercive force tolerated at best as an unfortunate necessity. As Sandel points out, Nozick's critique of Rawlsian redistributive justice rests on a view of the constitutive, possessive subject. Michael J. Sandel, *Liberalism and the Limits of Justice* (New York: Cambridge University Press, 1982), pp. 96–97. In the terms of the young Hegel, Nozick

is the latest version of the myth of empirical natural law. The mistake is the same—to confuse a description of civil society with a justification for its continuation as the only legitimate principle of social ordering.

14. See Heidegger, *Identity and Difference,* p. 47 (emphasis in original).

15. Ibid.

16. Heidegger, *Identity and Difference.*

> "For Hegel, the conversation with the earlier history of philosophy has the character of *Aufhebung,* that is, of the mediating concept in the sense of an absolute foundation.
>
> "For us, the character of the conversation with the history of thinking is no longer *Aufhebung* (elevation), but the step back.
>
> "Elevation leads to the heightening and gathering area of truth posited as absolute, truth in the sense of the completely developed certainty of self-knowing knowledge.
>
> "The step back points to the realm which until now has been skipped over, and from which the essence of truth becomes first of all worthy of thought."

Ibid., p. 49 (footnote omitted).

17. Ibid., p. 29 (emphasis in original).

18. See Jacques Derrida, *Writing and Difference,* trans. Alan Bass (Chicago: University of Chicago Press, 1978), pp. 251–60.

19. See Derrida, *Writing and Difference,* p. 275.

20. See Theodor W. Adorno, *Negative Dialectics,* trans. E. B. Ashton (New York: The Continuum Publishing Co., 1973), p. 350.

21. Georg W. F. Hegel, "Introduction: Reason in History," in *Lectures on the Philosophy of World History,* ed. Johannes Hoffmeister, trans. H. B. Nisbet (Cambridge: Cambridge University Press, 1953), p. 55. ("The *patriarchal* state is viewed, either in relation to the whole or to some branches (of the human family), as that condition in which, together with the legal element, the moral and emotional find their fulfillment." (emphasis in original))

22. Adorno, *Negative Dialectics.*

23. Ibid., p. 344.

24. See Georg W. F. Hegel, *Hegel's Science of Logic,* trans. A. V. Miller (Atlantic Highlands, N.J.: Humanities Press International, 1969).

25. Theodor W. Adorno, *Minima Moralia: Reflections from Damaged Life,* trans. E. F. N. Jephcott (London: New Left Books, 1974), p. 17.

26. Ibid., pp. 17–18.

27. See Hegel, *Natural Law,* p. 93.

28. See Adorno, *Minima Moralia,* p. 233.

29. See Jacques Derrida, *Of Grammatology,* trans. Gayatri Chakravorty Spivak (Baltimore: Johns Hopkins University Press, 1976), pp. 244–45.

30. Only an innocent community, and a community of reduced dimensions (a Rousseauist theme that will soon become clearer), only a micro-society of non-violence and freedom, all the members of which can by rights remain within range of an immediate and transparent, a "crystalline" address, fully self-present in its living speech, only such a community can suffer, as the surprise of an aggression coming *from without,* the insinuation of writing, the infiltration

of its "ruse" and of its "perfidy." Only such a community can import *from abroad* "the exploitation of man by man."

Ibid., p. 119.

31. Ibid., pp. 245–46.

32. See ibid., p. 125.

33. Ibid., p. 112.

34. Ibid., pp. 139–40.

35. Ibid., p. 246.

36. Ibid., p. 244.

37. See Mark C. Taylor, *Erring: A Postmodern A/theology* (Chicago: University of Chicago Press, 1984).

38. Robert Bernasconi, "Levinas Face to Face—With Hegel," in *Journal of the British Society for Phenomenology,* vol. 13, no. 3 (1982), p. 269.

39. Emmanuel Levinas, *Ethics and Infinity: Conversations with Philip Nemo,* trans. Richard A. Cohen (Pittsburgh: Duquesne University Press, 1st ed., 1985), p. 98.

40. Emmanuel Levinas, *Totality and Infinity: An Essay on Exteriority,* trans. Alphonso Lingis (Pittsburgh: Duquesne University Press, 1969), p. 101 (footnote omitted).

41. See Derrida, *Writing and Difference,* p. 127.

42. Ibid., p. 128.

43. Ibid., p. 107.

44. Simone de Beauvoir, *The Second Sex,* trans. H. M. Parshley (New York: Random House, 1974).

45. Derrida, *Writing and Difference,* p. 114.

46. Ibid., p. 141.

47. Sigmund Freud, *Beyond the Pleasure Principle,* ed. and trans. James Strachey (New York: W. W. Norton and Co., 1961).

48. Derrida, *Writing and Difference,* p. 259.

49. See Richard Rorty, *Philosophy and the Mirror of Nature* (Princeton: Princeton University Press, 1980).

50. Plato, *Phaedrus,* trans. R. Hackforth, in *The Collected Dialogues of Plato,* ed. Edith Hamilton and Huntington Cairns (Princeton: Princeton University Press, 1961).

51. Derrida, *Writing and Difference,* p. 80.

52. Adorno, *Negative Dialectics,* p. 191.

53. Adorno, *Minima Moralia,* p. 223.

54. Ibid., p. 247.

55. Jacques Derrida, "Of an Apocalyptic Tone Recently Adopted in Philosophy," *SEMIA,* vol. 23 (1982), pp. 84–85.

56. Jacques Derrida, *"Différance,"* in *Margins of Philosophy,* trans. Alan Bass (Chicago: University of Chicago Press, 1982), p. 18.

57. Ibid., p. 19.

58. Jacques Derrida, "Des Tours de Babel," in *Difference in Translation,* ed. and trans. Joseph F. Graham (Ithaca: Cornell University Press, 1985), p. 165.

59. See Adorno, *Minima Moralia,* p. 247.

60. Charles Levin, "La Greffe de "Zèle": Derrida and the Cupidity of the Text," in *The Structural Allegory: Reconstructive Encounters with the New French Thought,* ed. John Fekete (Minneapolis: University of Minnesota Press, 1984), p. 224 (emphasis in original).

61. Derrida, "Of an Apocalyptic Tone Recently Adopted in Philosophy," p. 94.

62. Jacques Derrida, "Of an Apocalyptic Tone Recently Adopted in Philosophy." There is no explicit connection drawn by Derrida between his use of dreaming and Walter Benjamin's reliance on a version of the collective unconscious in the *Passagen-Werk.* Yet the tone and the implication that we dream collectively is reminiscent of Benjamin. Benjamin tried to save the collective unconscious from its conservative appropriation in the works of Jung and Klages. In Benjamin, the ur-images have a transient rather than an ontological status. Benjamin uses his allegorical understanding of social history to free the dream images from their containment within an unchanging symbolism.

63. Alasdair MacIntyre, *Whose Justice? Which Rationality?* (London: Duckworth, 1988).

64. Ibid. MacIntyre essentially agrees with me here.

Chapter 3

1. Emmanuel Levinas, *Otherwise Than Being or Beyond Essence,* trans. Alphonso Lingis (The Hague: Martinus Nijhoff Publishers, 1981); Emmanuel Levinas, *Totality and Infinity: An Essay on Exteriority,* trans. Alphonso Lingis (Pittsburgh: Duquesne University Press, 1969).

2. Levinas, *Otherwise Than Being.*

3. Jacques Derrida, *Glas,* trans. John P. Leavey, Jr. and Richard Rand (Lincoln: University of Nebraska Press, 1986), p. 1.

4. Ibid.

5. Ibid., p. 115.

6. I am adopting the phrase redemptive criticism from Jürgen Habermas who uses it to describe Benjamin's project of salvaging the remains. Jürgen Habermas, "Consciousness-Raising or Redemptive Criticism: The Contemporaneity of Walter Benjamin," in *New German Critique,* vol. 6, no. 17 (Spring 1979), pp. 30–59.

7. It would be a mistake to read proximity as "closeness" in the usual sense of the word. As Levinas explains:

   Proximity as a suppression of distance suppresses the distance of consciousness of. . . . The neighbor excludes himself from the thought that seeks him, and this exclusion has a positive side to it: my exposure to him, antecedent to his appearing, my delay behind him, my undergoing, undo the core of what is identity in me. Proximity, suppression of the distance that consciousness of . . . involves, opens the distance of a diachrony without a common present, where difference is the past that cannot be caught up with, an unimaginable future, the non-representable status of the neighbor behind which I am late and obsessed by the neighbor. This difference is my non-indifference to the other. Proximity is a disturbance of the rememberable time.

Levinas, *Otherwise Than Being,* p. 89.

8. For example, Nietzsche associated action at a distance with the aura and the power of the feminine. "*Women [Die Frauen] and their action at a distance.* . . . The magic and the most powerful effect of woman is, in philosophical language, action at a distance, *actio in distans*; but this requires first of all and above all—*distance.*" Friedrich W. Nietzsche, *The Gay Science: With a Prelude in Rhymes and an Appendix of Songs,* trans. Walter Kaufmann (New York: Random House, 1st ed. 1974), p. 123.

9. Georg W. F. Hegel, *Hegel's Science of Logic,* trans. A. V. Miller (Atlantic Highlands, N.J.: Humanities Press International, 1969).

10. See the first three transitions of *Hegel's Science of Logic.*

11. Georg W. F. Hegel, *Hegel's Philosophy of Right,* trans. T. M. Knox (New York: Oxford University Press, 1952).

12. Ibid., pp. 152–58.

13. Karl Popper, *The Open Society and Its Enemies* (Princeton: Princeton University Press, 1971).

14. Georg W. F. Hegel, *Phenomenology of Spirit,* trans. A. V. Miller (Oxford: Oxford University Press, 1977), pp. 481–84.

15. Hegel, *Philosophy of Right,* pp. 23–36.

16. Hegel, *Philosophy of History,* trans. J. Sibree (New York: Dover, 1956), p. 100.

17. Emmanuel Levinas and Richard Kearney, "Dialogue with Emmanuel Levinas," in *Face to Face with Levinas,* ed. Richard A. Cohen (Albany: State University of New York Press, 1986), p. 27.

18. As Derrida has argued in his latest essay on Levinas, the ethical relation can be read to demand radical ingratitude. J. Derrida, "En ce Moment Même dans cet Ouvrage Me Voici," in Jacques Derrida, *Psyche: inventions de l'autre* (Paris: Galilée, 1987), p. 159. Gratitude, as a kind of restitution, would again appropriate the Other to the same.

19. Levinas, *Totality and Infinity,* p. 23.

20. Hegel's concept of the necessary relationship between the infinite and the finite has been rejected by recent mathematicians.

21. Derrida, *Glas,* p. 1.

22. Martin Heidegger, *Identity and Difference,* trans. Joan Stambaugh (New York: Harper and Row, 1st ed., 1969), pp. 50–51.

23. Heidegger in his later work crosses out ~~Being~~.

24. Derrida, *Glas,* p. 46.

25. Robert Bernasconi has eloquently argued that we should adopt the second reading of Levinas: "Derrida reads Levinas' 'transcendence' as standing outside history and concludes that the 'anhistoricity' of meaning at its origin is what profoundly separates Levinas from Heidegger." Robert Bernasconi, "Levinas and Derrida: The Question of the Closure of Metaphysics," in *Face to Face with Levinas*, ed. Richard A. Cohen (Albany: State University of New York Press, 1986), p. 193 (quoting Jacques Derrida, *Writing and Difference*, trans. Alan Bass (Chicago: University of Chicago Press, 1978), p. 148). Derrida's point here arises out of the apparent opposition of infinity and history in Levinas. Certainly the notion of "beyond history" dominates the preface of Levinas' *Totality and Infinity*, pp. 21–30. And yet it should be emphasized that Levinas has in mind here a theological conception of history, which he refers to Hegel, whereby history is constituted as a totality ordered by judgment. Bernasconi, "Levinas and Derrida," p. 181.

26. Jacques Derrida, "Acts," in *Mémoires for Paul de Man,* ed. Avital Ronell and Eduardo Cadava, trans. Cecile Lindsay, Jonathan Culler, and Eduardo Cadava (New York: Columbia University Press, 1986), p. 137.

27. Adriaan Peperzak has highlighted this potential difficulty in Levinas:

> What Levinas rejects most of all in Hegel's theory of being and nature is the thesis that the infinite itself reveals itself within and as the realm of the anonymous in which Leviathans are at home. As the element of magic forces, mythic gods, and delightful enthusiasms, nature cannot reveal the infinite, because it exists and "is" in another way than being, in its oscillation into and out of nonbeing. Levinas' hatred for this conception of relationship between the finite and the infinite is most clearly expressed in his polemics against Heidegger's attempt at resuscitating the gods of Greece and of Hoelderlin, through a celebration of the divine as it appears in the phenomena of the earth, with its places, woods, and rivers, in works of art, in the heroes of politics or thought, and in the time of destiny. It is, however, easy to adapt Levinas' criticism to Hegel's way of looking at nature and culture as the expressions of the absolute life unfolding itself through the hierarchy of stones and stars, plants, animals, and people, states and history.
>
> However, can we not defend Hegel against this criticism? Doesn't he say that the natural exteriority of the idea should not be isolated from its interior light and that, if it were isolated, nature would indeed be an ungodly, monsterly chaos without any meaning, structure, value, light? And couldn't Hegel ask Levinas how he can avoid a dualistic view, according to which part of the world—being or *il y a*—is essentially unholy and unredeemable? How can being thus be conceived of as created?

Adriaan Peperzak, "Some Remarks on Hegel, Kant, and Levinas," in *Face to Face with Levinas,* ed. Richard Cohen (Albany: State University of New York Press, 1986), p. 209.

28. Derrida, *Glas,* pp. 1–2.

29. Ibid., p. 115.

30. Jan de Greef has powerfully argued that Derrida's interrogation of Levinas should be read as the return of the skeptical critic. Although I disagree with his reading, he offers us a convincing argument for his own position. Jan de Greef, "Skepticism and Reason," in *Face to Face with Levinas,* pp. 159–79.

31. Jacques Derrida, "Mnemosyne," in *Mémoires for Paul de Man,* p. 21.

32. Rodolphe Gasché, in his excellent book, *The Tain of the Mirror* (Cambridge, Mass.:

Harvard University Press, 1986) has defended Derrida as a serious philosopher. I agree with him that Derrida is indeed a serious philosopher. Yet I disagree with his attempt to draw a rigid boundary between literature and philosophy. *Glas* is a reading effect and not a traditional philosophical statement for a reason. Derrida's literary experimentation is not just as an aside of a creative personality, but is instead essential to deconstruction itself which constantly shows us the limit of philosophy.

33. Derrida, "Acts," p. 132.

34. I put the end of metaphysics in quotation marks because I do not try to think there can be an end to metaphysics.

35. Levinas has explained his difference from Derrida in the following way:

> It is true that philosophy, in its traditional forms of ontotheology and logocentrism—to use Heidegger's and Derrida's terms—has come to an end. But it is not true of philosophy in the other sense of the critical speculation and interrogation. The speculative practice of philosophy is by no means near its end. Indeed, the whole contemporary discourse of overcoming and deconstructing the metaphysics is far more speculative in many respects than is metaphysics itself. Reason is never more versatile as when it puts itself in question. In the contemporary end of philosophy, philosophy has found a new lease on life.

Levinas and Kearney, "Dialogue with Emmanuel Levinas," p. 33. Yet, certainly, Derrida would be only too willing to recognize the "speculative" moment within deconstruction. The difference between the two thinkers is not that Derrida would deny that reason is never more versatile than when it puts itself in question, but rather that even this versatility runs up against the limits of philosophy in the attempt to faithfully pay tribute to the remain(s).

36. Derrida, "Acts," p. 145.

37. Jacques Derrida, "Des Tours de Babel," in *Difference in Translation*, ed. and trans. Joseph F. Graham (Ithaca: Cornell University Press, 1985), p. 191. Cf. Chapter 2.

38. Jacques Derrida, "The Art of *Mémoires*," in *Mémoires for Paul de Man*, p. 52.

39. Ibid.

40. Derrida, "Mnemosyne," p. 34.

41. Derrida, "The Art of *Mémoires*," p. 53.

42. Derrida, "Mnemosyne," p. 35.

43. Ibid., p. 38.

44. Derrida, "The Art of *Mémoires*," p. 75.

45. Derrida, *Glas*, p. 118.

46. Ibid.

47. Ibid., p. 209.

48. Derrida, "The Art of *Mémoires*," p. 58.

49. Derrida, *Glas*, p. 86.

50. Ibid., pp. 145–46.

51. Ibid., pp. 116–17.

52. James Joyce, *Finnegans Wake* (New York: Penguin Books, 1939).

53. See Walter Benjamin, "The Destructive Character," in *Reflections: Essays, Aphorisms, Autobiographical Writings*, ed. Peter Demetz, trans. Edmund Jephcott (New York: Harcourt Brace Jovanovich, 1978), pp. 301–3.

54. Derrida, *Glas*, p. 204.

55. Jacques Derrida and Christie McDonald, "Choreographies," in *The Ear of the Other: Otobiography, Transference, Translation*, ed. Christie McDonald, trans. Peggy Kamuf (Lincoln: University of Nebraska Press, 1985).

56. Derrida, *Glas*, p. 117.

57. Jacques Derrida, *The Ear of the Other*. Cf. Geoffrey Bennington and Jacques Derrida, *Jacques Derrida* (Paris: Seuil, 1991).

58. Derrida, "Mnemosyne," p. 34.

59. Derrida, *Glas*, p. 34.

60. Ibid., p. 35.

61. Hélène Cixous, "Sorties," in *The Newly Born Woman*, trans. Betsy Wing (Minneapolis: University of Minnesota Press, 1986), p. 84.

62. The "auratic gaze" is a phrase adopted by Walter Benjamin. Miriam Hansen has succinctly described the role of the auratic gaze in Benjamin's infinite task of salvaging the remain(s):

> The "gaze heavy with distance" that Benjamin reads in Baudelaire's *"regard familier"* turns on the same axis that, according to Freud, links *"unheimlich"* to *"heimlich,"* a psychic ambivalence which challenges the narcissistic complacency of the gaze: "The deeper the absence of the counterpart which a gaze had to overcome, the stronger its spell. In eyes that merely mirror the other, this absence remain(s) undiminished."

Miriam Hansen, "Benjamin, Cinema and Experience: 'The Blue Flower in the Land of Technology,'" *New German Critique*, vol. 14, no. 40 (Winter 1987), pp. 179, 217.

63. Nietzsche, *The Gay Science*, §60.

64. Derrida, *Glas*, p. 115.

65. Ibid.

66. Derrida, *Glas*, p. 65.

67. "His tomb, he loves only that: *Sa* falls, it loves only *ça* [*Sa tombe, il n'aime que ça*]. Ibid., p. 201.

68. Ibid., p. 229.

69. Ibid., p. 175.

70. Drucilla Cornell, *Beyond Accommodation: Ethical Feminism, Deconstruction and the Law* (New York: Routledge, 1991).

71. Derrida, *Glas*, p. 227.

72. Walter Benjamin, "On the Mimetic Faculty," in *Reflections*, p. 333.

73. It is important to note here that although they are obviously similar, Adorno's and Benjamin's conceptions of mimesis are not identical. As noted in the first chapter, Adorno borrowed the metaphor from Benjamin and Benjamin's influence on Adorno

should be noted. Benjamin is more explicit than Adorno in tracing the history of mimesis to the response of "primitive" human nature.

74. Theodor W. Adorno and Max Horkheimer, *Dialectic of Enlightenment*, trans. John Cumming (New York: Herder and Herder, 1972).

75. Derrida, *Glas*, p. 235.

76. Jacques Derrida, *Signéponge/Signsponge*, trans. Richard Rand (New York: Columbia University Press, 1984), p. 4.

77. Derrida, *Glas*, p. 215.

78. Derrida, "The Art of *Mémoires*," p. 73.

79. J. Hillis Miller, *The Ethics of Reading: Kant, de Man, Eliot, Trollope, James and Benjamin* (New York: Columbia University Press, 1987), pp. 104–5.

80. Ibid.

81. See, for example, the debate between Richard Bernstein and Reiner Schurmann which shows divergent positions. Richard Bernstein, "Heidegger on Humanism," in *Praxis International*, vol. 5 (Oxford: Basil Blackwell, 1985), pp. 95–114, and Schurmann's response.

82. Jacques Derrida, "Violence and Metaphysics: An Essay on the Thought of Emmanuel Levinas," in *Writing and Difference*, p. 79.

83. Ibid., p. 111.

84. Levinas and Kearney, "Dialogue with Emmanuel Levinas," p. 32.

85. Robert Bernasconi, "Deconstruction and the Possibility of Ethics," in *Deconstruction and Philosophy*, ed. John Sallis (1987), p. 135.

86. Ibid., pp. 135–36.

87. Derrida, "Acts," p. 137.

88. Derrida, *Signéponge/Signsponge*, p. 121.

89. Ibid., p. 125.

90. For a longer discussion of Lacan's analysis of the psychical fantasy of woman in the construction of the gender hierarchy, see chapter 1, "The Maternal and the Feminine," in my *Beyond Accommodation*.

91. Julia Kristeva, *Black Sun: Depression and Melancholia*, trans. Leon S. Roudiez (New York: Columbia University Press, 1989).

92. Luce Irigaray, "Questions to Emmanuel Levinas: On the Divinity of Love," *The Irigaray Reader*, ed. Margaret Whitford (London and Cambridge, Mass.: Basil Blackwell, 1991), p. 178.

93. Simone de Beauvoir, *The Second Sex*, trans. H. M. Parshley (New York: Random House, 1974).

94. Luce Irigaray, "Questions to Emmanuel Levinas," p. 182.

95. Jacques Derrida, *The Post Card: From Socrates to Freud and Beyond*, trans. Alan Bass (Chicago: University of Chicago Press, 1987).

96. Walter Benjamin, "Theologico-Political Fragment," in *Reflections*, pp. 312–13. I

would also trace Paul de Man's brilliant misreading of Benjamin to his failure to fully grasp the relationship between the nihilism that *must* result from the profane striving for happiness and Benjamin's own messianism. Benjamin's "nihilism" is the affirmation of the striving for happiness not only for its own sake, but because such striving forces us to reject what is and therefore helps clear the way for the messiah. De Man is right that in Benjamin history is not messianic. But the striving for happiness undermines the pure disjunction between history and messianic intensity that de Man finds in Benjamin's text. Paul de Man, *The Resistance to Theory* (Minneapolis: University of Minnesota Press, 1986).

97. Levinas, *Otherwise Than Being*, p. 151.

Chapter 4

1. Maurice Blanchot, *The Writing of the Disaster*, trans. Ann Smock (Lincoln: University of Nebraska Press, 1986), p. 144.

2. Jürgen Habermas, *On Human Values*, ed. McMurrin M. Sterling (Salt Lake City: University of Utah Press, 1987), pp. 217–19.

3. Stanley Fish, *Doing What Comes Naturally: Change, Rhetoric, and the Practice of Theory in Literary and Legal Studies* (Durham: Duke University Press, 1989).

4. Franz Kafka, "In the Penal Colony," in *The Penal Colony: Stories and Short Pieces*, trans. Willa Muir and Edwin Muir (New York: Schocken Books, 1961), p. 191–227.

5. Robert Cover, "Violence and the Word," *Yale Law Journal*, vol. 95, no. 8 (1986), p. 1600.

6. See John Stick, "Can Nihilism Be Pragmatic? (Buyer's Guide)," in *Harvard Law Review*, vol. 100, no. 2 (1986); Charles Yablon, "The Indeterminacy of the Law: Critical Legal Studies and the Problem of Legal Explanation," in *Cardoza Law Review*, vol. 6, no. 4 (1985).

7. Drucilla Cornell, "Institutionalization of Meaning, Recollective Imagination, and the Potential for Transformation in Legal Interpretation," in *University of Pennsylvania Law Review*, vol. 136, no. 2 (1988), p. 1135.

8. E.g., some Neo-Pragmatists have implicitly tried to appeal to what Hegel would have called objective spirit in order to justify moral and legal ideals. Hegel's own system, however, was based on the realization that an appeal to objective spirit could never justify the ideal. In order to justify the ideal, by showing it as the truth of the actual, Hegel had to culminate his system in absolute knowledge. See, for example, a Neo-Pragmatist who makes the mistake of reducing the justification to convention: Richard J. Bernstein, *Beyond Objectivism and Relativism: Science, Hermeneutics, and Praxis* (Philadelphia: University of Pennsylvania Press, 1983).

9. As we saw in the second chapter, Kant's problem in legal philosophy is that he cannot reconcile the realm of freedom with the realm of necessity.

10. Emmanuel Levinas, *Totality and Infinity: An Essay on Exteriority*, trans. Alphonso Lingis (Pittsburgh: Duquesne University Press, 1969), pp. 37–38.

11. Ibid., p. 21.

12. Ibid., pp. 21–22.

13. Ibid., p. 199.

14. Emmanuel Levinas, *Otherwise Than Being or Beyond Essence*, trans. Alphonso Lingis (The Hague: Martinus Nijhoff Publishers, 1981), p. 139.

15. Ibid., p. 139.

16. Blanchot, *The Writing of Disaster*, p. 2.

17. Cf. chapter 2.

18. See Gary Peller, "The Metaphysics of American Law," *California Law Review*, vol. 73, no. 4 (1985), pp. 1160–70.

19. Duncan Kennedy, "Form and Substance in Private Law Adjudication," *Harvard Law Review*, vol. 89, no. 8 (1976).

20. Ibid., p. 1685.

21. H. L. A. Hart, *The Concept of Law* (Oxford: Oxford University Press, 1961).

22. *Marbury vs. Madison*, 5 U.S. (1 Cranch) at 137. This case is the constitutional master rule of recognition, because it establishes the division of powers between the Supreme Court, the Executive, and the Legislative, in terms of who has the last word on constitutional interpretation.

23. Ronald Dworkin, *Taking Rights Seriously* (Cambridge, Mass.: Harvard University Press, 1977).

24. Cf. the "rule-following chapter" (§§138–242) of Ludwig Wittgenstein's *Philosophical Investigations* (New York: MacMillan, 1958), pp. 53–88.

25. See, for example, ibid., §§198–202 (pp. 80–81).

26. Levinas, *Otherwise Than Being*, p. 198.

27. Ibid., p. 151.

28. Jacques Derrida, *The Post Card: From Socrates to Freud and Beyond*, trans. Alan Bass (Chicago: University of Chicago Press, 1987), p. 441.

29. Martha Minow, "The Supreme Court, 1986 Term—Foreword: Justice Engendered," *Harvard Law Review*, vol. 101, no. 1 (1987), p. 10.

30. Ibid., pp. 90–95.

31. Robert Cover, "The Supreme Court, 1982 Term—Foreword: Nomos and Narrative," *Harvard Law Review*, vol. 97, no. 1 (1983), p. 16.

32. Ibid., p. 16.

33. Georg W. F. Hegel, *Hegel's Science of Logic*, trans. A. V. Miller (Atlantic Highlands, N.J.: Humanities Press International, 1969).

34. Levinas, *Otherwise Than Being*, p. 158.

35. Ibid., p. 161.

36. Virgina Woolf, *To the Lighthouse* (London: 1964).

37. See Ronald Dworkin, *Taking Rights Seriously* (Cambridge, Mass.: Harvard University Press, 1977). But cf. *Law's Empire* (Cambridge: Belknap Press, 1986), where he seems to have reversed his opinion that there could be one right answer precisely because of his understanding of the centrality of legal interpretation.

38. Cover, "The Supreme Court, 1982 Term—Foreword," pp. 4–5.

39. Cf. chapter 5.

40. Levinas, *Otherwise Than Being*, p. 165.

41. Jürgen Habermas, *Theory of Communicative Action*, vols. 1 and 2, trans. Thomas McCarthy (Boston: Beacon Press, 1984).

42. Jacques Derrida, "The principle of reason: the university in the eyes of its pupils," in the *Graduate Faculty Philosophy Journal*, vol. 10 (Spring 1984), pp. 5–45.

43. Hans Blumenberg, *Was ist Sakularisierung?*, trans. M. Stallman (Tuhngen: J. C. B. Mohr, 1960), p. 33.

44. Jacques Derrida, "Force of Law: The 'Mystical Foundation of Authority,'" in *Cardozo Law Review*, vol. 11, nos. 5–6 (1990).

45. Charles Sanders Peirce, *The Collected Papers of Charles Sanders Peirce*, ed. Charles Hartshorne and Paul Weiss (Cambridge, Mass.: Harvard University Press, 1934), § 587.

46. Jacques Derrida, *Of Grammatology*, trans. Gayatri Chakravorty Spivak (Baltimore: Johns Hopkins University Press, 1976), p. 112.

47. Cover, "The Supreme Court, 1982 Term—Foreword," p. 44.

48. Jacques Derrida, "En ce Moment Même dans cet Ouvrage Me Voici," in *Psyche: inventions de l'autre* (Paris: Galilée, 1987).

49. Jacques Derrida, "Violence and Metaphysics," in *Writing and Difference*, trans. Alan Bass (Chicago: University of Chicago Press, 1978).

50. Franz Kafka, "Vor dem Gesetz," in *Parables and Paradoxes* (New York: Schocken Books, 1975), pp. 60–79.

51. Cover, "The Supreme Court, 1982 Term—Foreword," p. 9.

52. Jacques Derrida, "Des Tours de Babel," in *Difference in Translation*, ed. and trans. Joseph F. Graham (Ithaca: Cornell University Press, 1985), p. 165.

53. Cover, "Violence and the Word," p. 1628.

54. Ibid., p. 1607.

55. Ibid., p. 1605.

56. Ibid.

57. Derrida, "Des Tours de Babel," pp. 202–3.

58. Cover, "The Supreme Court, 1982 Term—Foreword," p. 34.

59. Cf. chapter 2.

60. Jacques Derrida, "The Art of *Mémoires*," in *Mémoires: For Paul de Man*, ed. Avital

Ronell and Eduardo Cadava, trans. Cecile Lindsay, Jonathan Culler, and Eduardo Cadava (New York: Columbia University Press, 1986), p. 82.

Chapter 5

1. Niklas Luhmann, "Law as a Social System," in the *Northwestern Law Review*, vol. 83, p. 140.

2. Ibid.

3. For Luhmann's discussion of "deparadoxicalization," see ibid., p. 145.

4. I deliberately use the visual metaphor to underscore the importance Luhmann himself explicitly gives to the observer.

5. Niklas Luhmann, "Operational Closure and Structural Coupling: The Differentiation of the Legal System," in *Cardozo Law Review*, vol. 13 (forthcoming).

6. Ibid.

7. Jürgen Habermas, "What is Universal Pragmatics?" in *Communication and the Evolution of Society*, trans. Thomas McCarthy (Boston: Beacon Press, 1979).

8. See Jacques Derrida, "Force of Law: The 'Mystical Foundation of Authority,'" in *Cardozo Law Review*, vol. 11, nos. 5–6 (1990), p. 961. I am deliberately echoing Derrida's reference to Stanley Fish's expression "fresh judgment" from his article, "Force," in *Doing What Comes Naturally: Change, Rhetoric, and the Practice of Theory in Literary and Legal Studies* (Durham: Duke University Press, 1989).

9. See generally, John Rawls, "The Domain of the Political and Overlapping Consensus," in *New York University Law Review*, vol. 64, no. 2 (1989).

10. Luhmann, "Operational Closure."

11. See generally, Stanley Fish, *Doing What Comes Naturally: Change, Rhetoric, and the Practice of Theory in Literary and Legal Studies* (Durham: Duke University Press, 1989).

12. For a discussion of the conflict within autopoiesis between the autonomy of a normatively closed system and the dynamism of a cognitively open system, see Arthur Jacobson, "Autopoietic Law: The New Science of Niklas Luhmann," in *Michigan Law Review*, vol 87, no. 6 (1989).

13. Luhmann, "Operational Closure" (footnote omitted; my emphasis).

14. Jürgen Habermas, *The Legitimation Crisis*, trans. Thomas McCarthy (Boston: Beacon Press, 1975).

15. Niklas Luhmann, *Love as Passion*, trans. Jeremy Gaicresard and Doris L. Jones (Cambridge, Mass.: Harvard University Press, 1986), p. 85.

16. Luhmann, "Operational Closure."

17. Ibid.

18. Niklas Luhmann, "Closure and Openness: On Reality in the World of Law," in *Autopoietic Law: A New Approach to Law and Society*, ed. Gunther Teubner, trans. Ian Fraser (Berlin: de Gruyter, 1987), p. 337.

19. Ibid.

20. Ibid., p. 340.

21. Luhmann, "Operational Closure."

22. Ibid. (footnote omitted).

23. As Luhmann himself explains:

    First of all, with a comparable theoretical approach, it [the concept of autopoietic closure] replaces Kantian premises. This has chiefly affected epistemological questions. Autopoietic systems need not be transparent to themselves. They find nothing in themselves that could be regarded as an undeniable fact of consciousness and applied as an epistemological *a priori*. The assumption of an *a priori* is replaced by recursivity itself. . . . It may be that continuing application of the operations available to the system to the results of precisely those operations produces stable states (which means states that repeat themselves in further operations, so-called "eigenstates"), or it may not, and depending on the type of operation, many, or few, or only one of these self-referentially stable states may exist. How far the system itself possesses reflexive capacity to observe its own states and finds its own "identity" in them is another question.

    Ibid., p. 336.

24. Niklas Luhmann, *The Differentiation of Society*, trans. Stephen Holmes and Charles Larmore (New York: Columbia University Press, 1982), p. 274 (emphasis omitted).

25. Ibid., p. 283.

26. Ibid., p. 276 (emphasis in original; endnote omitted).

27. Ibid., p. 308.

28. Ibid., p. 292 (citations omitted).

29. Ibid., p. 272.

30. Ibid., p. 278 (citations and notes omitted).

31. Ibid., p. 307 (citation omitted).

32. Ibid., pp. 271–88.

33. Jürgen Habermas, *Theory of Communicative Action,* vols. 1 and 2, trans. Thomas McCarthy (Boston: Beacon Press, 1984). Cf. Jürgen Habermas, *On Human Values,* ed. McMurrin M. Sterling (Salt Lake City: University of Utah Press, 1987), pp. 217–19.

34. Luhmann, *The Differentiation of Society,* p. 318.

35. The concept of *Dasein* is one which is familiar to those who engage with German philosophy and especially with Heidegger. Generally, it is "[t]his entity which each of us is himself and which includes inquiring as one of the possibilities of its Being." Martin Heidegger, *Being and Time,* trans. John Macquarrie and Edward Robinson (New York: Harper and Row, 1962), p. 27 (footnote omitted). More specifically:

    [i]n everyday usage it [*Dasein*] tends to be used more narrowly to stand for the kind of being that belongs to *persons.* Heidegger follows the everyday usage in this respect, but goes somewhat further in that he often uses it to stand for any *person* who has such Being, and who is thus an "entity" himself.

    Ibid., p. 27, note 1 (emphasis in original).

36. Jacques Derrida, *"Différance," Margins of Philosophy,* trans. Alan Bass (Chicago: University of Chicago Press, 1982), p. 13 (emphasis in original).

37. Georg W. F. Hegel, *Phenomenology of Spirit,* trans. A. V. Miller (Oxford: Oxford University Press, 1977), p. 9.

38. Derrida, *"Différance"* (emphasis in original).

39. Ibid., pp. 21–22.

40. Derrida, "Force of Law," p. 943.

41. H. L. A. Hart, *The Concept of Law* (Oxford: Oxford University Press, 1961).

42. Derrida, "Force of Law," pp. 943–45 (italics in original, emphasis added).

43. Ibid., pp. 961–69.

44. Ibid., p. 961.

45. Ibid., pp. 961–63.

46. Ibid., pp. 963–67.

47. Ibid., pp. 96–65.

48. Ibid., pp. 967–69.

49. Lyotard is a much stricter Kantian than Habermas. See Jean-François Lyotard, *The Différand* (University of Minnesota, 1988).

50. Derrida, "Force of Law," p. 967.

51. What is defined as rationality may be sexist. See Susan Okin, *Justice, Gender, and the Family* (New York: Basic Books, 1989). Cf. Carol Gilligan, *In a Different Voice: Psychological Theory and Women's Development* (Cambridge, Mass.: Harvard University Press, 1982).

52. Derrida, "Force of Law," pp. 969–71 (emphasis added).

53. Emmanuel Levinas, *Totality and Infinity: An Essay on Exteriority,* trans. Alphonso Lingis (Pittsburgh: Duquesne University Press, 1969), p. 283.

54. Ibid.

55. Ibid.

56. Judith Butler, *Gender Trouble: Feminism and the Subversion of Identity* (New York: Routledge, Chapman and Hall, 1990).

57. Ibid.

58. Nancy Fraser, "The French Derrideans: Politicizing Deconstruction or Deconstructing the Political?" in *Unruly Practices: Power, Discourse, and Gender in Contemporary Social Theory,* vol. 69 (1989).

59. See again Butler, *Gender Trouble.*

60. See Drucilla Cornell, *Beyond Accommodation: Ethical Feminism, Deconstruction, and the Law* (New York: Routledge, Chapman & Hall, 1991).

61. Cf. Catharine MacKinnon, *Toward a Feminist Theory of the State* (Cambridge, Mass.: Harvard University Press, 1989), for her eloquent description of this reality.

62. Ibid., p. 176.

63. Ibid.

64. Ibid.

65. Ibid.

66. *Brown v. Board of Education,* 347 U.S. 483 (1954).

67. Jean-Pierry Dupuy, "On the Supposed Pleasure of Normative Systems," in *Autopoietic Law: A New Approach to Law and Society,* ed. Gunther Teubner (Berlin: 1988), p. 51–63.

68. Niklas Luhmann, *Religious Dogmatics and the Evolution of Society,* trans. Peter Beyer (Lewiston: Edwin Mellen, 1984).

69. Ludwig Wittgenstein, *Tractatus Logico-Philosophicus,* trans. C. K. Ogden (London: Routledge and Kegan Paul, Ltd., 1981), § 7 (p. 189).

70. Luhmann, *Love as Passion,* p. 85.

71. Luhmann, "Law as a Social System."

72. Ibid., p. 178.

73. Friedrich Rolf Huber.

74. Jacques Derrida, *The Truth in Painting,* trans. Geoffrey Bennington and Ian McLeod (Chicago: University of Chicago Press, 1987).

75. Cf. Luce Irigaray, *Le Temps de différence* (Paris: Librairie Générale Française, 1989).

76. Luhmann, "Operational Closure."

77. Ibid.

78. See, e.g., Stanley Fish, "Anti-Professionalism," in *Cardozo Law Review,* vol. 7, no. 3 (1986).

79. Derrida, "Force of Law," p. 945.

80. Jacques Derrida, "Acts," in *Mémoires: for Paul de Man,* ed. Avital Ronell and Eduardo Cadava, trans. Cecile Lindsay, Jonathan Culler, and Eduardo Cadava (New York: Columbia University Press, 1986), p. 145.

81. Emmanuel Levinas, *Otherwise Than Being or Beyond Essence,* trans. Alphonso Lingis (The Hague: Martinus Nijhoff Publishers, 1981), p. 184.

82. Jacques Derrida, "The Art of *Mémoires,*" in *Memoires for Paul de Man,* pp. 56–57 (emphasis in original).

83. Ibid., p. 58 (emphasis in original).

84. *Roe v. Wade,* 410 U.S. 113 (1973).

85. *Griswold v. Connecticut,* 381 U.S. 479 (1965).

86. Catharine A. MacKinnon, *Feminism Unmodified: Discourses on Life and Law* (Cambridge, Mass.: Harvard University Press, 1987), p. 93. Two separate state interests have been identified. The first is preserving and protecting the health of the pregnant woman. The second is protecting the potentiality of human life. "Each grows in substantiality as the woman approaches term and, at a point during pregnancy, each becomes 'compelling.' " *Roe,* 410 U.S., at 162–63. The Court consid-

ered these interests sufficiently compelling to authorize the state to override a woman's privacy interest.

87. For background on the history of, and demand for, reproductive freedom, see generally, Linda Gordon, *Woman's Body, Woman's Right: A Social History of Birth Control in America* (New York: Grossman, 1976); Rosalind Pollack Petchesky, *Abortion and Woman's Choice: The State, Sexuality, and Reproductive Freedom* (New York: Longman, 1984).

88. For a more complete discussion of the concept "collective imagination," see Drucilla Cornell, "Institutionalization of Meaning, Recollective Imagination and the Potential for Transformative Legal Interpretation," in *University of Pennsylvania Law Review*, vol. 136, no. 4 (1988).

89. "The fundamental aspiration of judicial decision-making [is] . . . the application of neutral principles 'sufficiently absolute' to give them roots throughout the community and continuity over significant periods of time. . . ." *City of Akron v. Akron Center for Reproductive Health*, 462 U.S. 416, 458 (1983) (O'Connor, J., dissenting) (quoting Archibald Cox, *The Role of the Supreme Court in American Government* (New York: Oxford University Press, 1976), p. 114).

90. Cornell, "Institutionalization of Meaning."

91. Derrida, "Force of Law," pp. 953–55.

92. I am using "integrity" here in the sense given it by Ronald Dworkin, *Law's Empire* (Cambridge: Belknap Press, 1986).

93. Derrida, "Force of Law," p. 955.

94. As Blackmun himself explained: "We need not resolve the difficult question of when life begins. When those trained in the respective disciplines of medicine, philosophy, and theology are unable to arrive at any consensus, the judiciary, at this point in the development of man's knowledge, is not in a position to speculate as to the answer." *Roe*, 410 U.S. at 159.

95. The trimester framework was set out as follows:

> (a) For the stage prior to approximately the end of the first trimester, the abortion decision and its effectuation must be left to the medical judgement of the pregnant woman's attending physician.
> (b) For the stage subsequent to approximately the end of the first trimester, the State, in promoting its interest in the health of the mother, may, if it chooses, regulate abortion procedure in ways that are reasonably related to maternal health.
> (c) For the stage subsequent to viability, the State in promoting its interest in the potentiality of human life may, if it chooses, regulate, and even proscribe, abortion except where it is necessary, in appropriate medical judgement, for the preservation of the life or health of the mother.

Ibid., pp. 164–65.

96. Ibid., p. 171 (Rehnquist, J., dissenting).

97. *Webster v. Reproductive Health Services*, 109 S. Ct. 3040 (1989).

98. Ibid., p. 3056 (quoting *Garcia v. San Antonio Metro. Transit Auth.*, 469 U.S. 528 (1985)).

99. Ibid., pp. 3057–58.

100. Ibid., pp. 3056–57.

101. Ibid., p. 3056.

102. Ibid.

103. *Missouri Revised Statutes,* §§ 1.205.1(1)–(2), 1.205.2 (1986).

104. *Webster v. Reproductive Health Services,* 109 S. Ct. 3040 (1989) at 3049.

105. Ibid., p. 5027. In his dissenting opinion, Justice Blackmun voiced an eloquent appeal for justice for women: "I fear for the future. I fear for the liberty and equality of the millions of women who have lived and come of age in the 16 years since *Roe* was decided. I fear for the integrity of, and public esteem for, this Court. I dissent." Ibid., p. 3067 (Blackmun, J., dissenting).

106. *Roe v. Wade,* 410 U.S 113, 156 (1973).

107. *Missouri Revised Statutes,* §§ 1.205.1(1)-(2) (1983).

108. *Roe,* 410 U.S. at 156–57.

109. *City of Akron v. Akron Center for Reproductive Health,* 462 U.S. 416 (1983).

110. Ibid., p. 458.

111. Ibid. p. 461.

112. For my discussion of the public/private distinction, and an alternative theory by which to address the abortion issue, see Drucilla Cornell, *Sexual Difference, Politics, and the Law* (New York: Routledge, forthcoming).

Chapter 6

1. Seyla Benhabib, "Deconstruction, Justice and the Ethical Relationship," in the forthcoming *Cardozo Law Review,* vol. 13 (1991).

2. Jacques Derrida, "Force of Law: The 'Mystical Foundations of Authority,'" in *Cardozo Law Review*, vol. 11, nos. 5–6 (1990).

3. Dominick LaCapra, "Violence, Justice, and the Force of Law," *Cardozo Law Review,* vol. 11, nos. 5–6 (1990).

4. Walter Benjamin, "The Critique of Violence," in *Reflections: Essays, Aphorisms, Autobiographical Writings,* ed. Peter Dementz, trans. Edmund Jephcott (New York: Harcourt Brace Jovanovich, 1978), p. 277.

5. Ibid., pp. 281–83.

6. *Bowers v. Hardwick,* 478 U.S. 186 (1986).

7. Benjamin, "The Critique of Violence," pp. 277–79; Derrida, "Force of Law," pp. 983–85, 989.

8. Benjamin, "The Critique of Violence," p. 277.

9. Benhabib, "Deconstruction, Justice and the Ethical Relationship." Seyla Benhabib misunderstands Benjamin here.

10. LaCapra, "Violence, Justice, and the Force of Law," p. 1077.

11. Derrida, "Force of Law," p. 919. I want to note here that this is also a reference to the title of the conference, "Deconstruction and the Possibility of Justice," held at the Benjamin N. Cardozo School of Law in October 1989. "Force of Law" was the basis of Jacques Derrida's keynote address at the conference.

12. Derrida, "Force of Law," p. 983.

13. Ibid., p. 945.

14. Ibid., p. 991.

15. Ibid., p. 993.

16. Ibid., p. 943.

17. LaCapra, "Violence, Justice, and the Force of Law," p. 1067.

18. See Stanley Fish, *Doing What Comes Naturally: Change, Rhetoric, and the Practice of Theory in Literary and Legal Studies* (Durham: Duke University Press, 1989).

19. Ibid., pp. 328–31.

20. In his essay, "Working on the Chain Gang," Fish notes:

> Paradoxically, one can be faithful to legal history only by revising it, by redescribing it in such a way as to accommodate and render manageable the issues raised by the present. This is a function of the law's conservatism, which will not allow a case to remain unrelated to the past, and so assures that the past, in the form of the history of decisions, will be continually rewritten. In fact, it is the duty of a judge to rewrite it (which is to say no more than that it is the *duty* of a judge to decide), and therefore there can be no simply "found" history in relation to which some other history could be said to be "invented."

Fish, *Doing What Comes Naturally*, p. 94 (footnote omitted; emphasis in original).

21. *Bowers v. Hardwick,* 478 U.S. 186 (1986).

22. In "Dennis Martinez and the Uses of Theory," Fish responds to Mark Kelman, quoting:

> It is illuminating and disquieting to see that we are nonrationally constructing the legal world over and over again. . . ." In fact, it is neither. It is not illuminating because it does not throw any light on any act of construction that is currently in force, for although your theory will tell you that there is always one (or more) under you feet, it cannot tell you which one it is or how to identify it. It is not disquieting because in the absence of any alternative to interpretive construction, the fact that we are always doing it is neither here nor there. It just tells us that our determinations of right and wrong will always occur within a set of assumptions that could not be subject to our scrutiny; but since everyone else is in the same boat, the point is without consequence and leaves us exactly where we always were, committed to whatever facts and certainties our interpretive constructions make available.

Fish, *Doing What Comes Naturally*, p. 395 (footnote omitted).

23. *Bowers v. Hardwick,* 478 U.S. 186 (1986) at 192–94.

24. *Hardwick v. Bowers,* 760 F.2d 1202 (1985), *rev'd* 478 U.S. 186 (1986).

25. *Bowers v. Hardwick,* 478 U.S. 186 (1986) at 189. The Ninth Amendment reads:

> The enumeration in the Constitution, of certain rights, shall not be construed to deny or disparage others retained by the people.

U.S. Const. amend. IX.

The Due Process Clause of the Fourteenth Amendment provides that:

> No State shall make or enforce any law which shall abridge the privileges or immunities of citizens of the United States; nor shall any State deprive any person of life, liberty, or property, without due process of law.

U.S. Const. amend. XIV, cl. 1.

26. *Griswold v. Connecticut*, 381 U.S. 479 (1965).

27. *Roe v. Wade*, 410 U.S. 113 (1973).

28. *Carey v. Population Services International*, 431 U.S. 678 (1977).

29. *Bowers v. Hardwick*, 478 U.S. 186 (1986) at 190–91.

30. The cases in this line include *Skinner v. Oklahoma*, 316 U.S. 535 (1942), which struck down a law requiring sterilization of those thrice convicted of certain felonies involving "moral turpitude," on grounds which included that the punishment interfered with the individuals' rights in procreation; *Loving v. Virginia*, 388 U.S. 1 (1967), in which the Supreme Court overturned a miscegenation law, in part because it interfered with the right to marry; *Griswold v. Connecticut*, which affirmed the rights of married persons to receive information on the use of contraceptives as part of their rights to conduct their family life free from state interference, *Eisenstadt v. Baird*, 405 U.S. 438 (1972), which addressed the right of a person, regardless of marital status, to make decisions as to her own procreative choices; Roe v. Wade, providing for the right of a woman to have an abortion; and *Carey v. Population Services International*, 431 U.S. 678 (1977), in which the Court disallowed a law prohibiting distribution of non-prescription contraceptives by any but pharmacists or distribution to minors under the age of 16.

31. *Bowers v. Hardwick*, 478 U.S. 186 (1986) at 191.

32. *Bowers v. Hardwick*, 478 U.S. 186 (1986) at 192–94 (footnotes and citation omitted).

33. Ibid., p. 194.

34. See Drucilla Cornell, "Institutionalization of Meaning, Recollective Imagination and the Potential for Transformative Legal Interpretation," *University of Pennsylvania Law Review*, vol. 136, no. 4 (1988); and chapter 5, "The Relevance of Time to the Relationship between the Philosophy of the Limit and Systems Theory: The Call to Judicial Responsibility," above.

35. See Fish, "Working on the Chain Gain," in *Doing What Comes Naturally*, pp. 93–95.

36. Derrida, "Force of Law," p. 997.

37. *Bowers v. Hardwick*, 478 U.S. 186 (1986) at 191.

38. *Bowers v. Hardwick*, 478 U.S. (making reference to Justice Goldberg's concurrence in *Griswold v. Connecticut*, 381 U.S.)

39. *Bowers v. Hardwick*, 478 U.S. 186 (1986) at 199 (Blackmun, J. dissenting; quoting *Olmstead v. United States*, 277 U.S. 438, 478 (1928) (Brandeis, J., dissenting)).

40. Ibid. (quoting, Oliver W. Holmes, "The Path of the Law," in *Harvard Law Review*, vol 10, no. 8 (1897), p. 469).

41. Derrida, "Force of Law," p. 943.

42. LaCapra, "Violence, Justice, and the Force of Law," p. 1069.

43. Benjamin, "The Critique of Violence," p. 286.

44. See LaCapra, "Violence, Justice, and the Force of Law," pp. 1071, 1077–78.

45. Derrida, "Force of Law," p. 971.

46. Ibid., pp. 943–45.

47. See *Hardwick v. Bowers*, 760 F.2d 1202 (1985) at 1211–13.

48. See Derrida, "Force of Law," pp. 961–63.

49. Oliver W. Holmes, "The Path of the Law," in *Harvard Law Review*, vol 10, no. 8 (1897).

50. Derrida, "Force of Law," p. 961.

51. For a more thorough exploration of the appeal to natural and unnatural conceptions of sexuality, see Drucilla Cornell, "Gender, Sex and Equivalent Rights," in *Feminists Theorize the Political*, ed. Judith Butler and Joan Scott (New York: Routledge, Chapman and Hall, 1991).

52. Derrida, "Force of Law," p. 971.

53. *Bowers v. Hardwick*, 478 U.S. at 186, 187, 199 (1986).

54. Derrida, "Force of Law," p. 955.

55. LaCapra, "Violence, Justice, and the Force of Law," p. 1068.

56. Derrida, "Force of Law," p. 993.

57. Benjamin, "The Critique of Violence," pp. 297–98; Derrida, "Force of Law," pp. 1029–31.

58. Benjamin, "The Critique of Violence," p. 294.

59. See LaCapra, "Violence, Justice, and the Force of Law," pp. 1069–70.

60. See Benjamin, "The Critique of Violence," pp. 286–87.

61. Monique Wittig, *Les Guérillères*, trans. David Le Vay (Boston: Beacon Press, 1975).

62. LaCapra, "Violence, Justice, and the Force of Law," p. 1070.

Conclusion

1. Derrida does not offer us a traditional sociological theory. This has been turned into criticism. See Thomas McCarthy, "The Politics of the Ineffable: Derrida's Deconstructionism," in *Philosophical Forum*, vol. 21, nos. 1–2 (Fall-Winter 1989–90). Cf. Peter Dews, *Logics of Disintegration* (London: Verso, 1987).

2. Jacques Derrida, *Glas*, trans. John P. Leavey, Jr. and Richard Rand (Lincoln: University of Nebraska Press, 1986).

3. Luce Irigaray, "Questions to Emmanuel Levinas: On the Divinity of Love," trans. Margaret Whitford.

4. Ibid.

5. Drucilla Cornell, "Gender, Sex and Equivalent Rights," in *Feminists Theorize the Political,* ed. Judith Butler and Joan Scott (New York: Routledge, Chapman and Hall, 1992).

6. Sigmund Freud, *Beyond the Pleasure Principle,* ed. and trans. James Strachey (New York: W. W. Norton and Co., 1961), pp. 8–11.

7. Eleanor Galenson and Hermann Roiphe, "The Impact of Early Sexual Discovery on Mood, Defensive Organization, and Symbolization," in *The Psychoanalytic Study of the Child,* vol. 26, no. 195 (1972).

8. Samuel Beckett, *Happy Days,* a play in two acts (New York: Grove Weidenfeld, 1961).

9. Deborah Tannen, *You Just Don't Understand* (New York: Ballantine, 1991).

10. Charles Sanders Peirce, *The Collected Papers of Charles Sanders Peirce,* vol. V, eds. Charles Hartshorne and Paul Weiss (Cambridge, Mass.: Harvard University Press, 1934), pp. 481–82.

11. Judith Butler, *Gender Trouble: Feminism and the Subversion of Identity* (New York: Routledge, Chapman and Hall, 1990).

12. See also chapters 4, 5, and 6.

13. Ibid.

14. Jacques Derrida, "Restitutions," in *The Truth in Painting,* trans. Geoffrey Bennington and Ian McLeod (Chicago: University of Chicago Press, 1987), pp. 255–382.

15. Peirce, *Collected Papers,* § 587.

16. Friedrich Schiller, *On the Aesthetic Education of Man,* trans. Reginald Snell (New York: Frederick Ungar, 1965).

17. Thomas Nagel, *Equality and Partiality* (Princeton: Princeton University Press, forthcoming).

18. Irigaray's sense of wonderment is close to Charles Peirce's conception of musement. For my discussion of Peirce's concept of "musement," see Drucilla Cornell, "Institutionalization of Meaning, Recollective Imagination and the Potential for Transformation," in *University of Pennsylvania Law Review,* vol. 136, no. 4 (1988), pp. 1135–1229.

19. Teresa Brennan, "History after Lacan," in *Equality and Society,* vol. 9, no. 3, pp. 277–313. This is Brennan's reading.

20. Ibid.

21. Max Horkheimer and Theodor W. Adorno, *Dialectic of Enlightenment,* trans. John Cumming (New York: Herder and Herder, 1972).

22. Richard Rorty, *Contingency, Irony, and Solidarity* (New York: Cambridge University Press, 1989). See also Rorty, *Philosophy and the Mirror of Nature* (Princeton: Princeton University Press, 1980).

23. Jacques Derrida, *Mémoires: for Paul de Man,* ed. Avital Ronell and Eduardo Cadava,

trans. Cecile Lindsay, Jonathan Culler, and Eduardo Cadava (New York: Columbia University Press, 1986).

24. Georg W. F. Hegel, *Phenomenology of Spirit,* trans. A. V. Miller (Oxford: Oxford University Press, 1977).

25. Thomas McCarthy, "The Politics of the Ineffable," in *Philosophical Forum,* vol. 21, nos. 1–2 (Fall-Winter 1989–90).

26. Jacques Derrida, "Du Droit à Philosophie" (Paris: Galilée, 1990).

27. Theodor W. Adorno, *Negative Dialectics,* trans. E. B. Ashton (New York: The Continuum Publishing Co., 1973), p. 3.

28. See, e.g. Thomas McCarthy, "The Politics of the Ineffable," p.158.

29. Jacques Derrida, "Force of Law: The 'Mystical Foundation of Authority,'" in *Cardozo Law Review*, vol. 11, nos. 5–6 (1990), pp. 960–73.

30. Cf. chapter 4.

31. Ibid.

32. John Rawls, "The Domain of the Political and Overlapping Consensus," in *New York University Law Review,* vol. 64, no. 2 (1989).

33. Cf. chapter 4.

34. Ingeborg Bachmann, *Malina* (New York: Holmes and Meier Publishers, Inc., 1990).

Index